ZAPPING CONFLICT
IN THE
HEALTH CARE
WORKPLACE

DR.
JUDITH BRILES

mile high
press

Also by
Dr. Judith Briles

The Confidence Factor—Cosmic Gooses Lay Golden Eggs
Stop Stabbing Yourself in the Back
Woman to Woman 2000
The Briles Report on Women in Healthcare
10 Smart Money Moves for Women
Smart Money Moves for Kids
GenderTraps
Confidence—How Self Esteem Can Change Your Life
When God Says NO
Money Sense
The Money $ense Guidebook
Raising Money-Wise Kids
Woman to Woman
Judith Briles' Money Book
Faith & $avvy Too!
Money Phases
The Woman's Guide to Financial Savvy
Self-Confidence and Peak Performance
Divorce—The Financial Guide for Women

Co-Authored Books
The Dollars and Sense of Divorce
The SeXX Factor
The Workplace

Free articles and information on Judith's books
are available on her web site at www.Briles.com.

ZAPPING CONFLICT

IN THE
HEALTH CARE
WORKPLACE

DR.
JUDITH BRILES

**mile high
press**

www.MileHighPress.com

Books may be purchased for sales promotion
by contacting the publisher,
Mile High Press at PO Box 460880 Aurora CO 80046
303-627-9179 ~ 303-627-9184 Fax ~ Info@MileHighPress.com

Library of Congress Catalog Card # 2002108940

ISBN: 1-885331-08-8

1. Conflict Management   2. Health/Business   3. Change

Second Edition   10/03   Printed in the United States of America

For Ellen Tryon . . .

An extraordinary health care
executive and leader—

A woman who walks her talk
and talks her walk.

Table of Contents

Exhibits, Figures and Tables

Preface

We all know it exists. Most of us have experienced it. And, some of us practice it. Conflict, sabotage, backstabbing, backbiting, gossip, and other undermining behaviors are alive and well in the workplace. That's the problem. Exposing these toxic behaviors and outlining how we can stop them is the purpose of this book.

For many years, I have been asking women and men to tell me about their experiences with sabotage at work. My primary interests are in learning more about women's experiences and how women stop destructive patterns. What I have found as I crisscross the country, speaking to approximately 30,000 healthcare professionals a year, is that women (and men) working in a variety of professions consistently report that they have been undermined more by other women than by men. They also report a substantial increase in the amount of conflict and sabotage as well as shortage of personnel in many areas.

Why might this be so? I believe that sabotaging is a learned behavior, in itself a misplaced attempt at workplace survival, not a genetic trick of nature. I also believe that with education, awareness, and commitment, sabotage cannot only change, it can be eliminated. Once sabotage ends and real support systems begin, women and men benefit emotionally, physically, and financially. Their co-workers do likewise. Conflict? It exists, is normal to some degree, and can be defused and resolved.

> **The increased levels of conflict and sabotage reported by the study used for this book is a key contributory factor to personnel shortage and retention experienced in nursing and dentistry.**

In this work, I turn once again to women and men working in health care, one of the most female-dominated work settings globally. The health care industry provided over 10 million jobs post 2000 in North America alone. Over 70 percent of those positions—7,000,000 jobs—will be held by women. Over 2.5 million nursing positions will be available, with 93 to 97 percent filled by women. In dentistry, staff and hygienists will fill an estimated 500,000 jobs. What might a look inside the health care industry tell us about surviving and thriving in any work setting? Read on.

The Origins of This Work

In the winter of 1992, I had just completed the second presentation of a two-part program at the Glens Falls Hospital, in Glens Falls, New York. After the evening program, several organizers and participants and I met at a restaurant in neighboring Sarasota Springs. The house specialty was pizza. It was delicious, but the conversation that followed was even better.

My dinner companions held various positions within their hospital. They were clinical specialists, staff nurses, and nurse executives. While sharing food and stories that evening, Kathleen Kennedy, vice president for nursing care at the time, encouraged me to undertake the study that was the basis of my first book, *The Briles Report on Women in Healthcare*.

The health field would provide quite a laboratory, we reasoned, when so many employees—especially those at the bottom rungs of the career ladders—are female. Here inside our hospitals, clinics, doctors' and dentists' offices, and the like—how did women (and men) really work together? Would they support each other because they saw themselves as caretakers with a vital, indeed, a life-and-death-public trust? Would the service aspect of working in health care make a difference? The question—would levels of conflict that I had found in other work settings be repeated in health care? Would women workers in health care undermine each other more than my earlier work in the generic workplace had found?

Several of the women sitting around the table eating pizza and talking about their work experiences that night in 1992 said they thought that backstabbing and undermining behavior had increased over the past few years. Terms like *abuse* and *assault* were used openly and freely. Neither of those words had surfaced in my previous interviews or surveys of the general workplace. I made a note to ask other women about this, too.

That note was the seed for my first book on the health

care field, and as I left my colleagues in New York that night, I was determined to begin a new nationwide study of working women, one focused on health care professionals. Over the next year, I continued to talk and listen to women in health care. I conducted interviews, a survey, and numerous workshops. The results of that study were the subject of the first book that exclusively focused on conflict, sabotage and workplace behavior, *The Briles Report on Women in Healthcare* (Jossey Bass, 1994).

Almost a decade later, it made sense to readdress the topic and take a pulse as to where the health care workplace was today. Over 1600 women and men participated in the new study for *Zapping Conflict in the Health Care Workplace*. To offer a quick overview, let me say that I found sabotage and conflict had increased, and that there were basically two reasons for the increase in behavorial sabotage: first, women were more aware of what sabotaging and undermining behavior was and were willing to identify it; and, second, women are the least likely to have seniority or authority in their workplaces, and so any reorganizing or changes within the organization will be likely to affect them first.The word, bullying, ws often cited.

The reasons for the reported levels of increased conflict varied—depending if you were staff or a manager. Managers viewed the primary reason for the increase in both as "change". Staff disagreed—they felt that the primary reason was that management didn't communicate clearly or effectively, that goals and objectives were indistinct. Staff also felt strongly that the significant reductions in training budgets were contributory factors; management didn't think it was a big deal.

The second part of the book offers tools and strategies to help stop conflict and sabotage and enable women (and men) to work together in a healthy environment.

It's Not the Shortage of Nurses . . . Stupid!

In 2002, the *Nurse-Physician Relationships: Impact on Nurse Satisfaction and Retention* was released by VHA, Inc., a Texas-based health alliance that represents 26 percent of the nation's community hospitals. The study included 1200 health care professionals—nurses, physicians and executives at various VHA facilities. Not only did respondents report that they had observed disruptive behavior by physicians toward nurses (92 percent), 30 percent of the nurses within the survey knew of at least one nurse resigning her position because of the behavior.

The VHA study found that disruptive physician behavior and the underlying institutions responses were key factors to a nurse's morale and her decision as to whether to stay in her position or not.

Since the early nineties, I've known from my previous studies and from the thousands of health care professionals interviewed and trained, that a large percentage of nurses had left employment because of sabotaging behavior and workplaces riddled with conflict. At every presentation and speech I made, nurses approached me and shared that they had left a previous workplace because of abusive behaviors. They had quit their jobs because they couldn't stand the level of undermining behavior from co-workers and managers.

Although this book was at the printers when the study was released, I felt it was important to do a follow-up survey of my own relating to terminating employment and the cause. The presses were stopped to process a new survey and reference it below (a costly venture for any publisher).

Over a two-week period in August of 2002, 1338 health care professionals replied to the survey generated from my website. The largest sector came from nursing (62 percent), followed by managers/administrators (28 percent), health care educators (4 percent) and dentistry (6 percent). The questions and responses were—

- Have you ever resigned from an organization or transferred to another department because of abusive behavior?—*45 percent said yes.*
- Was the behavior bullying, sabotage, harassment, other, or all of the above? *The greatest number said all of the above (48 percent).*
- Was the behavior generated from managers/ administrators, co-workers or both? *Forty-seven percent said it was from managers/administrators; 17 percent from co-workers and 31 percent from both (5 percent didn't answer).*
- Would you consider working for the organization again if the abusive parties were terminated? *Fifty-two percent said yes, and 48 percent said no.*
- Of the 48 percent who said no, a variety of reasons were given. *The majority (41 percent) reported that the problem was too invasive in the organization; 24 percent felt the problem was poor leadership, and management couldn't manage; 22 percent said that it wasn't worth it; and the remainder was split between the erosion of their confidence, tarnishing their reputation and the damage of their credibility.*

These responses are incredibly telling. First, the reported nursing shortage is not a shortage because of lack of personnel—*too many nurses choose not to work in nursing.* Second, if the leadership of an organization would acknowledge that there is conflict, sabotage and bullying within their organization, they could work at resolving it. And third, if they choose not to address it, deal with it and put an end to it, their organizations will continue to lose good people. The cost—millions of dollars a year in replacement and training costs.

> *ZAP Tip*
>
> *The key factor to the nurse shortage
> is NOT that there aren't enough nurses.
> The key factor is that there is too much
> bullying, sabotage, undermining and conflict
> in their workplaces. Until management,
> and nurses themselves, confront the abusive
> behavior and create a* no tolerance zone,
> *the shortage will only continue to increase.
> It's not the lack of nurses; it's the accepted and
> tolerated rotten behavior of co-workers,
> managers, and administrators. The health care
> toxic workplace must be changed.
> ZAP it . . . Now.*

Audience

This book is written for several audiences, including men. Employees and managers in all fields will recognize themselves and their co-workers. Women who work in nursing, medicine, dentistry, health care administration, medical insurance, health centers, hospitals, dentistry, and pharmaceuticals companies may laugh, cry, or get angry at the familiarity of the stories recorded in this work.

Women and men who read this work will want to

change their workplaces—for themselves and for others. They will be able to recognize conflict creating, sabotaging and other unacceptable behaviors in others (and sometimes in themselves) and identify appropriate ways to change destructive interactions. It is my hope that the readers of this work will truly believe that their voices do count and that together they can transform their toxic workplaces into thriving communities.

Part I:

What's What in the Workplace

I didn't want to believe it was happening. It was one of those times in my life that I didn't listen to myself. I kept pushing it down, saying, "This isn't true. It can't be happening. She's really not like this." When I finally opened my eyes and ears, I found that everything she did was for her own benefit. There really wasn't any effort to do anything as a team member or a partner.

Brenda, a Midwest RN

Setting the Stage

Conflict and sabotage are flourishing in today's workplace. The quote from the previous page was from a nurse that was surveyed for my first book that focused exclusively on the health care industry. The topics were sabotage and conflict. A decade later, not much has changed. The comment still holds true. Unfortunately.

Is there more conflict in today's workplace? Yes. Should (and could) there be less conflict in today's workplace? Absolutely. Could the workplace be more collaborative? Yes again. And, is there a reasonable, non-costly way to reduce the shortages that many fields under the health care umbrella face today? You bet, and you don't need to have a PhD in anything to figure it out. What is needed is common sense, willingness to acknowledge the components and players in the problem and a dose of guts to resolve it.

Since the mid-eighties, I've researched workplace issues—

some in a general workplace where there is a fairly equal number of males and females employed and others where one gender is in the great majority. One of the most prominent one-sided workplaces is health care. Within the health care umbrella, nursing is the most female dominated branch; dentistry highlights dental hygienists and assistants as being the most female populated category.

When I first explored that question of conflict and undermining activities in the workplace in the mid-eighties, I created a survey that went to 1,000 women and 1,000 men in 1987. The results were published in *Woman to Woman* (New Horizon Press). They produced a major brouhaha in working women's circles. Why?—they showed that when it comes to unethical, undermining, sabotaging behavior, men do not discriminate: they behave unethically toward both sexes, in equal measure. Their style of being unethical is also different from women's: men are more overt, and very direct; they let you know if they intend to undermine you.

But if a woman is going to be unethical and unsupportive, and if she displays other types of sabotaging behavior, her target is more likely to be another woman, and her style is likely to be covert. Sometimes her target doesn't even know where the sabotage has come from.

When these results were released to the media, such women's magazines as *New Woman, Working Woman, McCalls, Redbook, Family Circle, Ladies Home Journal* and *Cosmopolitan* ignored these findings. *Glamour,* to its credit, was different. The editors of *Glamour* decided to query their readers in a survey of their own. I supplied my data, the results, and the questions asked. They asked similar questions of their readers and their findings were published in June 1988. The editors were surprised. I wasn't. *Glamour's* readers agreed with my study.

With another source confirming my results, I felt that the problem of women's undermining other women would move from being a taboo topic to being one that could be addressed, discussed, and resolved.

Four additional national surveys have been completed since 1987. The latest was completed in 2002 and used as the basis for this work. All focused on women and men in the workplace. The surveys in 1994 and 2002 viewed health care exclusively. The first was generated when several directors of nursing from hospitals in different regions of the United States asked me to do a study that exclusively looked at them—health care and nursing. Those results, from over 1,000 respondents from the nursing sector were upsetting. Over 75 percent stated that they had been undermined by a woman in their workplace, a *45 percent increase* from the initial study done in 1987 of the general workplace.

These results were published in *The Briles Report on Women in Health Care* (Jossey-Bass, 1994), and negative comments surfaced, primarily from nursing-related journals. One in particular, *Rehabilitation Nursing,* questioned the data and the methodology. The editor, in her column, wrote,

> My initial reaction to what I was reading was uneasiness. Can it really be true that nurses sabotage other nurses? We've heard for years the saying that "nurses eat their young," but the undermining behaviors described by Briles were not reserved for the young!
>
> I tried to dismiss Briles' conclusions by disparaging the study methodology; it's easy to say that the study wasn't sound, therefore we can't trust the conclusions.

The whole book presents a dismal outlook on relationships between colleagues, whether on a peer level or in a supervision/subordinate situation. Can this really be the way things are in nurses' workplaces?[1]

She ended her column with a question: "How is it where you work? Your stories will help validate—or refute—the Briles study."

Taking Off the Rose Colored Glasses

To say that her readers' responses were overwhelming, and dismaying for her would be an understatement. In the following spring's journal (1996), she wrote,

Wow! What a response I received to my editorial about Judith Briles' book on the toxic work environments of women in health care professions. I wanted to believe that things are not as bad as Briles concluded. I asked, 'Am I wearing rose-colored glasses?' I urged readers of *Rehabilitation Nursing* to let me know whether conditions described by Briles are typical of nurses' workplaces. Apparently—and sadly—they are.

One individual who responded to my editorial assured me that 'this type of behavior started about 5 to 6 years ago and at this time is beyond belief.' Another noted, 'I could provide countless examples of backstabbing, undermining and manipulation.' Still another wrote, 'We both see and experience evil deeds by rogue nurses in the workplace.'

I read these accounts with a growing sense of disbelief that nurses in particular, or women in general, could be in the way described. But, I kept returning to example after example. Not once did I note a positive example![2]

The editor went on to say—get Briles' book and follow her suggestions and recommendations for dealing with sabotage and conflict in the workplace. Good news to any author. As a side note, I contacted the national office for this nursing group the same year, referred to the editorial and offered to waive my speaking fee and come to their annual meeting and do a hands-on workshop for their members. They said, "No, your topic doesn't fit with our program."

Another survey in 1996 contained the voices of 5,000 women; women who stated that being undermined by another woman and conflicts created by them in their workplaces were the third greatest problem they encountered (prejudice and miscommunications were numbers one and two.[3] These same results were reflected from another survey involving 5,000 respondents in *Woman to Woman 2000—Becoming Sabotage Savvy in the New Millennium* in 1999.[4]

> **No other industry has gone through the dramatic changes that health care has over recent decades. The words health care and change are synonymous. When change is in play, a greater degree of conflict surfaces and is energized in the process. Most people aren't thrilled with lots of change and certainly not with an organization that is riddled with conflict—going to work is not a joy.**

Health care has a problem—a major one. In the mid-nineties there was almost a slash and burn mentality—departments downsized, or were eliminated; mergers of facilities and departments at the drop of the hat (with many breaking up at a later date because of the wrong fit); administrators and executives replaced by bean counters; and for nurses—lay-offs were common-place.

Today, many look back and acknowledge mistakes. The wrong people were let go; certain departments weren't synergistic with each other; fancy names created by PR and marketing groups for the new marriage never took; as for nurses—more, please send more. During the Olympics of 2002, Johnson & Johnson rolled out a $20,000,000 campaign supporting nursing, encouraging viewers to choose nursing as a career. Nurses everywhere cheered, "Bravo!"

The field of dentistry wasn't blessed with a $20,000,000 boost in advertising from a pharmaceutical company as nursing was—there, too, a shortage exists, especially with support staff. Shortages are expected to grow over the next decade as more and more support staff (including dental hygienists, assistants and clerical) are choosing part time over full time work.

Summing Up

My speaking, training, consulting and writing in the health care field told me that lots had to be done in order to attract bright and dedicated women and men to nursing. I too exclaimed a "Bravo" to the folks at J&J, but nursing, dentistry and health care in general need more. Daily, I get e-mails from women (and men) nurses who are choosing to leave the profession. Why? Simply this—they can't stand the level of conflict and sabotage within their workplaces . . . from co-workers as well as supervisors. **They love their work; they hate their workplaces.**

From the beginning of my study of this national problem, the growing areas of conflict and sabotage needed to be addressed. As the pioneer of the topic of sabotage among women in the workplace, my first book focused on it, *Woman to Woman—From Sabotage to Support* (New Horizon Press 1987). That was after 28 rejections from other publishers who didn't think the topic was relevant or newsworthy. Fifteen plus years have passed, with international coverage from *The Wall Street Journal, Time, People,* even that bell-weather of gossipy news, *The National Enquirer* and 1000 radio and TV shows to date, those editors and their publishing houses were dead wrong. Sabotage and conflict among women was and is major news.

Post 2000, several books have been published by the same publishers who rejected *Woman to Woman: From Sabotage to Support*—from Susan Murphy and Patricia Hein's *In the Company of Women* and Phyllis Chesler's *Women's Inhumanity to Women*, each claiming to be ground-breaking and the "first". Suddenly, women's undermining other women is big news. One side of me welcomes the company to the small circle of courageous authors and publishers who are willing to tackle a dicey topic; the other side says, "What took you all so long?"

My only complaint is that it would have been nice to be acknowledged for being the first who did a study, published it and has spent over a decade increasing workplace awareness to the problem nationally and internationally.

At this point, I felt it was critical to "officially" revisit the health care scene, a female dominated workplace that has an added hot potato to the topic—patients. When women don't support other women, when women created conflict and sabotage because of old baggage and behaviors they create and embrace, patients are in jeopardy. With the completed new study, another book was birthed. It's now in your hands.

The Survey Speaks—What Respondents Say About Conflict

2

S ince my first book that focused on conflict, and undermining and sabotaging activities, I've criss-crossed North America speaking on the topic . . . and listening to women and men talk about their workplaces. I've heard the good, the bad and the ugly . . . the very good and the very ugly. Truth be told, comments about the ugly outweighed the good.

In the 21ˢᵗ Century, conflict is very much alive and unfortunately, doing quite well in its expansion activities. Most say,

> Yes, we know there is bad behavior and conflict among staff, doctors, administrators, even the patients and their families agree with us often.

Simple enough. I then ask what steps are they taking to reduce and eliminate rotten behavior and conflict within their facility. Silence. Stammering. I'll get back to you. Etc., etc., etc. You would have thought that I had asked them to strip naked and be the lead majorette or major in the local July 4th parade! Being snagged in the headlights of life is rarely fun. It's a defining moment for all—leader, manager, support staff.

Conflict **is when two or more people assume opposing and different positions in a situation or circumstance. The expression of the difference can be verbal or non-verbal and can be overtly or covertly presented. If** *conflict* **is not resolved within a timely manner, morale dives, loyalty diminishes, teams are splintered, distrust grows and turn-over increases.**

Ongoing *conflict* **costs an organization multi-millions of dollars a year in lost productivity, search fees and training costs for replacement of personnel.**

If conflict is not truthfully addressed, it can mean the difference between black and red—black meaning you have funds in the bank to continue your activities and work environment and red meaning . . . trouble; you are losing big money and your survival may be dependent on another's pocketbook, as in a merger and take-over.

All is Not Well in Health Care

The present results for this latest book again showed that all is not well. This time, focusing on conflict, some of the questions I asked included—

- Is there conflict in your workplace?
- Has it increased, decreased or not changed in the past five years?

- What do you think the reasons for the change (if any) are?
- Do different generations handle conflict differently?
- How does your manager or co-workers handle conflict?
- How do you react when conflict occurs?
- How do you rate yourself when handling conflict?

When it comes to conflict and sabotaging behavior, men do not discriminate: they behave unprofessionally toward both genders, in equal measure. Their style of creating conflict and undermining activities are also different from women's: men are more overt, and very direct; they let you know if they intend to undermine you. Few surprises are directed toward the intended target.

But if a woman is going to be unprofessional and a conflict creator, and if she displays other types of sabotaging behavior, her target is more likely to be another woman, and her style is likely to be covert, indirect. Sometimes her target doesn't even know where the sabotaging behavior has come from. Lots of surprises.

Survey Respondents

The 2002 survey respondents solely came from the health care field—nurses, doctors, directors of women's centers, vice presidents of nursing, educational departments, employees of pharmaceutical and other health related organizations, at randomly selected hospitals as well as on my website, *www.Briles.com*. At the time of the survey, 3,000 individuals received notice of a survey designed with ten questions. One set was for managers/administrative individuals to take and another set with the same questions for employees to take. Each questionnaire was accompanied by a cover letter.

Of the 3,000 surveys sent out, 1,670 were returned by the cutoff date. An additional five percent were received after the cutoff date but were not included statistically; in a post-evaluation, they, however, revealed the same type of responses as in the surveys received before the cutoff date. Of the 1,670 surveys, 317 were returned by men. The largest number of responses from individual states came from Colorado, California, Iowa, Florida, Louisiana, Michigan, Texas, and Ohio.

The Latest Findings

Back in 1994, 71 percent of our female respondents reported that they had been undermined by another female and 58 percent by a man; 20 percent of the male respondents reported that they had been sabotaged by a woman with an increase to 60 percent by another man. In 1999, I took another look at conflict and sabotage in the general workplace, this time with 5000 respondents from multiple work environments (*Woman to Woman 2000*, New Horizon Press). Only five years had elapsed and the level of undermining behavior had not decreased, it increased. In the health care sector of that survey, the percentage (34 percent) reporting undermining and conflict activities *increased to 81 percent*. As the 2002 survey showed, sabotage and conflict has not gone away, it has only intensified.

It's not unusual for potshots to be directed at any type of research. Purists would like to see multiple types of testing done that measure null hypothesis to populations that include mega thousands. I know, I've been there. In the past, I've done multiple national surveys that included testing for significant differences in various populations for both my Masters and Doctorate in Business Administration degrees. Elements included were engaging outside organizations that specialized in gathering data; random calling and mailings involving thousands using selected databases that were relevant to the population; distribution to all members of an entire association; and distributing written surveys during a six-month period to my audiences. At all times, respondents were able to use multiple selection of possible answers, including sections for writing fill-ins. Surveys were followed up with one-on-one interviews.

With advent of the Internet, times are changing. Researchers and probers like myself can reach thousands in a very short period of time. What's fascinating about the Internet is that surveys can get directed to more venues than can be imagined.

The *Conflict Survey* used for this book was distributed in three ways. First, it was posted on my website, *www.Briles.com* and announced to approximately 3,000 email addresses that had obtained various articles that I've written and are posted on the site. Second, I was routinely asked by managers within hospitals and offices if they could print the survey out and have their teams take it—the answer was always yes with a request to mail or fax results to my offices (many did). And third, many respondents emailed colleagues to go to the site and take the survey. At my cutoff date, 1670 women and men had responded. The responses received after the closing date paralleled the others already analyzed.

The theme of conflict was woven into every question of the survey. The first question asked was, *Has conflict increased, decreased or has there been no change in the respondent's workplace?* The overwhelming majority said yes, it had increased with 85 percent of the managers/administrators and 88 percent of staff reporting so. None of the staff had said it decreased (7.5 percent of managers/administrators replied it had) and 12 percent of the staff reported no change with 7.5 percent of the managers/administrators stating the same.

Has conflict increased, decreased or has there been no change in your workplace?

	Managers/ Administrators	Staff/ Employees
Increased	85.0%	88%
Decreased	7.5%	0%
No change	7.5%	12%

Figure 2.1

I've been speaking within health care for over 15 years and strongly believed that conflict and sabotaging activities had increased from the ongoing dialogues with conference and in-hospital personnel as well as from the input of several of the speaker-trainers that are in my network and whom I routinely encounter at health care conferences. Many of them have graciously taken their time to review the results and given feedback. Their thoughts and comments appear throughout this book as well as their contact information at the end of the book under *Speakers and Consultants Who Deliver Results.*

My next question was simply, *Why—as in why has conflict increased?* Respondents were able to choose multiple reasons and write in additional ones.

If conflict has increased, what is/are the key cause(s) of the increase?

	Managers/ Administrators	Staff/ Employees
Too much change	**40%**	**29%**
Mergers	31%	27%
Downsizing	**38%**	**22%**
Workforce not committed	31%	24%
Confusion	30%	34%
Too much turnover	**30%**	**41%**
Not enough turnover	15%	7%
Education training reduced	**4%**	**34%**
Employees unmotivated	**8%**	**27%**
Employees incompetent	**30%**	**15%**
Employees underpaid	**19%**	**39%**
Employees overpaid	15%	5%
Management unmotivated	**19%**	**34%**
Management incompetent	**8%**	**32%**
Management underpaid	**15%**	**5%**
Management overpaid	8%	15%
Management follows fads	11%	12%
Management unclear with goals, objectives	**19%**	**68%**
Poor retention	4%	12%
Nursing shortage	**4%**	**15%**

Note—significant variances are in **bold** type.

Figure 2.2

Comments on causes will be looked at in depth in other sections throughout *Zapping Conflict in the Health Care Workplace*.

Who's Who?

Who was who in our survey? Nineteen percent were male and 81 percent female, not surprising for a health care sampling. Of the entire total, 57 percent identified themselves as employees-staff and 43 percent management-administration. Very few of the physicians and dentists (5 percent) in the sample consider themselves as managers or administrators—they either were employees of an organization or they hired others to fill that function in their offices.

Breakdown of Respondents		
Male	19%	(317)
Female	81%	(1353)
Staff Nurse	43%	(719)
Physician-Dentists	5%	(83)
Manager-Administrator	42%	(701)
Other (technicians, educators, clerical dental hygienists, assistants)	10%	(167)

Figure 2.3

Women and Men and the Generations Are Different

When it comes to dealing with conflict and sabotage, women and men tackle the problems in different ways. So do the different generations. The GenXers and Yers (or Millennials or Nexters, depending on who you talk to) aren't afraid of confronting conflict and sabotaging behavior, where the Boomers and Maturers (aka Veterans) would rather it just go away. One of the biggest differences that was acknowledged by respondents was that the younger generations weren't afraid to deal with it, but their people skills were sorely lacking, thus offending many in their path.

Is there a difference in the way generations handle conflict?

	Managers/ Administrators	Staff/ Employees
Yes	85%	71%
No	15%	29%

Figure 2.4

Researchers see a significant difference within the generations. Robert Wendover is the CEO of the Center for Generational Studies in Colorado. Wendover reports that the generations, specifically the GenXers and Baby Boomers, have a very different take on handling conflict,

> GenXers are very outcome oriented, Boomers are task oriented. GenXers don't understand why Boomers put energy into tasks where an outcome isn't created and measured—it's a waste of time for them. When it comes to an issue that is generated from conflicts, their style is to jump in—decorum and diplomacy aren't their strengths.

With conflict, managers and administrators were more inclined to feel that it was caused and created in a variety of areas that they couldn't control—mergers, downsizing, workforce not being committed, too much change, turnover and confusion, and employees being incompetent.

Staff narrowed the primary cause of conflict to management being unclear with goals and objectives for the organization and their respective departments, followed by employees being underpaid, educational training reduced, management being incompetent, and confusion (see Figure 2.2).

Denial and Realty . . . Can They Co-exist?

We asked several questions about how conflict was handled—employee to employee, manager to employee and employee to manager. We also asked each respondent how they rated in handling conflict.

Beginning with, *How do your employees handle conflict?* and *How does your manager handle conflict?*, we found that a significant percentage of the managers felt that their staff and employees jumped in too soon before they knew what the facts were (46 percent) and 12 percent of the employees declared so. Employees and staff, on the other hand, thought that their managers ignored conflict (36 percent) where only 11.5 percent of managers admitted to ignoring it. Interestingly, 20 percent of the staff respondents believed that the managers and administrators created it.

When asked, *What happens when there is conflict within your area of management or workplace?*, variances also were apparent. The majority of the managers claimed that they acted as mediators (69 percent) and less than 10 percent reported they ignored it. Staff/employees had a different take about their managers, 36 percent said the managers

How do your employees handle conflict?
(For managers to respond only)
How does your manager handle conflict?
(For staff to respond only)

	Managers/ Administrators Say About Staff	Staff/ Employees Say About Managers
Ignore It	11.5%	36%
Create it	11.5%	20%
Thrive with it	11.5%	5%
Resolve it	8.0%	12%
Jump in too soon before knowing the facts	46.0%	12%
Tries to find out details before giving input	11.5%	15%

Figure 2.5

ignored conflict (see Figure 2.5). Fifteen percent of the managers told their employees to settle their differences.

Staff respondents had two areas that dominated their responses. They reported that they told co-workers to settle their differences (56 percent) and over a third of them confessed that they simply ignored it in their workplaces (34 percent). Staff was not inclined to act as a mediator with only 2.5 percent saying they took that role and very few of the staff respondents told co-workers to stop it by telling them what to do. None of the managers said that they told staff members how to stop it by telling them what to do.

> ### When conflict occurs within your area of management or workplace, I . . .
>
> | | Managers/ Administrators Say About Selves | Staff/ Employees Say About Selves |
> |---|---|---|
> | Ignore it | 8% | 34.0% |
> | Thrive with it | 8% | 5.0% |
> | Tell employees to settle their differences | 15% | 56.0% |
> | Act as mediator | 69% | 2.5% |
> | Stop it by telling them what to do | 0% | 2.5% |
>
> Figure 2.6

How you believe you personally handle conflict can be quite telling, especially when you get input from others. It's not surprising when the outside looking in doesn't mirror the inside looking out. When our respondents were asked how they personally handled conflict, most gave themselves an "OK" to "great" rating. In looking at the both Figure 2.5 and 2.6, it's clear that neither the managers or the staff get high marks.

The Cost Factor

A few years ago, I had a consulting contract with the mother ship of a hospital system. I was appalled at the level of duplicity among several of the staff, right under the noses of the senior administrators. The reported actions of the staff members toward others within the staff didn't surprise

How do you rate yourself in handling conflict employee to employee?		
	Managers/ Administrators Say About Selves	Staff/ Employees Say About Selves
Great	15%	10%
OK	54%	49%
Need Improvement	31%	34%
Not So Hot	0%	7%

Figure 2.7

me nor did the overall inattentiveness to the problem from bosses and administrators—nothing was really new. I'd heard about it, seen it, and experienced it repeatedly since I had focused on the health care workplace in the early nineties.

After multiple interviews and training sessions, I wrote a detailed report and made recommendations on how to deal with the three women who were the primary creators of the conflicting behaviors among the 15 women who worked there. The administrators were told that if they didn't deal with it fairly quickly, they would lose several key employees.

What happened? *Nothing, absolutely nothing.* Well, nothing with my recommendations. Within their office, several key employees tossed in the towel and said, "I've had it . . . enough is enough," and sought work elsewhere. When will management learn?

The costs are huge. Employees and staff members re-

How do you rate yourself in handling conflict with
your employee (manager) or co-worker (staff)?

	Managers/ Administrators Say About Employee	Staff/ Employees Say About Co-worker
Great	15%	10%
OK	65%	56%
Needs Improvement	20%	24%
Not So Hot	0%	10%

Figure 2.8

ported that it took them two to four times as long to complete their work, their morale nosedives, loyalty is diminished and their work becomes just a job and another paycheck. Recruiters will tell you that it could take an entire year's salary to replace someone.

Replacement is not pocket change—ongoing conflict and sabotage that is not acknowledged and dealt with costs individual health care organizations MILLIONS of dollars each year.

The Cost—His, Hers and the Organization

Significantly, men and women not only have different styles of conflicting and sabotaging behaviors, but the results of their action also are different. Male and female victims have different experiences. It's as if the men and women are playing in different ballgames; not only are the rules and players different, but so are the strikes and fouls.

How? When men sabotage or create conflict with another, the effects are usually fairly straightforward—a loss of money or a lost promotion. In our survey, women are much more likely to be guilty of other less tangible costs, including causing their victims embarrassment or damaged reputations.

Why such differences? Again, it probably goes back to the different agendas of men and women and what is more important to each. Men tend to be pragmatically oriented: when they decide to do someone in, they do so for what appears to be more practical reasons—to get more money or to get the other's job. They are, likewise, more sensitive to losing money themselves when they are the victim. Women focused more on emotional factors, and, to a greater extent than did men, caused their victims to suffer other losses, such as embarrassment and damaged reputations. Many women who are saboteurs leave their victims in financial binds or cause the loss of jobs. But after such a loss, the victim is more likely to feel other types of devastation than he or she would if betrayed by a man.

When it comes to damaging an organization, both men and women are successful. The biggest issue that these organizations are more likely to lose on are money, business and good employees. One of the best ways to eliminate the health care shortage gap and increase retention is to make an extensive effort to reduce the behaviors that create conflict and sabotage.

Gains and Losses from Conflict and Sabotage

Not only do men and women have different styles of undermining, the impact of their behavior toward women is different. Women reported that when they had been undermined by anyone, a man or a woman, the primary cost was embarrassment and loss of credibility. When undermined by another woman, 61 percent of the survey respondents reported so, while 74 percent reported embarrassment after having been undermined by a man. This discrepancy may be due to the male-female roles that society dictates. A woman may be more likely to feel that she must have done something to cause the other person to undermine her, particularly if the person has a higher status than she does. In most cases, the person with higher status, such as a physician, is a man. But when she is undermined by another woman, she will feel that they are on more equal footing; her reaction is more likely to include anger.

One cost area where there was a minimal difference related to gender, was in jobs and promotions. When women were undermined by another woman, 25 percent lost jobs or promotions. When undermined by a man, 23 percent lost jobs or promotions.

Women employers seemed to fare better. They stated that when the undermining behavior was performed by a woman employee, the primary cost was embarrassment, followed by low morale. When the undermining came from a man, the primary cost to the employer was perceived by women to be nothing; it was as though when a man undermined a woman, it was acceptable—no big deal.

Does society (or the workplace) expect men to display inappropriate, unsupportive, undermining behavior? Women's responses indicated that this may be so. Therefore, there may be less severe reactions or responses to inappropriate behavior by men: it comes with the territory, it's expected and accepted. In health care, the majority of practicing doctors, senior doctors, are still men, and most hospitals, health care associations, medical and dental practices subscribe to the premise that they are in the business of supporting the doctor's need.

When one person sabotages another, the saboteur seeks to gain something, while the sabotaged person may lose something. In the previous studies, we've found that the respondents said that when they were undermined by another woman, the primary benefit (and goal) to the saboteur was an enhanced reputation, more power, or getting a promotion or job.

If the saboteur was a man, enhanced reputation or more power was the goal. Very few reported men gaining jobs or promotions through sabotage. In health care, as in business, men already occupy most positions of authority; they may not see any other gains but enhanced reputations or visibility.

Nothing was the answer that 17 percent of the respondents gave when asked what an employer gained by a woman's unethical behavior. If an employer were to gain anything from a man's unethical behavior, 5 percent of the respondents stated, it would be the employer's enhanced reputation or visibility; otherwise, the majority of respondents said, employers gained nothing when men undermined them. Losses to the employer were another matter. Whether the saboteurs were men or women, loss of reputation, of employees' loyalty, of employees' productivity, of credibility, of team growth, and of effectiveness were all factors.

Money Talks . . .

The financial costs are unbelievable, ranging from lost productivity to placement fees for new personnel. Replacement experts and health care organizations report that replacing an employee, especially in a "shortage" environment like nursing, can range anywhere from $20,000 to $96,000, depending on location and speciality of the RN. If you have frontline turnover in a hospital of 15 percent (which many consider low and would actually like to achieve!) and have a minimum of 500 employees, turnover in the workplace can cost anywhere from $1,500,000 to $7,200,000 in replacement costs alone. A large percentage of that can be attributed to conflict and sabotage. Big, big bucks.

Now, add in the lower productivity issue. Employees reported that when unresolved conflict and sabotage are active in their areas and departments, it takes two to four times as long to get their work done. Using data from the Department of Labor for the number of women in the workplace coupled with the medium income and the reported percentage stating that they have or are experienced undermining activities, the problem grows to multi-billions a year.

> **Organizations are collectively losing a minimum of $38,000,000,000 a year due to lost productivity. Sabotage and conflict in the workplace is not a light-weight issue, nor should it be treated as one. Unfortunately, it is.**

Summing Up

If conflict is a situation when two or more people are at opposite positions in a situation or circumstance, then the results of the *Conflict Survey* are certainly confirmed. In the health care environment, it's not just co-workers who have conflicts and experience sabotage in their workplaces. Rather, conflict is woven throughout the organization. No level is immune. With the increasing levels of change that are fueled from multiple sources, conflict and sabotage will only accelerate within the workplace. Whether it's addressed and viable resolutions are implemented will be the choice of every member within the organization. If it's not, morale dives, loyalty diminishes, teams are splintered, distrust grows and turn-over increases.

You would wonder why an organization would choose to kiss off millions of dollars a year when investing in the "softer skills" of communicating more effectively and conflict resolution for both staff and managers could create a win-win environment. I contend that these skills are as important as the clinical ones.

The Survey Speaks—What Respondents Say About Sabotage

3

E veryone plays—women and men. Men don't discriminate, women do. The findings from all five of my surveys (1987, 1994, 1996, 1999, and 2002) indicate that women are more likely to sabotage other women than they are men and to allow conflict to simmer without dealing with it. If a man is a saboteur, gender is not an issue; the target can be either sex. Men and women also engage in different styles: women are more inclined to be covert and indirect when it comes to sabotage and creating conflict, while men are more overt and direct.

The Dark Side

Conflict and sabotage go hand-in-hand and no book about conflict, especially in the health care arena, can ignore the dark side of the workplace where shadow movements often dictate horrendous behaviors and outcomes. A contributory

Sabotage is the erosion or destruction of your personal or professional credibility or reputation. It can be administered intentionally or unintentionally through overt or covert methods. If *sabotage* is not resolved within a timely manner, morale dives, loyalty diminishes, teams are splintered, distrust grows and turn-over increases.

Ongoing *sabotage* costs an organization multi-millions of dollars a year in lost productivity, search fees and training for replacement of personnel.

factor to the dark side of the health care workplace is the overwhelming majority of women in specific areas (nursing, dental hygienists, assistants, clerical staff) and men in specific areas (administrators). A third of the women surveyed still report that if they had their druthers, they would prefer to work with men. As a woman working in health care—dream on, it's not going to happen, not in your lifetime.

For years, I've pondered why women say this. The survey used for this book represents the fifth national one that included the question, *"If you had your druthers, do you prefer working with men, women or it doesn't matter."* Each time, approximately one-third of the respondents say they would rather work with men, not women. I've come to the conclusion that it surfaces because of the differences between men and women when sabotage and conflict exists—creating it and dealing with it. When it is done by a male, it is usually out in the open, the perpetrator even openly taking credit for the behavior and letting the victim know ahead of time what is coming. As if it were a game.

Women are different. Conflict and sabotage is not something usually carried in the brag bag. No, when it is created by another woman, it's usually behind the scenes, similar to the wind. You can feel it, you just aren't sure where it starts from. So, when women often say they would rather work with men, it means that at least they know what's on the table. Still a game, but the rules are easier to understand.

Why?

Why should this be? Four key words summarize the findings: *change, opportunity, power* and *increased competition* in today's workplace. Women are more likely to sabotage each other simply because women are more likely to work together and because they are viewed as weaker due to their lack of experience, not knowing the rules, or being naive and too trusting. Women are also less likely to deal directly with conflict. Rather, their general preference is to take it back to co-workers by discussing, grumbling or complaining about it.

In addition to power and opportunity, the ramifications of fear, jealousy, envy, and low self-esteem surfaced in our interviews. Titles usually carry a form of power—some earned, some assumed. If a man or woman is in power but has a low self-esteem, it's improbable that subordinates or co-workers are going to be treated fairly. If a person doesn't feel good about who he or she is or confidence in what he or she is doing, then those feelings will permeate the work environment.

The question arises: do most women follow the same style of sabotaging and handling conflict that has been traditional in the male-dominated business world? Do they create, work through or avoid conflict in their workplaces? Those questions become particularly important now. Many women feel that they are at a distinct disadvantage in getting ahead because of years of prior disrespect, discrimination and prejudice. If additional barriers are added by women to restrict other women, the resulting blockades become almost insurmountable. It's not surprising that many in the nursing field feel that their only way to get ahead, to get paid more, is by unionizing. Maybe . . . and maybe not—it's not a black and white issue.

It also appears that women were more likely to be motivated to sabotage another out of fear, which usually can be traced to the power imbalance of men and women. Women are more fearful, more threatened because generally they are further down the power ladder. The most common reasons why many women commit sabotage were that they were jealous, envious, or even afraid someone was after their jobs.

Men, on the other hand, were more likely to undermine another to build up their egos, reflecting this traditional male push to be assertive. Men, much more so than women, failed to give someone else credit for their work or misrepresented it as theirs. Then, too, men were usually the ones accused of sexism or sexual harassment.

Women also sabotage for power reasons just as men do. Women's power is more generally over other women; if there is sabotaging behavior, the recipient is more likely to be another woman. Failing to give credit or taking credit for work completed by others was at the top of the behavior list, along with the spreading of wrong or malicious gossip. Victims of bullying behavior fight back, but rarely at the perpetrator. Instead, the employer is the recipient of vented feelings (or other co-workers).

Few of the male respondents reported this experience in their dealings with women. It's not always clear if their actions were intentional, yet the great majority felt that when sabotage was happening, it was *intentional* (90 percent).

The person who targets another individual for downfall does so to gain certain ends. As to the reasons for such behavior, the views of the men and women surveyed differed notably. Both men and women agreed on basic motivations for a man or woman sabotaging another. Most of the time they believed the man or woman wanted more money, more credibility or a better reputation, but not necessarily all three.

Differences suggest that men and women are coming to the workplace with dissimilar rules and motivations that affect how they act and what is important to them. The men surveyed were much more likely to think the individual acted to gain money. Men are more likely to be concerned about money, and they think other men are, also.

In contrast, for women, who have been spectators or second-string players within their organizations, the crucial elements of the game are quite different. Money may be central for some, but there are many other important factors that motivate their sabotaging behavior, when they are outside the main arena. Issues such as personal esteem, reputation, and embarrassment seem especially significant for most women. Women traditionally have been concerned about their images to others, so reputation and self-esteem are high on their agendas.

For men, the main goals of business success center on bottom line factors. Most men been traditionally brought up to measure success in material terms and this credo shows in the reasons why some men are unethical to others and the losses men experience when they become victims themselves. There are other issues that come up for men, of course, when sabotage surfaces, but men in the survey repeatedly mentioned money. Women felt that the motivation for sabotaging behavior was a better reputation and credibility, especially when a woman sabotaged another woman. The difference appears to relate to the different agenda men and women have. The exception is that women who head their own practices were the most likely to report about negative money issues rather than women who were hired employees.

ZAP Tip
Too many health care organizations—
from hospitals, educational institutes or offices
with a physician or dentist at the helm—foster
a lack of respect toward support and frontline
personnel. The result is substantial—
dysfunctional workplaces, low morale,
lack of trust and loyalty and high levels
of unresolved conflict—all a breeding ground
for sabotage and more conflict.

Saboteurs-by-Proxy and Serial Saboteurs

Two new terms/phrases were created after an interview with an East Coast based pediatric neurologist. Martha contacted me after reading my first book on health care's toxic workplace and shared a horrendous story about a nurse on her staff who was always the last person to find/deliver the "answer" or "missing item" when chaos was in play. After several months of keeping track of and documenting actions and behavior, the doctor concluded that the nurse was creating the chaos by hiding things, so that when they were found, she (the nurse) would be viewed as vital—important and very needed in the practice. She shared,

For several years, my workplace was fairly positive. We had our share of normal conflicts and they would get resolved. When cutbacks started about three years ago, my primary nurse was a case manager. Jackie did a good job. With the cutbacks, she took on the role of charge nurse for the entire floor plus her duties as the case manager.

Things didn't work well. After a year of requests to Administration for additional help, I finally got a Nurse Practitioner to assist me. Things were no longer efficient as they had been. At the end of the day, there were still 25-30 messages and phone calls not returned.

I took a family leave of absence for a few months. My Nurse Practitioner began to have problems with Jackie in my absence. Parents were complaining that neither she nor I returned calls—we never even knew that they had come in! The pharmacy would call my office about various prescriptions, including ones that no one could recall placing.

When I returned from my leave, I focused on making my practice better. I couldn't figure out why things weren't working well. After months of keeping track, and documenting, everything came back to my nurse. Information I would receive from her would be incomplete or wrong. Information that I sought was often withheld or delayed. She grumbled and complained about everything, including all personnel.

One day, documents and files were missing for Grand Rounds. Both the clerk and Nurse Practitioner ripped the office apart looking for it—it was nowhere to be found. Amazingly, Jackie found it 20 minutes later and said that it had been in the Nurse

Practitioner's office all along. We all knew that it wasn't true.

The straw that broke the camel's back was when the hospital pharmacist called me questioning the dosage for a prescription that he said my Nurse Practitioner had called in. If the child had taken it, most likely severe damage would have resulted. She hadn't called one in in this case, but her name was on it. Someone else had made the call using her name.

Munchausen-by-Proxy is where an adult physically harms her child by inducing illness and or injury to get attention. The Saboteur-by-Proxy only varies her (and it is usually a her in either case) action. The target isn't physically harmed or admitted for medical care as in Munchausen-by-Proxy. Rather, the action usually leads to the target questioning her mental health and professional competencies. The problem is the invisible target. In Martha's case, her patients filled that role. If the wrong prescription/ dosage had been given to the child, a crisis would have been created. Most like, severe damage, a possible death and a major lawsuit. A real attention getter.

Saboteurs-by-Proxy demonstrate a need to be needed— they're rescuers (creating a scenario that others need them—that they are the only competent people to fix/do it, whatever it is). They can do it themselves, or get someone else to do the deed(s), whatever the deed is.

In the case of Martha, repeated requests for help from her Administrator were made. She was continually told that the situations she reported concerns about were in her mind; that Jackie was the best of the best nurses and highly acclaimed by the male doctors. Martha finally threw in the towel and submitted her resignation. She refused to continue to work in an environment that would ignore the circumstances and put her and her patients in jeopardy.

Where Saboteurs-by-Proxy are individuals who constantly call attention to themselves as Serial Saboteurs do, the latter are women and men who create a situation—or situations—repeatedly. Getting direct attention isn't usually the goal—creating chaos and difficult situations for others is. These players (women and men who get others to create situations over and over again) usually make their workplaces so miserable that the good people leave, just as Martha shared.

Caron is a new director in a hospital that is in the process of expanding it's women and children's services. Under her umbrella, she oversees OB, L&D, NICU, Peds, general GYN needs and Mammography. Shortly after accepting the position, she noticed a series of activities that just didn't feel right. Reports were missing, some of the staff acted defiant, it was noted that unauthorized personnel information had been taken, and there was overall general unrest. As she probed, she learned that many of the activities could be directly tracked to Erica, a nurse who worked the evening shift in Labor & Delivery and had been employed for 15 years at the hospital. Caron's words,

> Working nights, especially L&D, can be grueling. There's less staff and the doctors rely heavily on the nurses to assist them in the assessment of a patient's progress during her labor. Erica was viewed as an essential member of the L&D staff and was held in a high respect (and gratitude) by many of the doctors.
>
> Our hospital is not union, but there have been union activities to organize, all of which have been unsuccessful to date. Erica believed that having union

representation within the hospital was a good idea and signed on to help organize it.

Initially, it started with the "whisper" campaign. Rumors about my competency, both as a nurse and manager, were bandied around the unit and circulated on all shifts. I found that remarks and suggestions I made at meetings were reworded on an ongoing basis. I would find that things would be missing from my office days and nights. I discovered that written memos I had created mysteriously disappeared. And, I was even told by one of the other directors that she was told that I had been fired from my previous position.

It was though I had become the "It Girl"—nothing I did or said carried any weight. Finally, one of the day nurses responded to my thinking-out-loud exasperation. She told me that Erica had approached several of the staff to "assist" her in a negative campaign against me. "Why?" I asked her. Her response, "She believed that you wouldn't support the union and if she could get others to give you a bad time and make you look bad, she could get rid of you."

Caron went on to share that she personally discovered that Erica had taken personnel records in her union organizer's cap that violated confidentially. She immediately suspended her.

When we began an investigation into Erica's activities, it was a Pandora's Box. Her skills as a nurse were excellent, and they may have been as a union organizer. Her ethics, we soon learned, were undeniably questionable. The doctors loved worked with her. After she was gone a few weeks, staff began to talk. A great deal of the talk wasn't too positive and eventually revealed that Erica had done a number of things that not only undermined the collaborative effort I was trying to create, but also jeopardized the integrity of the entire organization. After a formal hearing, Erica was terminated for cause.

Serial Saboteurs and Saboteurs-by-Proxy can now be recognized for the negative impact they create for all. These "Berts" and "Berthas" of the workplace are masters at creating disharmony among and within all levels of the organization. They are entrenched in most organizations and the cost is huge. Martha, the pediatric neurologist, estimated the cost of replacing a specialist in her field could run to a quarter of a million dollars. Caron estimated the cost of exposing and confronting Erica cost her organization in excess of $100,000 in legal fees and replacement costs.

Does It Matter Who Does What to Whom?

All of our previous surveys elicited information as to whether men and women differ in whom they choose to sabotage. Does it matter whether their victim is a woman or a man? It depends. There appears to be a big difference of opinion between most men and most women on this point. Most of the women in our survey believed that when a man sabotaged them it was because they were women, and, as already mentioned, many of the women accused men of sexism and sexual harassment. However, the men didn't think their sex had anything to do with it. They believed that those who sabotaged them did so because of other reasons, as in, they wanted my job or money.

Are There Preferences for Specific Behavior?

Are there any other connections? If there is so much sabotaging and conflict going on, can it be determined who is most likely to get hurt, the innocent victim or the saboteur? What about preferences? If the people who work together tend to both help and sabotage each other more, do people who prefer to work with one gender or the other differ from those who don't in their experiences with sabotaging behavior? And finally, do the reasons people for choosing to work with others have anything to do with what happens to them?

The results of our survey showed that to some extent sabotage begets more sabotage; either in the form of Serial Sabotage or retaliation. In other words, if sabotaged, a person most often fights back by using sabotage. Not many of the respondents said they had been accused of doing any sabotage themselves: only 14 percent of the respondents said so, and the vast majority of these—87 percent—said there was no basis for the accusation. As it turned out, those who were accused of sabotage were more likely to report that someone else sabotaged them. For example, only 2 percent of the respondents who said no one had sabotage them were accused of sabotaging another, but around 15 percent were accused of sabotaging behavior themselves.

But there was a much stronger connection between helpfulness and preference for working with men or women. Those who preferred working with a woman or a man were more likely to find that person helpful than those who had no such preferences. Over 70 percent of those with a preference for working with women found them helpful, compared to 63 percent with no preference; almost 90 percent of those expressing a preference for men felt this way, compared to 74 percent with none.

Some of the reasons given for preferences reflected traditional stereotypes about the way women can be as well as about the styles of sabotaging behavior talked about earlier. Those expressing a preference for working with women, did so because of emotional factors: They had a personal bias toward women or thought they needed support from other women.

But those women and men who expressed a preference for working with men often stated that they believed men were less petty, less likely to play games, or less prone to personality problems. They tended to convey opinions that many women display sabotaging behavior by being deceptive, vindictive, and covert in what they do.

With the increase in women studying medicine and dentistry, they now comprise 40 to 50 percent of medical and dental school students. We found that women doctors who had been trained in an authoritarian manner in medical or dental schools, internships, and residencies tended to display more verbal abuse and undermining of their general workplace relationships. Women doctors who had been trained in or practiced participative management were far less likely to engage in verbal abuse or to undermine work relationships. There was a greater degree of respect all around.

The most common types of this behavior reported were verbal abuse in front of colleagues and unprofessional conduct in doctors. This was followed by personal harassment (13 percent), discrimination (11 percent), and gossip (9 percent). Undermining of work relations was also the number one complaint about men (34 percent). Within that grouping, 43 percent of the respondents said they had been verbally abused, and 23 percent said they had been sexually harassed (the respondents separated derogatory remarks from verbal abuse, but most derogatory comments contained sexual innuendo).

The question arises of why women would purposely undermine and sabotage other women in an environment that is supposed to reflect nurturing, caring, and getting well. Do nurses (and other health care professionals) "eat their young," as many stated in the follow-up interviews?

What behavior causes sabotage?

By a woman:

Work relations undermined	65%
Personal harassment	13%
Discrimination	11%
Gossip	9%
Lies	7%
Taking credit	6%

By a man:

Work relations undermined	34%
Sexual harassment	23%
Unprofessional conduct	23%
Derogatory comments	15%
Discrimination	10%
Lies	7%

Figure 3.1

Why? In health care, men usually run things. Women may rise to a specific level (such as VP of Nursing, Chief Nursing Officer, VP of Patient Care, Director or VP of Human Resources or office manager) but then they stop. Most hit their salary ceiling within a few years after employment. Thus, in the "velvet ghetto" of health care, where 70 plus percent of employees are female, women's power is generally over *other women*. If there is going to be unethical behavior—whatever it is, the object will most likely be another woman. Therefore, while women and men may be equally unethical, women are more likely to sabotage other women because other women are the co-workers whom they have the *opportunity* to undermine.

Different Visions

Men and women come to the workplace with dissimilar rules and motivations that affect how they act and dictate what is important. Usually, for men, the main focus is on bottom-line factors: success in material terms, doing a job or task for money. Historically, women's work was often a stopgap measure, or simply something to do. Money is now a factor for women, of course, but there are others: reputation, visibility, and self-esteem all rank high.

In health care, people can be viewed as players on a field. The main players are key hospital administrators and doctors. The doctors do most of the "scoring." Their focus is on what the score is (how many patients, how much revenue generated), how to increase the score for themselves (higher fees, bigger payouts), and how to keep others from making gains (greater clout within health care's exclusive specialties).

The spectators and supporting players, nurses (93 percent plus female) and dental hygienists (99 percent female), don't usually have the same focus on scoring. They become more interested in tangential things. The main players gain satisfaction from seeing or interacting with other spectators (the "old boys" network). The supporting players are interested in being noticed, so that they can build up their own reputations and be chosen more often to play in the game. Since so many of the supporting players are women, the bigger fees and payouts are not their primary focus, as women are less likely to be in important executive positions.

Conflict Creators & Saboteurs in the Midst

One question that arises is whether a female saboteur would purposely target another woman. In the 1994 survey (health care professionals only), I asked whether the saboteur's action had anything to do with the respondent's being a woman or a man. I found 52 percent who said yes—that the action directed against them by a woman was a direct reflection of their gender; 38 percent said no, and 10 percent were not sure. Of the same respondents, 76 percent who stated that a man had sabotaged them because of their gender; 20 percent said men had not, and 4 percent were not sure.

In the 1999 survey (general workplace with one-third of the 5000 respondents from the health care professions), the results were basically a mirror to the 1993 results.

In 2002, the health care professionals pushed the envelope. An *increase to 81 percent* said that the action was directed at them because of their gender, 16 percent said no and three percent weren't sure.

Since my original survey in 1987, I found a big difference of opinion between most men and women on this point. Most of the women in the original survey believed that when a man treated them unethically, he was taking advantage of them because they were women with the primary charge being that of sexism and sexual harassment. Men didn't think that their gender had anything to do with being sabotaged; they believed that those who acted unethically toward them did so because of other reasons.

Support, Lack of Support and a Mentor or Two . . .

There are always two sides to every coin. The flip side of not supporting someone is helping someone in the work-place. In the study, I looked for connections between who supports and who doesn't support another. Those who usually have the power to help also have the power to hinder.

In the interviews, it often appeared that the same people who were unsupportive also offered help at times. Although the majority responded that other women had undermined them, there is good news: the majority also said that they had been actively helped by a woman (89 percent), and actively helped by a man (68 percent). With a greater female population in the health care field, it's logical that more women would report being helped as well as harmed by other women.

When we asked if gender had anything to do with the amount of help received, 71 percent said it did not when the help came from women, and 89 percent said their gender had nothing to do with help from a male.

Mentoring is important for both women and men. Neither gender got high marks in this area. Only a quarter of our respondents reported that another had actively mentored them, be it a male or female. The good news is that the percentage increased from 14 percent in 1994 to 24 percent in 2002. Men reported little mentoring as managers and frontline staff (10 percent); those in upper management reported a greater percentage (36 percent).

Preference

Since health care is predominantly women working to-gether, some might assume that women would choose to work in health care because of that factor. Our respondents stated that they do choose to work with women (30 percent), or that they have no preference for working with either sex (36 percent). An alarming 34 percent stated that they preferred not to work with women. This is no different from our previous study of the health care field. Women said they did not care to work with women because women are untrustworthy, backbiting, backstabbing, covert, gossipy, unsure of themselves, and not business-like.

In workshops I conduct for both managers and staff, backstabbing is one of the most common phrases used when associated with females. Men didn't carry the backstabbing tag. They were more inclined to be identified as front-stabbers.

The reasons they gave for preferring to work with men were that men are more straightforward, businesslike, job-oriented, and clearer about what the rules are.

For 15 years, the above percentages, with a percent or two varying, have stood in each of the surveys done—workplace populations were incidental—be they mostly female, or mixed.

Giving and Getting

There was a connection between helpfulness and preferences. Those who had a gender preference were more likely to find that the preferred gender was more helpful than those who had no such preference. It's important to note that some of the reasons given for preferences do reflect traditional stereotypes about how women behave, as well as the styles of unethical behavior discussed earlier. Respondents who prefer to work with women may have a personal bias toward women or feel they need support from other women.

Those respondents who expressed a preference for working with men stated they believed men were less petty, less

---

Do you prefer to work with men or women or does it matter?

Women reporting:

Prefer to work with women	30%
Prefer to work with men	34%
It doesn't matter	36%

Figure 3.2

---

likely to play games, or less likely to have personal or emotional problems (no one in the returned surveys referred to premenstrual syndrome or menopause). They also tended to say that women who act unethically and undermine others do so by being deceptive, vindictive, and covert.

Friendships

Every survey questionnaire has asked the respondents if they had developed friendships at work. In 1993, 70 percent said yes. In 2002, the affirmative response increased to 76 percent. Reasons given by those who said no included needing to be more careful, needing more time to develop friendships, preferring only professional relationships with co-workers, thinking friendships should be avoided with employees, and being shy, selective, or too busy.

Respondents were also asked whether they regretted having befriended a woman or a man at work. We found that 45 percent regretted befriending another women and 13 percent regretted befriending a man in the workplace in 2002, no change from the previous survey. In training workshops, I find that the response is greater—more than half routinely say that they have regretted befriending another woman.

Do You Develop Friendships Quickly at Work?

Women reporting:

Yes	76%
No	20%
No response	4%

Do You Regret Developing Friendships at Work

Women reporting:

With women	47%
With men	11%

Figure 3.3

Reasons given for regretting friendships with women included misuse of personal information, being stabbed in the back, false friendship, manipulation, and getting too personal. With men, the reasons included sexual harassment, personal harassment, dishonesty, and being manipulated. One woman psychiatrist said that she had befriended a woman, invited her home, and introduced her to her family. The new "friend" ended up having an affair with her husband, which led to a divorce. Having a friend pursue my spouse sounds like pretty blatant sabotage to me.

Summing Up

All our studies suggest that men may be better able to strike back, and do strike back (or others perceive that they do). In contrast, women who are less powerful are often less likely to be accused of action directed at men, since there are fewer men at their level. Others are less likely to perceive women as aggressors. If a woman is going to be an aggressor, she will direct her attention at an individual who she believes or perceives to have less power in the workplace—another woman. If an individual feels oppressed, they act out by creating conflict, by becoming saboteurs in the midst. Horizontal violence becomes a reality and Serial Saboteurs and Saboteurs-by-Proxy multiply.

The bottom line is that it's a power game. Unfortunately, our culture translates success into dollars, and inappropriate behavior becomes part of it. To change conflicting and sabotaging behaviors, we must come to terms with power issues. Their dynamics need to be investigated and explored. Finally, a method of dealing with power needs to be established in ways that will be beneficial to both women and men in the health care field.

Both genders create conflict and practice the art of sabotage, although their styles and methods are different. But sabotaging behavior is not genetic. It is learned, and it can be unlearned. Resolving conflict can be learned; creating it, unlearned.

The Workplace in Conflict— Caution: Women (and Men) at Work

4

Throughout this book, you will hear voices that show the darker side of women and men—the side that is not nurturing, caring, or supportive as many assume the health care workplace would create. You will read about vengefulness, secretiveness, backstabbing, gossip, behind-the-scenes manipulation, and activities that can undermine a career. You will read about misuse of power, verbal abuse, and other kinds of pain that individuals inflict and undergo as they try to maintain their sanity in the workplace.

The Difference . . .

Initially, I thought that the increase in sabotage and conflict reported from the 1987 general workplace study up to and including the 2002 health care exclusive study meant that there was increased awareness among women of having been sabotaged or undermined by other women. Awareness is a factor, but so is the economy. With the shakiness of the health care industry, fear and concern have increased, and territorialism has become a major factor: "I will do anything to protect my job, and that includes making someone look bad or undermining another." The "another" is likely to be a woman, for the reasons I have been discussing.

Men do it, women do it, but men and women do it differently. In health care, women's sabotaging behavior will definitely be directed toward other women. Men's behavior will be directed at either sex. Mayhem, damage, destruction, betrayal, treachery, and seduction are synonymous with it.

Men react to it, women react to it, but again, men and women react differently. When conflict occurs, men are more inclined to react one of two ways: either confront it directly when it occurs and basically say, "The hell with it, it's not worth my time and effort" and drop it and move on.

Women are more inclined to react one way: not confront it directly and then go back to co-workers and friends and grumble and complain about the perpetrator and his or her action. The perpetrator isn't confronted, the conflict isn't dealt with directly and the silence factor enables it to fester and erupt again . . . and again.

In all of my survey responses, I found that when women were undermined by other women, those actions included the following:

- Lying
- Spreading rumors about personal matters and professional abilities
- Making comments about a subordinate's evaluation to other staff before conferring with the subordinate who was evaluated
- Stealing research ideas
- Taking credit for another's work, directly or indirectly
- Telling staff not to be helpful to others
- Interviewing people for a job and not telling interviewees that the interviewer's position is the one to be filled
- Advising a friend not to take an "awful" job, and then applying for it oneself
- Before a weekly office meeting, designating someone as "It", the target of gossip and backstabbing before and during the meeting
- Verbally abusing someone in front of colleagues, patients, and patients' families

So Eager to Help, So Eager to Please

Sara had the ideal job. She was the director of a successful women's health center, known for its innovative programs for women and families in the community. The center was also an important factor in the financial well-being of the hospital Sara worked for. Ken, her boss, was someone who had come up through the ranks and whose personality was very different from hers.

Sara was determined to work hard and make things positive. Whenever she approached Ken, he would listen. When he nominated her for the state's Woman of Achievement Award, an award she later won, she reached a pinnacle of her career. She developed considerable respect for

Ken, although there were times she didn't agree with him. She ran things by him, let him know what she intended to do, got his input and feedback, and then implemented the latest program for the center.

One week, when Sara was out having surgery, Ken's open-door policy became her downfall. As it happened, Sara was a great believer in teamwork. The three primary employees of the women's center were the office manager, the education coordinator, and herself. They all made management decisions and worked closely together. Sara was pleased that she could empower her staff to make decisions that she would stand by. What she didn't realize is that she had empowered her enemy.

One of her staff members, Rebecca, begged Sara to let her do more. Rebecca was happy to screen her calls and resolve disputes between other employees. She told the other employees that she was close to Sara, and that she knew she could help them. Initially, Sara thought that Rebecca was being very helpful. She was very nice and made a great "right hand."

In most communities where there is a women's health center, the director often receives a lot of local attention and press. Sara was no exception to this rule. She was well known and well liked and was viewed as a role model for women in the community.

Sara's power was challenged when she took a few weeks off after surgery and her "right hand" decided she could run the office as well as Sara. When Sara entered the hospital, Rebecca started a strong campaign to prove to other employees that she could run the office, and that they should align with her. At the same time, Rebecca told Sara that she was handling various problems and things were running smoothly. She was able to work through problems and solve them, she said; Sara should just get well.

Initially, Sara thought it was others who were creating the hassles and problems that Rebecca had to solve. Rebecca was friendly with Martha, another employee. As Sara continued to recover, Rebecca and Martha began to verbally abuse another employee, who happened to be a neighbor of Sara's. That employee did not want to take advantage of her relationship with Sara, and so she didn't tell Sara about the others' behavior. After three weeks, Sara returned to work. It was an eye-opener for her.

In her position, Sara was required to attend various meetings and conferences. Upon returning from one, she went to see Ken. Sara found out that he had initiated several interviews with her staff while she was at a conference without her knowledge. She confronted him and he responded,

> Well, Sara, I was just trying to nip it in the bud and talk to them. For the most part, your staff really doesn't like you. There are a couple of them, and you know who they are, that are mad at you. I don't know what you've done to make them upset, but they have a folder two inches thick of things that you have done.

When Sara asked about the contents of the folder, Ken said that they were petty things. The next day, she returned to the office and asked him if he still respected her, trusted her, and still held her in high esteem. After all, this was the same man who had nominated her for an award. He said that he had "all the confidence in the world" in her. He added that she may have made a poor decision somewhere along the route, and that he had made some poor ones himself. Sara said she needed to think about what had been done, and she asked Ken what he wanted her to do. Ken gave Sara a week to work things out with Rebecca. After that, he said, one of them would have to go, and he would decide who.

After a week, Sara touched base with Ken. She said she felt that her phone was being tapped and her office was bugged. She was being treated with disrespect in front of other employees and patients. She was also receiving letters from Rebecca, who refused to meet with Sara in Sara's office because she was tired of Sara "harassing" her. Sara wanted to fire Rebecca, but Ken wouldn't let her.

The following week, she told Ken,

> You have to do something. I can't work with the woman anymore. You are going to have to make a decision.

Three more weeks passed. Sara then gave Ken a memo that said she no longer wanted Rebecca in her department. Problems continued. Sara wanted Rebecca removed within three working days. Then Sara went to a meeting in another state. When she returned to her office the following Monday, she was fired.

Many times, when a staff member sets out to undermine and sabotage her boss, her primary motive is to grab the job. Rebecca didn't get Sara's. A new director was hired instead, and Rebecca didn't last another month. Sara shares,

> She thought she would get my job. I didn't have a clue why she thought so, as she had no education or training for the position. Within a month, the new director had fired her. Rebecca had been caught tape recording conversations with her, Ken, and other employees.

Hindsight is always accurate, and Sara says there are two things that she would not repeat: she became too friendly with her employees, and she gave up her power too early. Rebecca's initial strategy for usurping Sara's authority and position was covert and indirect. Rebecca became more overt when she made direct statements to Sara, refusing to meet with her in her office. But she never said directly to Sara or Ken that she wanted Sara's job, or that she could do it as well. Ken kept blinders on during the whole time, failing to support a key employee. Too often, men don't want to get in the middle of what they perceive as conflict among women.

The Disappearing Mentor

Usually, it's not the employee who undermines the employer; rather, it's the other way around. When a manager or supervisor sets out to belittle or undermine an employee, our research has shown, it is primarily from feelings of low self-esteem and insecurity. The boss feels threatened, and the threat can come from a variety of areas: an employee may let others know that her goal is to be the boss, or an insecure boss may be threatened by up-and-coming employees who are talented and may actually be a peril to the boss's position.

Nancy was a regional manager for a large pharmaceutical company based in Pennsylvania. She began as an administrative assistant to Bob. He was her mentor, and she learned a lot about the business. Areas of growth where she could expand her career were pointed out to her. He made her his pupil. Nancy remembers,

> I put Bob on a pedestal. I was his mentee. I was very young and green, and he wanted me to succeed. As I did. Within a year of my starting with the company, one of Bob's direct reports was promoted to another position. He decided that one of his female managers

would take the man's place, and Debbie was promoted.

At first she was great. She was strong and competent and had a wonderful sense of humor. I liked and admired her a great deal.

When she was still being considered for the job, she had come into my office and said, 'What's the deal here? Am I the token woman being considered for this job?' She was very forthright. I responded that I didn't know exactly who all the candidates were, but to my knowledge she was the only woman. I also told her that Bob was very impressed with her and that she should take that as a good sign, because he would say that only if he meant it.

After she had the new position, things changed. I was to report to her instead of to Bob. That was fine with me. I saw her becoming my new mentor and was very excited about that possibility.

Later, Bob and I went to dinner, and he approached me about the possibility of my taking Debbie's previous position out in the field, as a regional manager. I told him I wasn't ready and needed to learn a lot more.

At another dinner, this one with Debbie, she took me into her confidence. She asked me a lot of things about working with Bob. She disclosed that she saw some weaknesses and some things that she thought might be somewhat difficult. When she asked if he was a patronizing manager, I said no. I told her that I admired Bob. His shortcomings were that he was a bit of a procrastinator and let things go to the last minute. Debbie encouraged me to take the management position in the field that Bob had offered me. She felt that I was competent and that her district would be in good hands. She would help me. Well, that's all I needed. I jumped in.

Before long, I realized that I was on my own, and that the promised support was nonexistent. I began to feel that Debbie had pitted herself against me. I realized that at any opportunity she would stab me in the back, with any information she could use. She worked at driving a wedge between Bob and myself. My once close relationship with him, as his mentee, was deteriorating. Many times when I sat down with him for performance reviews, the only negative input came from Debbie. I began to wonder who was ranking my performance. Was it my director and manager? Or Debbie, who was second in charge?

Nancy confided that the reports and files that Debbie had turned over to Nancy were incomplete, pages and sections appeared to be missing. Not having been a manager before, Nancy was unaware of all the requirements and due dates. When Bob asked for a series of reports, Nancy knew nothing about them, much less when they were due. She continues,

Debbie got away with an awful lot. She knew that she had left me in the lurch by not telling me about the things that were required, and which she had not been doing. I could have gone to Bob and ranted and raved, but somehow I didn't think he would hear me. From what I could see, she had snowed him pretty well.

Many times when people are promoted, they fear that their lack of skills will be uncovered. Nancy felt that she was not totally qualified for her new position, but Debbie saw that Nancy was a quick learner and capable of doing the job. In fact, Debbie may have perceived that there was the possibility of Nancy's advancing into Debbie's own position in the future. For a position to open up, it means either that someone gets advanced/promoted or they get the boot. There's always the fear of the latter. Nancy thinks back,

> I was literally out there flying by the seat of my pants, learning as I went along and looking to some of my peers for guidance and help in what I should be doing. I didn't get it from Bob, my former mentor, and I certainly didn't get it from Debbie. The only feedback I was getting at this point was that I wasn't doing it, whatever "it" was supposed to be. I felt like I was in a Catch-22 situation but was bound and determined to make it on my own and get through it the best I could.
>
> I told myself that I would treat her and work with her the best way I knew, because she was going to make or break me. It finally dawned on me that I was a threat to her—that she would do nothing to help my career or support it. I learned from my reps in the field that she had taken them aside in confidence and asked them a lot of questions about me. Fortunately, I had a good reputation and a good relationship with them.
>
> I think she would be perfect for the FBI. She has this way about her that makes you want to like her as a person. She wins you over and then starts to probe with questions. Before long, you realize you've been interrogated.

Our research shows that when someone who is in a supervisory position perceives a threat from someone else, either at the same level or below, the most important rule for survival is to align with someone higher up. Debbie secured herself by her relationship with Bob. Nancy felt that Debbie had learned how to manipulate him and take full advantage of his weaknesses. One time, Nancy approached Bob for guidance.

As her mentor/former mentor, she felt he could give some insight to the situation. Instead, he was defensive. It is not uncommon for anyone to act defensively when their judgement may be in question. With men, it's an extra challenge they aren't thrilled with. If it appears to be on personalities or a "girl thing," their preference of handling it is distance. Nancy told him that she felt she had a personality conflict with Debbie,

> It wasn't getting any better. In fact, it had gotten worse. I told him that if he had any comments that needed to be made about my work, it might be best if they came directly from him. That way, I would hear them firsthand instead of secondhand.
>
> He was very defensive. He trusted Debbie's judgment because she was in contact with me more than he was. He did admit that if her opinion of me was biased or prejudiced, then that wasn't very helpful. Recently, a man who had worked with the company for thirty years retired. He told me that if the company was going to promote individuals like Debbie, he didn't want to be around. He had had numerous run-ins with her.

When a manager feels threatened by an employee, one of the ways to keep her in line is not to give credit for work she has done, to deny that she did any of the work in the first place or to play team members against each other. Nancy experienced all three,

I worked on a task force that had four members—
three of us to do the work, and Debbie as the leader.
My style is to delegate assignments quickly, and so I
just wanted to get in. I began to implement what we
were going to do. Debbie wanted to gab and be the
center of attention. In fact, she is famous for that. My
style was to keep us on track. The three of us ended
up dividing the work equally.

As time went on, I would get glowing voice mail
messages from Debbie, thanking me for my
contributions and saying that my contributions were
greater than those of the other two members. She also
said that the things I brought to the table were of high
quality, very relevant and valid, and that she
appreciated the extra effort. She said that she was
going to pass all her glowing comments along to Bob.

I did a stupid thing by not saving her messages.
When I sat down at review time with Bob, the issue
of the task force came up. I expected to hear all these
wonderful things about my participation. He
informed me that Debbie said that I really hadn't
held up my end of the deal, and that I didn't do as
much as the other members.

This stunned me. I was told that I had done a
great job, and I knew I had. And then Bob told me
I hadn't, and I was devastated. I told Bob that I
didn't understand: Debbie had given me several
compliments and had left them on my voice mail. I
was sorry I hadn't saved them, so I could play them
back to him.

Finally, though, I thought luck was on my side.
The division I was with folded into another division
within the company, and I was given a couple of
options, including staying on as a regional manager

for the new division. I felt that I could finally get off of Debbie's coattails. Unfortunately, she was made the new area director, and I had to report directly to her. Bob was no longer in the picture.

Women are known for hanging on to a job. If you go to your supervisor, or to the supervisor over the person you are having problems with, your options begin to narrow. You can get the word out about your capabilities and qualifications and look for a transfer, or you can get ready to jump ship. Nancy got ready to jump ship,

> I decided I was going to grin and bear it until I could find another job. Then opportunity knocked. The company decided to expand into new geographical regions. Because I had seniority as a manager at the time, I was asked if I would be willing to relocate. I couldn't say yes fast enough. Several regions were offered. I packed my bags, ready to report to a new manager and was out of there.

The Kendall Attack

Insecurities can pop up in any type of setting. When the boss feels insecure and perceives that employees are stepping into her territory, she may act out her frustrations, both indirectly and directly.

Jeannie was assistant director of a research program at a medical school. Kendall was the director. Her story,

> Kendall perceived that I was trying to act as though I was director of the program. At a meeting with an outside agency representative, we talked about program plans and how another group might be able

to help, to be a cosponsor of the events that we were doing. After this meeting, Kendall told me that she wanted me to come to her office to go over the budget again.

When I got to her office, I had no idea that there was anything wrong, or that she was angry. After working on the budget for about ten minutes, she pulled out a job description. She told me that she was upset about what I said to the other person in the meeting and about the way I had presented myself. Kendall accused me of giving the impression that I was heading up the program, when she was the person who was in charge.

I had gone to her office to talk about the budget. I did not know there was a hidden agenda. She really wanted to talk about my job, and about what she did and did not want me to do. She had written a new job description. I felt that she had lied to me about why she wanted me there. She should have just been direct with me, so that I could have had the opportunity to support myself.

My experience had been that we were open with each other and talked about things, especially things like this change in my job description that she was laying out to me. It really angered me. I had been in the community longer and had helped connect her to many professionals she would end up working with and needing for her research and programs. I didn't think the connections I had built up over the years were threatening. I thought they were something we could tap and use for the education department.

One of the things Kendall asked me to stop doing was networking. She did not want me to talk to

others in the conferences or workshops that we
planned. She wanted me to do registration and any
detail work, cover for her until she got to the event,
and then leave. She would then introduce the
program and work with the participants. I had
thought that we were going to work as a team, and
that she would involve me in areas where I could
utilize my skills. When I found out that I was only to
be there as a gofer, and that there had never been any
intent on her part to include me in developing
professional relationships, I felt used.

Like Nancy, Jeannie resolved to grin and bear it and
began to look for a new job. She didn't find one until after
she had a scary encounter that almost led to a physical
confrontation. She continues,

Kendall had interfered with something that was my
responsibility. I had made a decision about a program
being cancelled and based my decision on the number
of people who had signed up.
  Normally, we have many women responding to
the programs we do. But in this case, we only had 10
participants. I had informed Kendall that I had to
make this decision, and that there was the possibility
of cancellation. She took it upon herself to contact the
speaker and tell her that there would be no
cancellation and that she would be back in touch. She
then came to my office. She was furious with me for
making the decision to cancel the program.
  I explained to her again what I was doing and why
the program was being cancelled. She told me to
contact the speaker and tell her that the program was

still on. I responded that since she had already told the speaker she would be in touch, it made sense for her to make that contact. Basically, she had already taken it out of my hands and had indicated by her actions that she should take care of it.

Her anger was apparent, but I stood my ground. We started getting louder and louder. Finally I said, 'I think you need to leave, and we will talk about it later.' Kendall would not leave, and I finally told her to get out of my office, that I wouldn't talk with her since we were not getting anywhere. She still would not leave, and so I left. She followed me down the hall, right on my heels. I then turned around went back into my office as our secretaries watched the scene unfold.

I closed my door and stood against it so that she could not force it open. But she put her foot on the door frame, forcing the door open and pulling me out. At that point, we were nose to nose. She told me that the deputy director of the program was going to hear about this.

I wish I had called security or had the secretary do it when Kendall refused to leave. To this day, that conflict is known as the *Kendall Attack.* People remember where they were and what they were doing when it occurred. It was obvious to all: she was the aggressor, out of control.

It's been 10 years since the *Kendall Attack.* Jeannie reports that it is still painful. With time, she feels she has been able to empower herself after feeling so defeated and manipulated. In the past, women usually don't have the fear of a physical attack by another woman, this is usually male territory. More and more women are reporting that they feel physically threatened when they get into conflicts and confrontations with other women.

Not Letting Go

Sometimes when a boss is put in charge of a totally new area, it's difficult for her to let go of old ties. She is seen as trying to straddle the fence. Mary Ellen was hired as program director for a school of nursing. The previous director had been promoted to the office of dean. But the new dean just couldn't let go of the old territory. Mary Ellen describes the situation,

> Everything I did was tied up with her. I wasn't able to manage my program the way I thought it should be done. People had been encouraged to report to her on anything I did that displeased them. It was a horrible thing. After three months, I felt it wouldn't work, and I started to look for other employment.
>
> The same thing seemed to happen at other campuses affiliated with this university. I had a lot of support from the dean at the school of nursing on another campus. She had always been there for me, but at that time she was forced out by a political power play. It was very disillusioning, the way people went behind her back to get her ousted.

As Mary Ellen discovered, sabotage doesn't happen solely at the lower levels. It also happens in top positions. She felt that conflict was not dealt with fairly or directly. The way individuals at higher levels dealt with others was very indirect and behind the scenes. She also learned an important lesson—when your advocate leaves or is in disfavor, it's as though you have cooties. You are orphaned and left hung out to dry as Jill learns in the next situation.

Promises Not Kept

Insecurity can lead a manager to reprimand subordinates for unimportant or even illusory things: "If I can put you down and make you feel miserable, I'm bound to feel better."

Jill works in oncology. Normal shifts are twelve hours, from 7:00 PM to 7:00 AM. Jill didn't know that her own boss's job was on the line, and that the support she had been offered would eventually evaporate. She adds,

> I've been in nursing since 1984. People didn't stay on our floor long, for a number of reasons. Six or seven years ago, we had a head nurse whose job turned out to be on the line. At the time, I was in a master's program, and she chose me to advance along the clinical ladder. After I had completed all the necessary paperwork, she sat on it. It was held for several weeks. I kept asking her what was going on, and she would respond that she was working on it.
>
> It turned out that she was not doing anything. Instead, she was under the gun because she wasn't functioning well as a nurse manager. She had made several poor decisions and never told me that her position was in jeopardy, nor could she pay any attention to my application. So it just sat there.
>
> After she was dismissed, it was given to another person. By then, it was too late. I had missed the due date. The previous nurse manager had never looked at it, nor had she sent it to the committee. I missed out.

When someone has actively sought your participation in a situation, and you have performed the requested task, you feel undermined when she or he is not there to support you. The sting in this case would have been reduced substantially if communication had been open. Jill continues,

When a nurse puts in an application to begin the move up the clinical ladder, it augments the nurse manager's position. I think she was doing whatever she needed to do to save her job. She used me and my application as an instrument to help fill her needs. I wish I hadn't got into the situation, because I was very motivated and I really wanted the promotion.

She left me hanging in the wind. She never bothered to come to me and confide that her position was bumpy and that she might not be able to put it through. I was the first person to attempt a climb up the clinical ladder. My success would have enhanced not only my own career but also the reputation of our department.

Welcome to the Floor

Cindy is a practicing RN working in internal medicine. She has been with her hospital for five years, and wasn't always an RN—her first two years, she was a nursing assistant. Her story,

Our floor had just received a new boss. The previous one had been fired, and a nurse from the orthopedic floor had been transferred over as the new nurse manager.

I've always prided myself on reaching out and helping new people. When she called me into her office, she said that she knew that women tried to sabotage other women in the unit. I told her I had been aware of that, and she said that she did not want it to be a factor on her floor. I agreed.

At the same time, a new nurse was hired. Previously, she had been a patient in a psychiatric hospital. One of my tasks was to orient her. When I discussed the distribution of the work load, other nurses thought it would be a good idea to give problem patients to the new nurse. I didn't.

The new nurse could not handle the work. She complained, and I was written up. The new nurse was also treated badly by the nurse manager. I had spoken with four other nurses on different occasions, after that they had been talked to by the nurse manager. They were crying and had been written up for things they hadn't done. The new nurse eventually quit because she could not fit in, and because of the stress.

It was not long before our new nurse manager's reputation was well known. She had a bad temper and treated everyone like garbage. I remember telling her that turnover on our floor was substantial; people didn't stay around, and we needed more help. All she could do was scream at me and tell me how hard everyone was working to get new help. She accused me of only thinking of myself.

Granted, I was thinking of myself, because I did carry a great deal of the work load, but so did the other nurses on the floor. We just didn't have enough help. The hospital ended up closing beds.

Cindy actually had several strikes against her in this situation. First—she was one of *them,* an outsider as a nursing assistant who has to really earn her stripes to be accepted by the *regular RNs*; second, she has stumbled upon one of the *unwritten rules*—give the worst cases to the new nurse (or the floater); and three, she has encountered the *Patty Principle*—her manager had risen to a position that exceeded her skill level.

Not All Feedback Is Good

Sharon has been in nursing for several years. For the past five years, she has been director of surgical services. After one year, she had her first evaluation. The outcome was a surprise. Her words,

> I was called into the vice president of nursing's office for an evaluation. It turned out to be the worst one of my career. When I asked for specific examples, she was unable to cite any. I had been given no warning during the year and had never been told that there were any problems. Being given a poor evaluation, unexpectedly, negated any increases in salary for the coming year.

Unfortunately, the failure to support or document a poor evaluation is all too common. It takes time and energy. It was poor management on her manager's side— no one should give critical feedback, whether at a co-worker or supervisory level, that is not accurately documented. Whether the criticism of Sharon's job performance was accurate or not, documentation needs to be in place. Otherwise, as an employee, I would be prepared to write a written challenge and place a written denial in my personnel file.

Your Job Is Theirs to Support and Not to Support

When women act out of low self-esteem, insecurity, and fear, the women they direct their actions toward may find themselves in a difficult scenario.

Ursula was a head nurse for her floor but was moved out of her job, without any warning. She got a phone call from the vice president of nursing's office and was asked to meet with her and the new director of nursing. They had some ideas they wanted to discuss with her. She shares,

I went to the office, and the new director of nursing was there. I barely knew her, just her name, as I had not had the opportunity to meet her personally and spend any time with her.

The vice president of nursing said that they had a job they thought I would be good in. She wanted me to apply for it. I responded that I was flattered, but I really liked what I was doing and did not want to move into another position at that time. They replied that maybe they hadn't made themselves clear: they had a position that they wanted me to apply for.

The bottom line was that I had no choice. I was the director of the unit and enjoyed my work, but when it finally dawned on me that they did not want me to remain in the unit, I was shocked.

I had been sitting in on interviews with individuals who, I understood, were being considered for director of the unit. All during that time, I was assured that I was doing a good job. At no time did I know that it was *my* position people were being interviewed for!

I was trying to get to the bottom of what was going on, and so I called the vice president of nursing and begged for an interview. She refused to discuss it. The new director of nursing felt that she was really too new to the hospital to take a position on the matter. At the time, being newly divorced with a family to support, I didn't feel I could just say, "Take this job and shove it." I felt that I really needed to get out of there. I began to look for another job.

By the time I found something I was suited for, I had actually developed a relationship with the director of nursing, who took me under her wing and became my mentor. I got a new job, which was structured as a lateral move without any loss in pay.

It was three years before they hired someone else to replace me, going through three other people until they finally found someone to fit in—a man, and not a nurse. The position I have today is one that I developed from scratch. I have been here 15 years. Both the director and the vice president of nursing have left the hospital.

Ursula was fortunate: the director of nursing became a mentor, someone who envisioned Ursula's skills and was able to direct them. Too often, however, women feel that a situation is hopeless, that they are stuck and can't escape.

The Shoe Is on the Other Foot

In workshops, I always throw out the question with the caveat that participants don't have to raise their hands, "How many of you have undermined another or created conflict in your workplace?" Very, very few women and men will admit to being conflict creators or saboteurs. The reality is, that most of us at some point in time (or for that matter, repeatedly) have undermined or created conflict with another. Sometimes intentionally, but usually unintentionally.

Ursula herself had been accused of sabotaging behavior and was willing to talk about it. She continued,

When I was a head nurse, I had a staff nurse who I felt was unprofessional in some of her conduct. She would come to work and constantly flirt with the physicians. My main concern was that at times I observed her being disruptive with patients. I felt that she was there more to boost her own self-esteem than to have any positive interactions with the patients and the physicians. I would counsel her, reminding her that she had a specific job to perform.

Rather than put up with pressure from me, she decided to switch to the second shift, staying in the same unit. When the charge nurse on the second shift asked me about her, I told her of my concerns and described some of the behavior I had noted. Unknown to me, this charge nurse and the staff nurse were close friends. The charge nurse repeated my concerns to her friend.

The staff nurse was furious. Letters were written, and a verbal campaign commenced, saying that I talked about personal and private things, sharing information and evaluations with others. I responded that I had and would do it again. I believe that I was not unethical in MY behavior, but the charge nurse was unethical in sharing the information that I passed on, manager to manager.

In the end, both the charge nurse and the staff nurse resigned.

For Her Eyes Only

The aggressive changes and reorganizations of the nineties were like being caught in the middle of a hurricane for many. Hospitals, facilities, and offices that competed with one another for patients were now "together," now one big family. Anyone knows that not all members of a family are of the same mindset and if they are, they may not all be there at the same time. When organizations and systems merge, there are changes, often drastic. Employees feel anxious and uncertain. Difficulties often aren't dealt with straightforwardly. Staff reported in the *Conflict Survey* that the biggest conflict creator was the simple fact that management didn't communicate effectively.

Pearl is an administrative assistant in a Fortune 500 pharmaceutical company based in New York. She found a memo about herself in a file that was left out in the coffee room. Sometimes, one wonders—is something intentionally left out for others to see, or was it accidentally left out? For Pearl, it didn't matter, the contents were devastating,

Our department had gone through a series of changes. In fact, it seemed like there was some type of reorganization every week. It all started with a merger with another corporation. New supervisors, managers, and other personnel were brought together.

Lydia, one of the secretaries who worked part-time, quit. Lydia told me that she hadn't been able to stand the politics and infighting since the merger. She had found a job with another company, for less pay and less stress. I didn't blame her. It seemed that everyone was complaining, even calling in sick when I knew they really were well.

After Lydia quit, my supervisor told me that I would have to cover for her post. I was already taking work home—and not declaring any overtime. I have a preschooler and need at least an hour to get to my home in New Jersey. When I told my supervisor that I couldn't cover for Lydia, she wasn't happy. She even implied that if I didn't like it, I could find another job.

One morning, I took a coffee break. No one else was in the office kitchen. By the coffee machine was a bright red file. It was labeled THINGS TO DO. I assumed that one of the secretaries had laid it down and left it by mistake when she went back to her station.

I opened the file, to identify whom it belonged to. The first page was a memo that identified whom the file belonged to—my supervisor. By her name was the topic of the memo—I couldn't have avoided it. It said, "Memo to Bernie Re: Terminating Pearl." Bernie was the manager of our department. I didn't know what to do and decided to leave the "hot" file on her secretary's desk.

After a few weeks and many sleepless nights, I decided to make an appointment to talk with Bernie. He didn't say much. He gave no support or recognition for the work I had produced and the dedication I had given to the company. And my supervisor was furious with me for looking in her personal file.

After her meeting with Bernie, the stress escalated. Three months later, Pearl declared, 'Enough.' She now works where Lydia does. Granted, her pay is a little less. But she enjoys what she is doing. She gets off at 3:30 and is able to catch an earlier bus and spend more time with her young daughter. And she no longer takes work home. Pearl figures that she got a raise.

Pearl's supervisor was what I call an Old Bertha. She had been there for a long time and had seniority. It was improbable that she would be moved or terminated in the near future. When these situations develop, upper management often turns away and does not deal with the problem. In the end, businesses lose billions of dollars annually because so many employees decide that employers can "take the job and shove it." They move on to greener pastures, as Pearl and Lydia did.

The Right Credentials and the Wrong Fit

Theresa is a nursing manager in one hospital within a chain of hospitals on the West Coast. She has a BS in business and is an RN. She is also working on her master's degree

---

ZAP Tip

One thing women need to bear in mind is that the job does not love you. Women tend to be loyal to a job, when the job really isn't loyal to them. Women are often in a very unhealthy and toxic environment. It's an environment that, with continued exposure, reduces your self-esteem to nil and can literally make you sick.

An unhealthy workplace breeds poor health for its employees, both mentally and physically.

---

in health administration. She was definitely interested in moving up. She shares,

> I was up for a promotion that I didn't get. I had all the right knowledge but the wrong degree, at least from the decision makers' perspective.
>
> When I was turned down for the promotion, a competing hospital in a nearby community expressed interest in me. All of a sudden, they stopped calling. I then heard from three separate recruiters for similar positions in neighboring communities, the same position for which I was turned down at my own hospital. I had been told by the recruiters that each of the hospitals wanted me. And then I heard nothing. When the third recruiter contacted me, I said that I had heard from someone else that I was 'off limits.'

The recruiter said that was impossible. But I was beginning to feel that I had been blackballed.

When another directorship opened up at the hospital, I again applied for it. I definitely had the right credentials, but not the right degree. I was turned down with comments from the interview committee, asking when I would get my BSN.

I told them that I wouldn't. Instead, I was now working on my master's degree. They were startled that I was able to bypass a BSN and go straight to a master's program. It was like if you didn't play by their rules, you weren't going to play in the game. The master's program is wonderful, bringing me a great deal of satisfaction. It turns out that several of the people who were involved in turning me down for the directorship are now my classmates.

Although Theresa had the "wrong" bachelor's degree when she was being considered for the two promotions, it may well be the right degree in today's health care environment. It makes sense for a manager to have a business background. In Theresa's case, as a nurse manager in the operating room, she has a budget in excess of $8,000,000. Having a little business savvy certainly makes sense.

Summing Up

The voices throughout this chapter expressed great pain over these incidents from the past. All the stories turn on a single question: "How and why could someone do this to me?" Most of the women felt that they had done little to provoke the sabotaging behavior that led to heightened conflicts. Otherwise, they wouldn't have felt so hurt.

As expected, women were more likely to hang in there when unacceptable behaviors permeate the workplace—

the patients need me, I need the job, the location is ideal, my best friend works there, etc. etc. Men don't carry the "needs" with them, are more willing to relocate and don't mix the need to be with friends with environment to the depth that women do. They've learned that the job doesn't love them and that if it's a wrong fit, it's a wrong fit. Move on . . . and mostly likely up.

The next chapter continues these voices. From withheld information to rampant displays of verbal abuse, women who work in health care suffer from many of the same symptoms recognized in battered women. From a health-oriented perspective, this is bad news.

Why There is So Much Undermining, Undercurrents and Conflict

5

Health care is synonymous with caring and nurturing. Undermining, undercurrents and conflict should be out of place, but they aren't. Why was there a greater reporting of women's undermining women in both studies that focused exclusively on health care (1994, 2002) than in the 1987, 1996 and 1999 studies of men and women in the general workplace? This chapter explores why women undermine other women, why there has been an increase in reports of women's sabotaging behavior and why there appears to be more conflict in an environment such as health care.

The Problem

The problem of increased reporting of undermining activity and conflict has multiple facets:

✓ The female dominated workplace;

✓ Women working with women;

✓ Women not wanting to work with women;

✓ A rapidly changing work environment that is technology challenged at times—many report that IT departments in hospitals are 10-15 years behind the corporate workplace;

✓ The huge cutbacks, layoffs, mergers, downsizing and closing of facilities of the nineties juxtaposed with the expansion and building of new facilities and scrambling of hiring of personnel the following decade;

✓ Increasing resentment among older and/or senior employees when upfront moneys—bonuses—are paid to new hires; and

✓ Increased Union organization activities among nurses.

The 2002 study indicated that one-third of the women respondents did not want to work with or for another woman, whereas two-thirds of the respondents had no objection. Since 70 percent of overall health care employees are women, a potentially dangerous environment for both patients and working personnel occurs.

Women traditionally have been drawn to the health care field, and their percentages are expected to increase during the next decade. Today, women are still society's caregivers. With Baby Boomers now approaching their sixties, they will move into the forefront of needing care, as their parents did before them. The difference is that there are so many more Baby Boomers than there are/were Veterans or Matures as the senior population is identified as today.

The pay is reasonable, although it was interesting to note that both managers and staff each added that the other was underpaid (19 percent of the managers and 39 percent of the staff reporting about employees; 15 percent of managers reporting and 5 percent of the staff reporting about managers being underpaid). Depending upon which part of the United States you live in, pay ranges from $30,000 to over $100,000 for registered nurses. In Canada, RNs make far less. They are further hampered by the value of the Canadian dollar in relation to the American. The Canadian nurse becomes an active target for recruitment for hospitals and their personnel shortages.

Dialogue with the various segments within health care points to a widespread fear of the unknown. Its members don't know where the industry is going with the reforms, much less where it will take them.

HMOs were hot in the nineties, not looking so hot post 2000. The nursing shortage was not a big deal a few years ago; it's gargantuan today. In the past, hospitals actively supported education offerings of personnel; it's now one of the first places to be slashed. Nurses from the study (34 percent) stated that it was one of the main reasons conflict had risen in their workplace. Managers and administration reported that it was no big deal in why conflict had increased (4 percent reported it as a contributory factor). Organizations that offer education have turned to more of an "in-house" program, forgetting that outside voices bring new energy and often new ideas for resolution. Ironically, hospitals that have successful and ongoing education budgets have fewer turnovers than those that don't.

This could prove to be a classic situation: the survival

of the fittest, with battles being fought by both overt and subtle manipulations. Many players will be rendered obsolete, some will come away dismayed and distressed, and others will look at it as an opportunity to grow and expand in whatever they are now doing. In addition to fear of the unknown, demographics, history, psychology, and sociology reveal twelve major reasons why there are greater levels of conflict and sabotage in the workplace and why women are inclined to undermine their own gender:

1. There is greater competition among women within the workplace today. This is due to both demographic and social trends. Women struggle harder to obtain their positions and get ahead, many being the primary source of income for their homes.

2. The downturn of the economy during the 1990s pitted woman against woman when it came to layoffs. As a rule, women are not in senior management; they are employed in middle to lower management, if in management at all. When layoffs and terminations are presented, women are often the first to go.

3. The upturn/need for health care personnel in the 2000s has put women in an interesting driver's seat. All of a sudden bonuses for new hires are the norm, upsetting long-term employees.

4. Present-day society is continuing to experience crises of unethical behavior. Traditional morals and values have declined. The impact seems to be greater on women; they have traditionally held the family together (however the family is defined), setting the tone for its values, its ethics, and its morals.

5. The workplace is still a jungle, with the players struggling to take advantage of various opportunities and to form alliances. Hospitals that were fierce competitors in the previous decade are now owned by the same health system. Cultures clash.

6. Women are known to be practitioners of a participative management style. Their personal style works successfully at times. At other times, it can backfire because of its greater personal interaction with colleagues and employees.

7. If discipline, a reprimand, or criticism is warranted in a specific situation, one may feel betrayed because there was a perceived personal relationship with the supervisor. This is far more common with women than with men. Women are more likely to develop personal relationships with other women in the workplace. Men don't view personal relationships as a priority.

8. Women are overloaded. They have extra pressures from balancing their family and workplace responsibilities, as well as their personal lives. When women are overloaded, attempting to balance work with family and personal life, they worry more. Their worry loads cover relationships, appearance, pleasing, making wrong decisions, health, kids, lack of time, aging, parents, job performance, and even world affairs. The impact of the terrorist attack of the United States on September 11th has added a huge worry to families nationwide. Men are much more myopic in their concerns.

9. Women are still held back from upper-level management positions because of old stereotypes.

A woman still has to do and accomplish more before she is viewed as someone of competence. In health care, there are over two million nursing positions of which in excess of 1.8 million are held by women. Nurses quickly hit the "glass ceiling." Their ability to advance, as well as to enhance their income, is severely limited.

10. Upbringing's always a factor. Women have been raised differently from men, and they bring a more flexible and situational approach to relating the *world* to the workplace. Those approaches and methods are consistently passed on to the next generation. Legacies are difficult to break.

11. Women and men are split on their psychological realities. Each gender relates to the world differently, and so each has different ideas about dishonesty and deception, competition, self-esteem, and the impact of relationships. Men deal differently with their feelings of anger and hostility than women do. When most men encounter conflict or betrayal, they usually do one of two things—confront it directly or decide to kiss it off, it's not worth their time or energy. Women are more inclined not to confront it, but allow the "issue" or "situation" to resurface over and over again. They are also more inclined to share whatever the situation is with friends and colleagues, including them as almost a third party in the situation.

12. Women today are acknowledging that other women have undermined them. In the past, women ignored it, didn't talk about it, or denied that another woman had displayed sabotaging behavior toward them or others. If a woman

spoke up and spoke out, she could be misinterpreted as not supporting other women.

Denial Is In Vogue . . .Still

With the publication of *Woman to Woman* in 1987 (New Horizon Press), many women's groups and associations were angry that I had pointed out the fact of these differences. They suggested that women in the workplace should be viewed as the equals of men, and they believed that any discussion about differences or disparities would only hurt women in the end. For some strange reason, that all changed in 2002. Publications such as *Woman's Inhumanity to Woman* by Phyllis Chesler, *In the Company of Women* by Pat Hein and Susan Murphy, *Queen Bees & Wannabes* by Rosalind Wiseman, and *The Secret Lives of Girls* by Sharon Lamb become the "talk" of the media town . . . and were met by denial by many professional women and organizations.

To deny these differences is absurd. There is no question that women should have equal opportunity, and that women have the ability to do virtually any job on the same *level as* their male counterparts. That is a separate issue, however. The issue that I'm addressing is the fact that many women don't support other women. This appears to permeate female-dominated professions, including nursing, dentistry, social work, teaching, secretarial services, real estate, banking and cosmetology.

Social Trends

Demographics and social trends are major factors in the status of women (and men) in the health care workplace. Recent decades have seen a rapid overall transformation in their workplace. Women have moved in growing numbers into higher-level positions. Their employment has been a key factor in the shift toward services and away from manufacturing and industry.

Parity in the paycheck has not yet occurred. It will only change when women are in sufficient numbers and are in the "pay-assignment" driver's seat—it doesn't matter what the industry is. Only a few occupations within health care pay at the same level for the same grade type for men and women—nursing and hygienists! In the eighties, women's earnings ranged from 60-64 percent of men's; in 1990, it increased to 70 percent; and in 2000, slightly higher. Women are continually getting more education, experience and recognition and are moving into higher-level jobs. As women perform well in their new jobs, doors will continue to open. Recent statistics support this.

Working in Health Care, Shortage and All

Since 1970, the number of women in management and professional jobs has escalated; women are moving into professions formerly dominated by men. During the 1970s, women held only 18 percent of executive, administrative, and management positions. By the eighties, the percentage had increased to thirty. Employment in the health care field grew by more than 2.5 million jobs in the 1980s, to 7.8 million in the nineties. It is estimated that by the year 2005, 11.5 million women and men will be full time employed in this field.

Registered nurses compose the largest segment of employment in health care. As the largest health care occupation, RNs held 2.2 million jobs in 2000 with three out of five of those positions in a hospital. Present estimates from various nursing associations estimate the number to exceed 2.5 million by 2005. The new Millennium brought a renewed cry of shortage—the nursing shortage—same cry that was heard in the late eighties to early nineties. This time, though, no one was talking about lay-offs that became the norm in the last shortage a decade ago. Today, signing bonuses are the norm, some of them quite hefty.

The particular need for increased nursing personnel is largely a function of the aging population and the acuity of the patient. In the early nineties, 80 percent of patient care was internal—you checked into the hospital, stayed overnight(s) and had your procedure done. No more—80 percent of all procedures are done on an out-patient basis. It will only increase. Patients who are admitted are sick, really sick. Long gone are the days when someone would be admitted for "exhaustion."

The demand for RNs continues to rise, but the supply decreases. In the fall of 1986, 20,000 female college freshmen planned to become nurses, compared to 43,000 in 1983. The University of California at Los Angeles reported a 50 percent decrease since 1974 of women interested in pursuing a nursing career, as opposed to an almost threefold increase among those interested in business. The National Student Nurse Association reported that enrollments had increased in 2002 to 30,000. Most likely, the support of Johnson & Johnson's program advocating nursing as a career was a contributing factor. Nursing represents the largest segment of the health care workforce with over 2.2 million licensed to practice as RNs and over 1.8 million employed as such in 2001.

Today, many women are choosing to become physicians instead of nurses, because they now have this option. In 1991, American colleges awarded 14,500 Bachelor of Science in Nursing (BSN) degrees, compared to almost 16,000 Medical Doctor (MD) degrees to women. The last numbers are eye opening. They place the much-discussed physician surplus and nursing shortage in an interesting and very different light. In the early nineties, many hospitals created hiring freezes, even though there was a definite need and positions were available. Few were being filled because of the uncertainty of health care reform and the uncertainty of HMOs. In 2002, it was common to see billboards advocating nursing as a career, with men featured as nurses.

The dental field is really no different—there's not the 24/7 call that is routine in a hospital environment. But there is a shortage. The number of hygienists is significantly less than that of nurses. Presently, approximately 150,000 jobs are filled. Dental assistants hold another 250,000 jobs.

Both nursing and dental hygienists are considered prime career choices due to demand and are projected to be in the top ten fastest growing occupations. Part time and flexible schedules for both are common (and part of the solution to the shortage issue). Johnson & Johnson Health Care Systems website *[www.DiscoverNursing.com]* reported that by the year 2020, it is estimated that there will be a shortage of 434,000 nurses. On the June 2002 website, it added that signing bonuses range from $5,000 to $14,000 for experienced nurses at many hospitals.

In the nineties, it was common for a RN to make $37,000. In 2002, the average income range was $47,759 for those working full time in a hospital environment and the average age of a nurse was 45.2 years.[1] In places, such as Northern California, many nurses make in excess of $100,000. Before you plan to relocate and book a flight, consider that the cost of living matches the income—it's not uncommon for a small three bedroom, one bath home to price out at $500,000!

According to the American Dental Association, income for hygienists ranges from $31,000 to $75,000 a year and for assistants, from $16,500 to $37,000. Lesser ranges than in the nursing spectrum, but respectable moneys that have far less stress than what nursing environments create.

Many women work because they have to. They are heads of households, or their earnings are needed in two-income families. The social changes that propelled women into the work force have created other pressures. Divorce rates have increased, and more women choose to remain single.

Women are gaining more responsibility in the workplace, but they also have more responsibilities outside the workplace. Women have more freedom and choice in their lives, but freedom and choice also bring risk.

Women have increased financial responsibility for themselves and their families. This is enhanced by the increase in divorce rates and is statistically supported by the fact that a great majority of women who are awarded child or spousal support do not actually receive it. They become financially overburdened because of these non-payments. Many women feel alone. When they concentrate on their work, careers, or family, especially if they are heads of households, they often don't have the time or the energy to develop other relationships.

The ongoing income gap between men and women adds pressure. Women are often trapped into lower-paying, routine jobs in the "Pink-collar Ghetto." In 2000, 99 percent of all secretaries were women; 93 percent of all nurses were women; and 99 percent of all dental assistants and hygienists were women. These numbers have not changed for several decades. Granted, there are women who will break away from the pack—switching hats for administrative and management rolls or even that of physician or dentist. When they do, it often becomes a source of resentment and hurt to those left behind.

The need for nurses in medicine, hygienists and assistants in dentistry is not going away. The projected shortfall of 500,000 plus between the groups will most likely grow with the added factor of attrition.

Outcasts from Within

Many of the women I interviewed in 1994 and again for this book reported that when they received promotions involving title and responsibility, they often found themselves in an "out group" environment. No longer were they in the inner circle, privy to shared confidences or even what would be construed as "girlfriend chat." They were now considered outcasts: women who had broken out were not to be trusted . . . they were now considered to be "one of them", whoever "them" is.

According to statistics released by the Department of Labor and the National Association of Women Business Owners (NAWBO), women-owned businesses employ more individuals nationwide than the *Fortune* 500 companies combined. Women started their own businesses at a ratio of three-to-one over men as the 20th Century came to a close. The 21st Century is projected to be no different. For many women, leaving an organization and starting a business is a direct response to some form of discrimination. They often feel blocked from advancement, and so their only way out is to do their own thing. Health care professionals are doing more consulting and creating a variety of new businesses, both service oriented and new products, than ever before.

Once in business for themselves, however, women face more pressures. Since men have been creating businesses for a long time, women now run smack into the "old boys network" and the new "old boys network"—the next generation. As more and more women jump into the entrepreneurial mode and start their own businesses, they are developing their own support networks. My homebase is Aurora Colorado, part of what is known as the Metro-Denver area. Presently, there are over 60 professional women's groups that offer networking support under the Colorado Women's Leadership Coalition. Several are health care related.

Like these businesswomen, many nurses have broken away from a traditional employee-employer relationship with hospitals and formed their own co-ops, negotiating directly with hospitals for their services. Within their co-ops, they have associates and junior and senior partners. They are creating their own businesses, tapping into the needs of the health care consumer. These entrepreneurial nurses have found that they are more in control of their own destinies and their own dollars.

Because women gravitate toward the service types of businesses, their competitors are usually going to be other women, especially in the beginning stages. Therefore, they are more likely to direct their competitive actions toward other women than toward men, who have been out there longer, are more established, and are more entrenched.

Stereotype Overload

Women are still burdened with expectations and stereotypes of what they should do and how they should behave. These stereotypes specify that women should do certain types of work. They are expected to emphasize their nurturing skills and their domestic abilities, as well as their physical attractiveness. Women are brought up to believe that they should be friends with everybody, and that friends don't usually compete with other friends. But it is naive to assume that everyone will be a friend or should be; the reality is that not everyone is friend material.

When a woman opens up too soon about her hopes and dreams, her fears and concerns, she may be opening up to the wrong person. That person, usually another woman, may use this newly gained information against her. A woman who is open, in the spirit of girlhood-inspired niceness, may come to feel personally betrayed.

Men learn something different. They are taught as boys

to concentrate and to expand their technical skills and physical abilities, as well as to be domineering and authoritative.

Old habits, patterns and attitudes die-hard. Today's women play a different and newer role in the workplace as they break from the old stereotypes of being supporters and caregivers. Many people, men as well as women, feel uncomfortable with the role changes. As I write this section, I'm reminded of a conversation that I had with the producer of a video series I did for a health care TV channel. We were talking about nursing in general. I shared that I had just been in Johnstown, Pennsylvania and had observed several billboards promoting nursing as a career—the models were all male! His comment . . . "When I think of a nurse, it's always a woman, never a man."

The women's movement has definitely been a force in creating new roles, perceptions, and realities for women in the workplace. It also helped create the present situation, which contributes to women's undermining of other women. Our survey revealed that when women are under a great deal of stress, they are far more likely to sabotage each other, since they have to compete for a finite number of positions. At the same time, women's vulnerability opens up. These factors all contribute to women's sabotaging each other and constant conflict.

Women and the Decline of Values

The war on values and the decline of values is broadcast daily in the newspapers, on television, and on the radio. Examples are everywhere: religious disputes, drugs, guns, and ethical debates over developments in science and medicine. The movie *Jurassic Park* stimulated a debate on whether science should leave well enough alone followed by cloning Dolly the sheep and as the Millennium birthed, talk of actually cloning a human.

In 2002, several women were featured in the "whistle-blowing" arena—they spoke up. Enron's Sherron Watkins, a company Vice President led the charge that something was sour in Texas. FBI Special Agent Coleen Rowley sounded the horn on the mishandling of a suspected September 11 terrorist and California State Department of Insurance lawyer Cynthia Ossias leaked documents that showed her boss had coerced insurance companies into paying over $12,000,000 to non-profits he had created.

In health care, much of the increased union activity is a form of/result of whistle blowing. Collectively, many nurses have "had it" and sought what they believed to be a more powerful voice to speak for them—the union.

Still, apathy seems to be everywhere. Whistle-blowing is the exception, not the rule. Many people just don't care, or they feel that if they are not directly involved in a situation, it is not their problem. In an article published in *Fortune* magazine almost thirty years ago, Peter Berger traces how religious education and scientific institutions have been hit hard by ethical decline. One of his main points is that the values of the secular and the religious cultures alike in America have been undermined and weakened. Even as they claim to support these values, people have lost faith in traditions and institutions. It sounds as current today as then.

The impact on women is substantial. Historically, they have been constrained by traditional values. As values change, so do the constraints on women. People become confused about what to do when beliefs about what is proper break down.

Individuals may have one standard of ethics, and the company they work for may have another. The employees jointly may have a group ethic that is different from the ethics of the separate individuals as well as from the ethic of the company. The end result is that it's impossible to achieve/seek out a single moral standard to follow. It doesn't exist, confusion and conflict is the result.

Many businesses and hospitals actually create an environment that can contribute to unethical actions. Multiple departments lead to conflicting institutional goals, or there may be a disparity between short-term and long-term profit goals. If problems arise in one unit of an organization, some within the unit may seek to shift the blame to another unit. After all, it's not uncommon to hear, "If something goes wrong, blame it on the other (group, person, nurse)." In fact, it's an unwritten rule in many workplaces.

This pervasive breakdown of values is nothing new. Vast technological and social changes have disrupted traditional roles and relationships. As society has let down its hair and as morals and values have loosened, everyone is freer to act on his or her own "druthers." No one is immune to these social changes, including women. Their position in society has changed the most over the past two decades, and they may be more at risk because of their own roles and relationships.

Social and Cultural Dynamics in the Workplace

Are there competitive pressures in the workplace that are especially stressful to women? Men? Are there special circumstances that make women even more likely to undermine other women, or is it just office politics?

The Corporate Barrier

Most large corporations and health care systems are highly complex, with many levels of power, and power encourages a variety of coalitions and factions to form. These groups serve two purposes: they provide a source of strength and nurturing, and they offer a power base for people working their way to the top. As individuals move from one group to another, they can easily step on others. The ones stepped on become hostile and resentful.

Thus, one of the results of a more altruistic environment is that pathways and communication routes to top management are more open, and individual creativity is encouraged. And there are more opportunities for employees to develop power groups, factions, and coalitions to achieve their personal goals. A consequence is that women are more apt to be exploited or to prey on other women in the ensuing power struggles. Why? When a woman preys on or stalks someone else, the target will usually be someone with less power, most likely another woman.

In *Corporate Cultures,* Deal and Kennedy identify the obstacles that make it hard for women to merge into a corporate culture. The majority of corporate women they interviewed felt excluded from important events at many stages in their careers. The men already in power tended not to see them.[1] The first edition of the book was published in 1982. Its reflection of the early 1980s is similar to what goes on in the 2000s, especially in large companies.

Women commonly react to such barriers by feeling frustrated and powerless. It's difficult to act out their hostile feelings toward those in power—the men. That leaves the less powerful-women as the targets. Women know these barriers are in place and may struggle even harder to get into the inner, more powerful circles. If it means they have to push other women down to get there, that's the breaks.

Underground Players

Subcultures spring up in companies for a variety of reasons. Most likely, they develop around work differences. Examples are groups centered on sales, research and development, dentistry, critical-care nursing, and surgery. They also develop around common economic, educational, and gender characteristics. Once formed, groups create their own cultural environments and worldviews. Anyone with low power in these groups feels disappointed when her own values and opinions are not recognized. She in turn penalizes those who have even less power, and the pecking order go into effect.

Administrative assistants, secretaries and clerks are examples. They sometimes get caught up in power struggles. It is not uncommon for a secretary's status to be linked to that of her boss. Secretaries of the higher-level bosses would dump on the secretaries of the lower-level bosses when they saw their bosses feuding. Undermining one's own bosses when they had designs on the bosses' jobs is not unusual. This scenario was likely to occur when the boss was a woman, since the position seemed more attainable if another woman already held it.

In one organization I consulted with, it was clear early on that status had a great deal to do with conflict and undermining in the all female administrative assistant work area. If one woman worked for a Senior Executive Vice President and another who worked for just a Vice President needed a file, the higher status administrative assistant would drag her feet in getting the info to her.

In health care, this commonly happens in the male doctor-female nurse relationship. A nurse may identify her power with that of her employer, the chief of staff, or even the doctor who generates the most revenues for the hospital.

Getting ahead requires skills, including the skill of maneuvering through the resentment of those left behind. Getting ahead is like a game. Doing it is important, and therefore it is stressed for both women and men. But women don't know all the rules, still, and have fewer resources and fewer skills for playing the game than men do. Until they learn the rules, they may be more likely to engage in questionable conduct against each other.

Another problem surfaces: since there are fewer women at the higher organizational levels, women in these positions are more visible. Some may view women's behavior on the way to the top as tricky or devious. It can be a no-win situation if they want to survive. The game is now harder and has more constraints. Women haven't learned all the rules, nor have they passed them on to other women when they have learned them. Their actions can be construed as more calculating than men's. In the end, women are more likely to be accused of foul play.

Politics at Work

Political game playing can also result in women's resorting to more covert tactics. It is still not as acceptable for women as it is for men to exercise blatant power. Women aren't as open and aggressive about wanting to get to the top as men are, and so they are more likely to engage in behind-the-scenes actions. If covert methods don't work and they find themselves blocked, feelings of hostility can arise out of disappointments. According to Harvard University's Rosabeth Moss Kanter,

> Previous research has found that high-mobility situations tend to fester rivalry, instability in the composition of work groups and comparison upward in the hierarchy.[2]

Since women are more likely to be in this type of situation than men are when they try to advance, they may be more likely to express hostility and anger.

Women who choose not to aspire higher are not necessarily more ethical than those who do. According to research, including Kanter's, these women also may be deceptive, sometimes even malicious and vengeful. When they exhibit these tendencies, they often pick on people outside the group, as a way of fortifying their own low aspirations and group bonding. If someone within the group decides to promote herself and aspire higher by leaving the group, she may end up being ostracized by the others, who then assert the values and power of the group. Joking, ridicule, and taking credit for the accomplishments of the resented outsider are normal responses. All of our studies affirm these postures.

Women are not the only practitioners of this type of behavior. Men in low-status positions may be deceptive, too, but people who act this way are more typically women. As Kanter found in her research, women are usually in the low-status, blocked jobs, and their victims are most likely the women who have moved up the ladder. Finding fewer and fewer female peers and supporters on the way up, they are most susceptible to an assault. As men move up, they find peer groups at every level. The opposite also happens: those who move up sometimes sabotage those left behind in the trenches. It's a method of gaining revenge for past resentments and hostilities, or of affirming connections. An example would be a woman who has been with the new group is promoted and gives negative references for women who helped move her along.

When women are in a routine low-power setting, where the majority of women are still found, they are likely to engage in covert political activities.

The Bees

The *Queen Bee* is well known in any workplace. She is the woman at the top who got there by hard work. She will claim her position is due to her efforts and hers alone. Her attitude is one of non-mentoring and nonsupport of other women. She is extremely territorial and feels that any woman who wants to advance has to do it the hard way—just as she did, with no help.

In the 1980s, she was joined by the *Princess Bee*, who is supportive of other women within her own work environment—that is, as long as the other women do not invade her territory, her hive. In a hospital, if she is in marketing and another woman is in education, she will actively support the other woman as long as the latter shows no desire to move into marketing. The Princess Bee openly supports women moving up. She is an active mentor of other women, as long as she believes that her job and her future work are non-claimable.

The 1990s introduced the next generation, the *Phantom Bee*. She is a woman who, when asked if she knows of any women qualified to fill a position that she is about to vacate, responds, "There is no one. There is not another woman who can do the job as well as I do. I will keep my eyes open and let you know when I have found a woman who is qualified." The result is that a man often gets the promotion, and the pipeline for bringing women to the top narrows.

The 2000s has created the *Bumbler Bee* and the *Wanna Bee*. Because of the shortages and aggressive expansion that has hit health care with the turn of the Century, the *Bumbler Bee* is promoted too quickly and without the appropriate skill level. She is someone who has minimal competencies but has a title. She is fearful of many, primarily because their competencies exceed hers and she doesn't want to be exposed. The *Wanna Bee* is usually a whiner, wants everything NOW and will almost harass whoever is in her way to get it, especially by grumbling, complaining and whining.

What's disturbing about the Bees is the shift in attitudes among younger managers. It is not uncommon to find that women forty and older believed that women have a responsibility to help other women climb the ladder. Those younger, don't carry that philosophy. This could mean that newer, younger managers may be closing the pipeline before other competent and qualified women have an opportunity to advance.

Some individuals use their connections with an advocate higher up to undercut a boss whose position ranks lower. As a strategy, a woman may act to ensure her own power base by making alliances with more than one mentor. Then if one sponsor falls, she won't go down with the ship. This hedging strategy has become common among women. A woman's power may be more tenuous than a man's, and her position is at risk. If another woman chooses to turn on her, she usually can be undercut. It makes political sense to have more than one advocate.

Power Squeezes

The woman manager is in much the same situation. She has fewer power links. She has to carry out the demands of higher-level managers. At the same time, she has to contend with the resistance of employees who resent being stuck in their low-opportunity positions and who are bitter that she got ahead. In order to sabotage her, they may engage in passive-aggressive actions, such as slacking off and not being available. Her response to these actions may make her look demanding, critical, and pushy. These reactions help to perpetuate the cycle as additional hostility and resentment lead to more criticism and efforts to dominate.

The basis of this problem is that women have much less power than men. Until there are several generations of women in power, and until a norm is established, women will have more difficulty handling their power. An environment is created that encourages women to undermine other women. The same dynamics contribute to the unethical actions of men, but women have a much smaller arena in which to play. Women's targets are usually other women, because women are less powerful and less likely to fight back.

Different Management Styles

Women in management positions tend to use a more personal management style. Coupled with the discrimination and opposition that they may have experienced in the workplace, it can enhance and contribute to sabotaging behavior and conflict.

The good news is that women managers are more likely to be concerned with the feelings of others. The bad news is that women often lack the political savvy that men have obtained through years at the controls. A more personal management style results in a closer interaction with others; people simply feel better about working together on a specific task. But when things get bumpy, closeness can turn into hostility and personal conflict. Men have been criticized for years that they don't expose or share their feelings with others. The fact is that they've learned that it is sometimes unwise to divulge too much, too soon.

Kids at Play

Psychologists say that one of the reasons for differences in management styles may be that men and women, as children, learn to play by different sets of rules. Carol Gilligan has concentrated her work on how children play. She has found that boys tend to play more competitive games with defined rules, while girls tend to enjoy turn-taking games. Through these games, girls learn to develop more empathy with others and regard rules as being more flexible—something they can readily change if the rules don't work.

Boys learn to be independent and yet better able to work on a team and handle competition. They can play with their enemies and compete with their friends, according to the rules of the game.

In her latest book, *The Birth of Pleasure* (Knopf), she affirms that the quietness and non-aggression of females is totally influenced from the close circle of adults and that if a girl is going to fit in, she will need to recast who she is so that others are pleased. In other words, the encouragement to be authentic is squelched by society. This doesn't pertain to females only; boys get pushed (sometimes shamed) into masculinity, whether ready or not.[3]

Adults at Work

These learned patterns are carried over into adulthood. If women are more willing to change the rules, it means a more flexible and adaptive working environment when times are good. It can also mean that when things aren't going well, women will not be bound by the traditional rules of the workplace. The result is a manager who may act unethically, changing the rules when it is expedient to do so. If women are less compliant with team play, in the spirit of competition and compromise, they may be inclined toward revenge against a perceived enemy rather than inclined to regard rivalry for a position as part of the work game. Men lean more toward playing by the stated rules, holding back feelings of rivalry for the overall sake of the team.

Another major difference in women's management style is women's tendency to be critical and controlling. It appears to come about because women may feel more threatened when they use their power. Having power is newer to women. They are more likely to face challenges or resentment from those they manage. Their inclination is to control too much, at times not even realizing they are doing so. Another major difference originates in childhood, when little girls are taught to use persuasion and manipulation, rather than direct orders, to get someone to do something. As managers, women tend to retain and use these techniques in dealing with colleagues and employees. Covert versus overt.

In today's workplace, management leans toward a more personal and participative style, creating a more humanistic and supportive environment for workers. One benefit is productivity and increased loyalty, but this environment can also be a breeding ground for sabotage. Every workplace has difficult people who vent their feelings and hostilities at one another. They are more likely to reinvent the rules, forming them into whatever seems to be expedient and effective at any given time. The combination of a personal, less rule-bound style with the tendency to be tough and even over-controlling can lead to chaos. In fact, it can be a time bomb that explodes into a no-holds-barred attack when a woman manager feels threatened and goes after the person who threatens her or is perceived as a threat.

When Men and Women Use the Same Styles

Ongoing pressures and problems occur for women managers because they face a laundry list of stereotypical perceptions and expectations of how they should behave. It isn't unusual to find that the members of a work group will judge women more harshly when the women acted in a more instrumental and analytical way, a style that is more characteristic of men. The same work group will be more positive when women act in a more expressive way, the expected female style.

My continuing research shows that many women feel compelled to downplay their strengths but must display a tough shell in order to shake off the stereotypical view that they are too soft. What they are doing, in effect, is supporting the traditional male business method view that a rational, analytical style of management is always best—a style that, over time, will most likely be out of style.

Most women say they tend to do best with some form of the participative style of management, and current research continues to support that premise. Yet women who adopt it, and do what appears to work best, risk being stereotyped, since this is identified as the primary style of feminine leadership. Other observers believe that women do know how to work with people but lack important leadership skills: emotional stability, aggressiveness, self-reliance, analytical ability, and objectivity—all qualities traditionally associated with men. It's no wonder that women managers feel great pressure to perform.

The Balancing Act

Four main areas of stress exist for women, starting with the "second shift" and performing the majority of home and child responsibilities. Women are also likely to receive less pay for work equal or comparable to men's, and anger escalates. Discrimination and differential treatment is another reality that builds resentment. Finally, women can be their own worst enemies: as one woman seeks to get ahead, others may attempt to pull her back.

Most women who work outside the home are under a great deal of stress. Arlie Hochschild, in *Second Shift*, reports that when women go home from their for-pay jobs, they come home to another shift, but the woman's male partner or spouse usually comes home to a more "rest and recreation" status. Meanwhile, women proceed with the domestic shift—kids, cooking, cleaning, and errands.

Certainly, couples do more sharing in household duties

than they did ten years ago. The days of Ozzie and Harriett are long gone. But, many women actually play a mental game upon themselves—insisting on doing the majority of the house related chores. Why? Most likely, they, too, are stuck in the stereotypes that society so easily labels. Someday, women will give themselves permission to hire help for domestic obligations, or just say, "Later..." Unless they love housework (and some do), it makes sense to get some help.

What Women Get Is Not What They Are Worth

When it comes to receiving equal pay for equal or comparable work, women are still shortchanged. Women make seventy cents for each dollar a man makes for the same work. Besides the economic strain that this injustice creates, women's self-esteem is impaired. Women work the same number of hours as men do, and they get less pay. This is a key problem for women who are the primary support for themselves and/or their children.

In the study done for my book *The Confidence Factor,* I found that a group of "Accomplished Women" felt the amount of money they made had an effect on their confidence. It can be assumed that women who make less may have lower feelings of self-esteem. Those feelings can become a breeding ground for resentment against those who are doing better by making more, including women in management and supervisory positions, or women who are beginning to move up the career ladder and out of the lower-status groups.[4]

Women who feel held back and underpaid also resent others whom they see moving ahead. If they act on their resentment, the victims are likely to be other women: women are more immediately accessible than upper management and other decision makers, and there are almost always more women beneath a female manager or administrator.

Women as Subordinates

If a woman is going to be a saboteur or conflict creator and she is a subordinate or staff member, there are a variety of ways to undermine a woman manager's power. Typical actions designed to challenge a woman's use of power include going over the woman's head to a male authority, purposely disobeying or ignoring instructions, pretending not to hear directions, and attempting to entice a female manager to abandon the authority role.

At times, female employees may challenge the authority of a male manager, but when they do, they usually use the tactic of open confrontation. When they challenge women, their efforts are much more devious. Through scheming and plotting, they attempt to subvert the woman in the authority role. The rationale may be that they just don't like working for another woman.

One reason why there may be so much conflict between women subordinates and their female managers is that women are normally socialized to take the number two position, with a man in the number one position. As a result, many women resist being accountable to other women because they have been conditioned to compete with other women for coveted positions. It doesn't fit the expected procedures for women to support, acknowledge the worth of or defend another woman.

Subordinates may also resist more directive leadership from a woman because they are used to her playing a more expressive and supportive role. They think she should do things that are helpful and understanding, and they feel a sense of emptiness or abandonment when she plays a more forceful role. They may react with anger and resentment.

On the flip side, the number of managers and executives who believe men would be uncomfortable working for women has declined significantly over the past thirty

> **Researchers have found repeatedly that men, more than women, were willing to accept women as colleagues and competent equals. Our study showed that over a 15-year period, approximately one-third of the women respondents said that their preference was not to work for or with another female—an almost impossibility in the health care system of today.**

years. These researchers feel that adversarial relationships between women superiors and their female subordinates may be developing and expanding for a number of reasons.

- First, a female boss may be demanding more now of her female subordinates, in order to mold them into competent managerial women.
- Second, a subordinate not only may resent the additional demands but also may be disappointed that she isn't getting the warmth, support, and encouragement commonly associated with a female boss.
- Third, female subordinates may suspect that there are a limited number of slots open to women, and so they feel competitive with their female bosses.
- Finally, there appear to be more difficult conflicts when a younger woman is supervising an older woman.

Women (and men) who challenge managers and executives usually operate from a position of low-confidence and self-esteem. They rarely have any positional power, but view themselves as powerful and act out to display their power.

With men, it will mostly likely be in an overt delivery; with women, covert.

Are You Sabotage-Savvy?

Women's preponderance to undermine other women is not a genetic disorder. It is a learned behavior, created from years of ingrained stereotyping and societal pressures, and it can change. In fact, it must change if the workplace is to be truly collaborative. The *Are You Sabotage Savvy? Quiz* (Exhibit 5. 1) has two parts and forty questions. Few will be able to answer *no* to every question.

Most of us have participated in some form of sabotaging or conflict creating behavior, whether it was taking credit for someone else's work, not speaking up when someone else took credit for another's work, or just passing along everyday gossip. Each of these actions constitutes a form of sabotage and conflict in the workplace. Take the *Are You Sabotage Savvy? Quiz* before going on to the next chapter.

Are You Sabotage Savvy? Quiz©

Part I

To check whether you are Sabotage Savvy, answer *Yes, No,* or *Not Sure* to the following questions.

	Yes	No	Not Sure
1. Have you ever given a name as a reference, later to find out that the reference gave you a neutral to negative referral?	___	___	___
2. Have you ever felt that information that would make your job easier or clarified has bypassed you or been withheld?	___	___	___
3. Have you ever felt that files or personal items in your office or workspace have been opened or used without your prior knowledge or consent?	___	___	___
4. Has a group of co-workers or friends ever ceased talking or changed a subject when you approached them (assuming that a surprise event in your honor was not being discussed)?	___	___	___
5. Has anyone ever passed on or exchanged information about you that was untrue?	___	___	___

Are You Sabotage Savvy? Quiz©

Part I (continued)

	Yes	No	Not Sure
6. Has anyone ever taken credit for work you have completed?	____	____	____
7. Has anyone ever not acknowledged you or given you credit for work you have participated in or completed?	____	____	____
8. Have you ever been reprimanded or confronted by someone in front of others?	____	____	____
9. Has someone ever threatened you with a consequence if you did not meet and/or support demands that you felt were contrary to your values?	____	____	____
10. Has anyone ever forgotten to give you important messages or phone calls?	____	____	____
11. Has anyone ever made a commitment to do something for or with you and then reneged on the commitment?	____	____	____
12. Has anyone ever expected you to behave, react, or work in a specific way or according to a specific method,			

	Yes	No	Not Sure

without telling you what
the way or method was?

13. Have you ever been with
an individual or a group of
people who have identified
a problem and made the
commitment to seek a
solution, only to discover
that there was no one to
support you in "your"
problem when you
discussed it with the boss?

14. Have you ever been stuck
with doing a co-worker's job
because she or he is often
late or spends work time
doing personal things?

15. Has anyone consistently
criticized areas or items
of your work without
acknowledging or applauding
the positive areas?

16. Has anyone ever tried to
reduce or destroy your
credibility?

17. Have you ever been
terminated without cause?

18. Has anyone ever told
someone else personal
information that you had
shared confidentially?

19. Has anyone ever called or
planned a meeting that

Are You Sabotage Savvy? Quiz©

Part I (continued)

	Yes	No	Not Sure
involved you, your ideas, or your plans, without including you?	____	____	____
20. Has anyone ever lodged a complaint against you to your supervisor or others whom you work with, without first discussing it with you?	____	____	____

If you answered *Yes* to any of the above, you have been sabotaged by someone. If you answered *Not Sure,* the odds are that you have been undermined by someone. If you answered *No* to all of the above, you lead a reclusive life.

Are You Sabotage Savvy? Quiz©

Part II

To determine whether you have ever sabotaged another, answer *Yes, No,* or *Not Sure* to the following questions.

	Yes	No	Not Sure
1. Have you ever offered to be a reference for someone and not given a positive reference when asked?	____	____	____
2. Have you ever withheld information, intentionally or unintentionally, that would have clarified someone else's job or task?	____	____	____
3. Have you ever used someone's files or personal items without prior permission?	____	____	____
4. Have you ever participated in or led a discussion about someone else and quit listening or talking when that person or the person's friend or colleague entered the room where you were?	____	____	____
5. Have you ever shared personal information about someone that you did not verify as accurate?	____	____	____

Are You Sabotage Savvy? Quiz©

Part II (continued)

	Yes	No	Not Sure
6. Have you ever taken credit for work that someone else completed?	____	____	____
7. Have you ever not spoken up when someone else took credit for work that you know he or she did not do?	____	____	____
8. Have you ever confronted or reprimanded someone when others could observe and/or hear your actions?	____	____	____
9. Have you ever intimidated someone with a demand or a perceived threat if she didn't support you when your demand was contrary to her values?	____	____	____
10. Have you ever delayed passing on important messages or phone calls?	____	____	____
11. Have you ever reneged on a commitment?	____	____	____
12. Have you ever expected someone to behave or react in a specific way to a situation or problem, without telling her beforehand what your expectations were?	____	____	____

	Yes	*No*	*Not Sure*
13. Have you ever told someone that you supported her, her idea, or her desire to solve a problem and then not spoken up when someone in authority was willing or ready to listen?	____	____	____
14. Have your co-workers ever had to do your share of work because you spent work time on personal matters (such as phone calls, making appointments, or just being away from your desk)?	____	____	____
15. Have you ever directed negative criticism at a co-worker or employee, without acknowledging some of the positive things that she does?	____	____	____
16. Have you ever put someone down or belittled her authority or presence?	____	____	____
17. Have you ever fired someone without cause?	____	____	____
18. Have you ever passed on confidential information about someone without her permission?	____	____	____
19. Have you ever planned or called a meeting that involved someone else's			

Are You Sabotage Savvy? Quiz©

Part II (continued)

	Yes	No	Not Sure
ideas or plans, and not included her?	____	____	____
20. Have you ever made a complaint about someone without first approaching her with your concerns?	____	____	____

If you answered *Yes* to any of the above, you have sabotaged someone. If you answered *Not Sure,* the odds are that you have undermined someone. If you answered *No* to all of the above, you are a saint.

Source: *Zapping Conflict in the Health Care Workplace,* by Judith Briles. The Briles Group, Inc. 2002. Permission to reproduce and distribute material (with copyright notice visible) is hereby granted. If material is to be used in a compilation to be sold for profit, please contact publisher for permission.

Exhibit 5.1

Sabotage is: the undermining or destruction of personal or professional integrity; malicious subversion; damage to personal or professional credibility. Any of these can lead to the erosion or destruction of self-esteem and confidence.

Conflict Creators, Saboteurs, Bullies & Toxic Co-Workers

6

Change is the middle name of health care, as in health *change* care. *Downsizing* is a catchall phrase for reducing or reorganizing a work force that was frequently bandied about throughout the nineties. The previous decade had seen facilities shut down, departments and services eliminated, and staff reduced. Some acknowledged it openly. Others sidestepped the issue.

When the 21st Century reared its head, the *nursing shortage* became the new catchall for why health care was limping along. Work within health care looked liked a safe haven as the economy reshuffled the deck. Billboards throughout the country beckoned women and men (in a small city in Pennsylvania, I spied three billboards featuring men only) to begin a career in nursing.

In reality, any time there is a strategy to change the size of the work force, from expansion to depletion and back to expansion, there is a major impact on all players. Everyone feels the force. Those who are let go experience fear, anger, and disbelief. Their morale is at rock bottom. Surprisingly, so is that of those who are not cut. They are fearful that they will be let go in the next series of cutback rounds. They can't believe that their environment is as it is, and they are angry—angry that friends have been let go, and that management has little loyalty or respect for years of dedication. At least, that's the perception. Remaining employees can't help wondering when their turn will come.

The level of concern regarding adequate care for patients expressed by health care professionals, both in management and on the staff, rattled organizations as the Millennium birthed. The media started publishing reports about internal concerns as the nineties wound down. All of a sudden, a new cry popped up—There aren't enough nurses . . . Where will they come from? . . . The average new nurse is in her 30s versus the 20s . . . Nurses are leaving traditional nursing! . . . The Boomers are aging and who will care for them? . . . What shall we do . . . The sky is falling in health care!

The Impact

The end result of these wild gyrations is a loss for all. Management points to reduced expenses from all the cutbacks, but were they truly reduced? The biggest expense in a hospital is nursing—the obvious place to begin to reduce financial bleeding. And that's what happened in the nineties, it became slash and burn time—forget about the number of patients to care for, forget about the acquity of the patient . . . we are saving money! Thousands of excellent nurses said the heck with it, I'll find another way to support myself and my family. When morale and loyalty are at rock bottom, productivity slides—in good times and in bad.

The impact of the downsizing trends has led to an aggressive scrambling by managers and administrators in the next decade. Not only were new facilities being built, but lures were put out to get nurses back, or to entice them from leaving their current employer for them. The lure?—money, bonuses, and attractive bonuses at that. The nursing personnel who weren't put out to pasture through downsizing or who chose to stay out of loyalty, age or whatever reason now felt a tad resentful. Why? Money again—no sign-on bonuses, only new nurses got them.

The end result is that hospitals are woven with unhappy employees. Be it a shortage, what is perceived as unfair distribution of moneys, or an attitude of "we" versus "them", hospitals are now dealing with a challenge that they would prefer not to deal with—unionization. Some hospitals have done fairly well in working with unions, Kaiser Permanente is at the top of the lists; others are battlegrounds. Breeding grounds for conflict and sabotage.

Meanwhile, everyone is looking out for number one—herself or himself. Confidences are betrayed, discrimination is more prominent, different types of unethical behavior become commonplace, and tongues sharpen.

Women and men who are assertive usually don't get caught up in game playing. They prefer factual information and don't like to waste time. When someone asserts their positions, through body language, speech, and actions—communications are less muddled.

Through the Camera's Eye

Clear communications are a requirement for building teams within the workplace. Louise should know. She has taught assertiveness training for several years and is a nursing educator for a large hospital.

One of the formats Louise uses in her courses is that of

> **ZAP Tip**
> *Many report that verbal abuse is increasing. Some have used the phrase verbal assault and ward rage. Individuals who put down or betray others, discriminate, and act unethically all display bullying tactics. The critical way to deal with bullies is to be assertive and confront them. It's an ideal way to let others know that you stand behind your opinions and statements and that you are not easily plowed under. The most effective way to deal with conflict is to acknowledge it and address it.*

videotaping participants. This is for their own personal use, so they can evaluate how well they apply what they have learned in the course. In order for people to open up and allow themselves to receive a critique from the class leader, it is necessary to offer confidentiality. That was part of Louise's normal practice. She explains,

In my classes, I normally use a role-playing format. The first time I introduced video to record the role plays among participants, I listed a series of behaviors. In turn, I would watch as well as use the camera for different signs that would show assertiveness, nonassertiveness, eye contact, body position, and tone of voice. They would work up a script with a partner and then role play it. The camera rolled. The purpose would then be for me to sit down with each of them and discuss what I saw, as well as what they saw. Their strengths and weaknesses were pointed out, with suggestions for changes in behavior, so they could be more assertive. Everyone felt the whole process was very beneficial.

Somewhere between the time the class ended and the time I began to make appointments to evaluate the videos with each participant, the manager of the staff came to me and said that each person had OK'd her viewing of the videos. When I asked her if she had talked to the participants directly, she assured me that she had. I then sat down with the manager and showed her the tapes. Now, these videos are very revealing. They show weak areas, especially when you are nervous or hesitant. She made a lot of comments about each of them.

I then began to have my individual appointments. I mentioned to one of the staff that the manager had already looked at it. The staff member was horrified and asked why I hadn't asked her for permission to allow another to see it. I told her that the manager had said that she had already given it. I then went back to each of the people involved with the videos and asked if the manager had indeed sought permission. None of them had been asked, nor would they have allowed her to see them. I then went to my director and said that there was a breach of confidence and told her what the manager had done.

When I confronted the manager, at first she made an offhand comment: "Well, I guess my staff didn't realize I was going to look at them." Then she denied their denial. I then proceeded to apologize to each

participant in the class. I told them I hadn't realized
that this would happen. Their response was that they
were not surprised; that was the way she treated
everyone.

I learned a lot from the situation. I felt that I had
been manipulated to get information that could be
used against individuals within the course. My
credibility had been significantly undermined, and I
learned that I would never allow anyone to see a
video or anyone's work product without first getting
direct authorization to release it.

Louise was fortunate that the participants in the course
understood the situation. They didn't like it, but the action
of the manager came as no surprise.

Confidentiality Is Not Sacred

When inappropriate actions are taken by supervisors or
people in higher positions, and when the targets speak up
in their own defense, there are usually two basic responses.
One is nonresponse, "How dare anyone question my authority?" The other is outright denial.

Barbara is a marketing coordinator for women's services with a hospital in the Pacific Northwest. She has an
MBA degree and maintains a high profile within her community. She can recall several occasions when supervisors
took credit for work she had done, ideas she had created
and put in place. But the one item that sticks in her mind
involves what she believes was misuse of personal employee information. She shared,

We had just opened our breast center. My supervisor
thought it would be a great idea for female employees
to have mammograms. I thought she was going to

offer it to all employees. Instead, she took it upon herself to identify all women over the age of forty, contact them, and tell them they needed to come in and have a mammogram. This was without even knowing whether or not they routinely had them with other doctors or even hospitals.

It created a considerable disturbance among the employees, who felt that their personal files and their privacy had been invaded. When I brought it to my supervisor's attention that there was a great deal of friction and anger among the female employees, she merely shrugged it off. At that point, I didn't feel there was anything else I could do.

Many of the women respondents to our first survey exclusively of health care professionals stated that personal information did not stay confidential. Even when personal information was obtained through a confidential doctor-to-patient relationship, it was exposed to co-workers.

Kathleen is the educational coordinator for a women's care facility in the Southwest. She is an RN working on her MSW degree. Through the years, she has been affiliated professionally with psychologists and psychotherapists. She found that personal information regarding her family background and the way she makes decisions, information she had revealed to a psychologist, had ceased to be private. Her words,

I had accepted a position within a hospice environment. My primary goal was to develop a strong cohesive team. One of the team members was a psychologist, Sherri, with whom I had sought counseling with a few years back. Another was a social worker who was close to her.

At first, I welcomed them as team members. As time went by, however, I became uncomfortable and then devastated. I was shocked that Sherri was using information about my psychological makeup, information she had obtained through past counseling sessions. Here I was, the leader of the team, and during meetings they would whisper, talk, and carry on about their own agendas while others were presenting information. They were rude to me, to everyone.

What mortified me so much is that I had trusted Sherri professionally. For her to use the information that I had revealed during therapy sessions was unethical. Back then, I didn't have the skills or the knowledge that I have today. I was very naive.

Initially, Kathleen had viewed Sherri as a mother figure; she was safe—matronly, nurturing, and caring. Over time, though, there was a shift. Other traits surfaced—Sherri could be stern, authoritarian, dictatorial, even cold. Kathleen said that like most therapists, Sherri knew all her vulnerabilities.

Now Kathleen was wedged in a power play. Neither Sherri nor her social worker friend, had any respect for Kathleen's leadership. They may have had their own agenda, which could have included leading the team themselves. Kathleen believes that neither one felt she had credibility or deserved the leadership position.

Unfortunately, when undermining is blatant, as in Kathleen's case, and is not confronted or understood, it continues unchecked. Being vulnerable opens one up to both betrayal and conflict. Today, Kathleen is more experienced and much wiser.

> ## ZAP Tip
> *When individuals obtain personal information under a professional umbrella and then reveal it inappropriately, they are either unconscious or totally unethical. Unethical use of information is often tied in with envy, power, and low self-esteem. Both management and staff reported that confusion was a leading factor in the increase of conflict.*
>
> *The misuse of personal information, even the seeking of it, is a surefire way to stir up the confusion pot. With just a few changes or omissions about another, passed on to others, will guarantee high levels of conflict and sabotage. Employees must collectively agree that they won't be players in the gossip mill.*

Closing the Circle—The Honored Guest Isn't Honored

Kim transitioned from being an RN to an MD years ago. She will never forget the going-away party given by her nursing colleagues as she began medical school. It wins my meanness award: a party to which everyone was invited except the honored guest, Kim. She shared,

> I was excluded. I wasn't even invited. I knew a party was going on. I didn't know the reason.

I was still working in the operating room. They just didn't invite me!

Initially, I couldn't believe what I had heard Kim say. To my knowledge, this was a first. I have spoken to thousands of women and men over the years, hearing story after story. Some stories were so absurd I couldn't help laughing. Others communicated the teller's deep pain. Kim continued,

> I had worked in the operating room for five years. On my last day of work, I was involved in a very intricate plastic-surgery case. Normally, my shift is over at three o'clock. At that time, I should have gone to the party. That's when it began. At least, that's what I was told later.
>
> No one was sent in to tell me or relieve me, so I stayed and finished the case. It lasted until six o'clock that evening. On my way out of the operating room, I picked up my "surprise" going-away gift, a piece of cake, and a note that said, "Good luck" that was left for me on the desk. I was ready to begin a new life.

Kim had moved from an "inner circle"—we are the same, to another environment—we are the same (and therefor OK), you are different (and not OK). For Kim, one consequence was exclusion and invisibility. She was leaving, the circle is closed to her.

Belonging to the "Wrong" Group

Lynn is a physician specializing in family practice. She felt that she had been discriminated against because she was the wrong color, the wrong race. Lynn continues,

Part of the problem was being an American female and being white. I worked in the Bahamas, which is 90 percent black. My purpose in going there was to work with Planned Parenthood. It had been a pet project of several people there. They had made many attempts to get it started but were unsuccessful.

When I came, it finally got off the ground. Because of my ties with the United States, I was able to get funding. That was okay on the inside. But, externally, the original committee wanted the public credit. They were openly angry and hostile toward me and others who had been actively involved in bringing funds to the island.

As an observer and participant, I thought the success of the project was secondary to their own personal glory. The majority of the committee was female. They would bicker over small things, from the decor to types of flowers. There appeared to be more cruel and snide remarks from the women than there were from the male members. When men started joining the committee, there was still conflict, but there was not the level of bickering that I had experienced with the women.

It's not that women are incapable of getting things done—to the contrary. But women report that when committees have a predominance of female participants, a lot of time is wasted on the "small stuff." Jobs that eventually get done could have gone a lot faster if people had cut to the chase.

Since I started doing workshops and trainings in the mid-eighties, I've found that men can make the difference in moving projects forward. They are less likely to get caught up in the nitty gritty of things and more likely to just want to get it done. The side issues and stories that many women get distracted by are rarely as issue for the men.

Chairwoman of the Board

Lisa Marie is the marketing director of a women's center on the West Coast. Her primary credential is life experience. Several years ago, she was chair of the board of the biggest hospital in her area. Her experience has been that many women don't help each other advance. They are harder on other women, more demanding, and sometimes unpleasant to work with. She found that the levels of conflict created by other women who desired to be the top dog were unbearable. When they eventually achieve power, many of them feel that they have to behave like one of the guys. According to Lisa Marie,

> Women try very hard to achieve the place where they think they should be. When they get there, they feel accepted by the male world. In one respect, they do not want males to think they are siding with females, because they interpret that as a weakening in their position. I also see women worry about how something gets done, rather than if it gets done.
>
> My experience has been that men are more apt to give you a deadline. They tell you what they want and leave you alone so you can do it. I think that women are not taught early on that more than one person can be right at the same time, and that things can be accomplished in different ways.
>
> When I first joined the board at the hospital, other women would caution me not to be too aggressive. It wouldn't look good for women. If I had been a man, it would have been assumed that I was acting assertively and decisively. I had a man on the board

who would argue with anything that I brought forward, even when I stated it was at the direction of a committee that consisted primarily of men, such as the executive committee. Because the message was delivered by me, a female, he would argue with me, sometimes even insulting me.

As the first woman chair of the board at this hospital, Lisa Marie found herself in a unique position. She did not fit the female stereotype, nor was she a male. Yet as she came forward with decisions and recommendations, whether her own or those of a committee, she risked being discounted because she had broken the traditional mold. She was seen as too assertive by some members. She continues,

Women sometimes don't accept the fact that you can be soft and caring and be assertive. I found that several women envied the position I found myself in, especially at my age, as chair of the board. They felt that they had done all the right things, agreed with the men on the board almost always, and been ladylike, and yet they hadn't been considered for or offered the position. Several of them were older than I.

During my ten years as chair, the hospital made significant inroads into expansion and presence within the community. Although a lot of the ideas were mine, many of them were brought forward by some of the heavy-duty men, so that it appeared the ideas came from them. That way, the women on the committees would support them.

One of the differences Lisa Marie found between men and women was that, once she had learned the rules, tasks, and whatever else was expected of her, the men accorded her greater respect than the women did. Many of the women still saw her in a competitive mode, as woman versus woman, rather than in terms of her responsibility for the team—the board. Respect was not automatically accorded her when she gained her influential position. It had to not only be earned, the women had to feel they "liked" her too.

> I found the women to be less supportive. The more I was respected by the men, the more the women became unfriendly and uncooperative. The men, especially the older men on the board, gave me the greatest amount of respect. Once they saw me work, saw that I had learned what I needed to learn and would accept some of their advice and input, I found they accepted me as the chair.
>
> One older doctor on the board was not an ally when I first joined. He openly campaigned to keep me out. When my name was brought up in nominations for vice chairman, when he was the nominating chair, he put everyone's name on the ballot but mine: I was a woman. His son-in-law later joined the board as a trustee. It was with great pride that I heard that his father-in-law had told him sometime later that I was the best chair the hospital ever had.
>
> Eventually, he became my mentor and acknowledged that I had a great deal of value to bring to the board. Once he realized that, he spent hours and hours educating me about the background of hospital policy, about the hospital's responsibility to the community, and about the health care industry in general. Ironically, as I became more accepted by the men on the board, the women distanced themselves

from me. It was like they couldn't accept the fact that I could do what I did. I believe that my power was unacceptable to them.

Don't Get Too Excited . . .

Cam is a relief nursing supervisor at an intermediate-size hospital in the Northeast. She remembers the time when a new nurse came into her department, a woman she characterized as a "Sherman tank." She reveals the lack of professionalism,

> For some reason, I felt that she had singled me out as competition. She likes power and control. I'm not really a competitive person. I drop back. But she wouldn't let up. She continued to needle me, at least when our boss wasn't around. She was very abrupt, condescending at times, treating me like a child. For example, when she was the charge nurse and I stated my concerns about the condition of specific patients, she would minimize my concerns, 'Now, honey, don't you think you're getting a little bit too excited?'
>
> Rarely did I feel that I was treated as a professional. I'm not as particular as some of the other nurses on the floor were at that time, so I would clam up and walk away. My primary concern was that I did a good job—that everyone was pink and breathing when I left. Power wasn't my thing.

Whose Credit Is It, Anyway?

One of the criteria for identifying any saboteurs in the midst is to ask the question, "Does anyone take credit for another's work?" When someone takes credit for someone else's work, there is a feeling of betrayal and anger. Sue Anne is a clinical educator specializing in surgery. She has completed her BSN degree and is now working toward her master's. She recalls a time when a colleague took credit for her work, rather backhandedly. Her experience,

> Fifteen years ago, I was a staff nurse. We were beginning patient education in the hospital. Our surgery nurses would actually go and see pre-op patients after they had checked into the hospital. Because it was something new, I decided that it would be beneficial to develop a training video for the nurses to use.
>
> One of the other nurses, who was in the education department, attended the annual meeting for the operating-room nurses. In the meeting, there was a special section that acknowledged and gave various awards for new educational programs that had been developed. I did not attend this meeting. My colleague took the video that I had written and produced, and she entered it as her work. Not only did she enter it, she won an award!

To make matters worse, another person who attended the meeting was aware of the deception but said nothing. When the plagiarist was finally confronted, she merely shrugged,

> No one spoke up. There were no repercussions for this unethical behavior. She is still in nursing, and she kept the award.

When Sue Anne shared this experience with me, I felt angry about the situation and for her. . . and at her. Her "colleague" denied that taking credit for Sue Anne's work was intentional. She said that it was such a good video, it deserved to be considered for the award, and since Sue Anne wasn't attending, the colleague might as well enter it. When I asked her if she confronted the other woman, she said, "No."

Wrong, wrong, wrong. Silence condones inappropriate behavior and needs to be confronted. Sue Anne felt that the woman would get justice some day. I suspect not soon enough, if ever.

Sue Anne has learned her lesson. She still produces educational videos, but she makes sure she puts at the beginning of each video, as well as the credits, her name as coordinator and producer. Anyone who views her work now knows it's hers. What happened to the thief? Nothing.

When Trust Is a Bust

Nicole, an RN, wears multiple hats as an associate professor, director of a university nursing program, and director of a state alliance for nursing. Nicole's hindsight tells her that a former colleague and friend used her. She revealed,

Anna, a friend and colleague in the nursing field, planned a series of papers with me. One of us was to be the lead author of the first paper, and then we would rotate on the second, and on the third, and so forth. What started with the best of intentions ended in a huge argument. I agreed that Anna could be the lead author the first time around, and then ended up writing more than 80 percent of our paper. Anna, of course, got the main credit. Along the way, it became clear to me that she was more concerned about her own advancement and credentials than about our collaborative agreement.

It got to the point where I didn't feel that she was trustworthy. We were both at different universities and, with this publication, she was able to get the necessary ranking she needed at her institution. In effect, what she received was enhancement of her reputation, which would lead to promotions and more income.

According to the terms of their agreement, Nicole was to receive lead-author credit for the second paper, but it wasn't worth it to her. She refused to continue the collaboration, and Anna lashed out, calling people all over the country and pleading with them to intervene and make Nicole write the next paper. She continued,

> It was a very bad experience for me. I finally made the decision not to work with her any longer, after she called other professionals I knew, which ended up impairing my credibility. She caused me an enormous amount of embarrassment. Her insensitivity ended up terminating our professional and personal relationship.

Kellie is a nurse manager on the East Coast. She and a peer have similarly structured units that involve budgeting in clinical areas. They function with the same patient population and under the same physicians. Each manages a staff of forty to fifty employees, with departmental budgets of over $1,000,000. Kellie and her colleague are well respected, and both maintain a high profile within the hospital.

An associate surgeon of long standing was retiring. They both had a good relationship with him and were looking forward to the dinner in his honor. Kellie shared,

> We met formally, to discuss how we would present our units in terms of his retirement. We wondered if

we should give a gift or make a speech. My counterpart told me that she had met with the chief of surgery, who was organizing the dinner. We were invited and welcome, but in his opinion, it wouldn't be appropriate for us to recognize his achievements; other doctors would be doing that.

My colleague said she told the chief of surgery that it would be fine with the two of us, and that we would get together as department heads and organize something more personal within the hospital, like a luncheon, where we could do our own presentations and gift giving. That seemed reasonable to me, and I agreed.

The night of the dinner, I went down to pick her up. There was a huge gift in her office. When I asked her whom it was for, she told me it was for the retiring surgeon. She said the staff had already collected the money and purchased this gift, and they wanted to give it that evening.

After dinner, she stood up and made a little speech and gave her unit's gift. It quickly became obvious that my unit had nothing. It was horrible. I can't remember a time when I've been so embarrassed in front of 150 people. My entire staff had been invited as well, and they were furious with me for making them look stupid. They thought I had purposely planned this situation.

I stood there with my mouth open, apologizing to everyone and saying that this was not what we had agreed to. I said I had learned just a little while ago that she was going to present a gift on behalf of her unit.

When I talked to the chief of surgery later, I found out that he had told her that it would be fine for both of us to recognize him and present gifts. I think her motivation was to make herself look good and make me look awful.

Like Nicole, Kellie no longer trusts her colleague.

The Cost of Withholding Information

When Jo, an office manager for a large dental practice in Illinois, was new on the job, she was asked to do a task that required the printing of brochures and flyers. The person advising (or not advising) her was someone who didn't want her in the position for which she had been hired. She added,

> I had worked with this person a few years prior to my promotion. We didn't get along real well, but in this new position, I felt things were going well. I asked her help in planning a flyer, from the layout to where the postage would be placed in the corner, along with the designated bulk-mail description required by the post office. I also wanted her input on other items that would make this a winning and successful flyer, versus one that a recipient would get and throw in the trash. She had a great deal more experience than I had in formatting.
>
> After I put it together and laid it out, I showed it to her. She didn't suggest any changes, and so took it to the print shop. I assumed I would be getting a mockup or proof before the print run started. When the mockup came back, I would be able to fine-tune and then present it for the final run.
>
> I was wrong. The shop called to tell me to pick up the completed run. It was only then, through the input of others, that I discovered that I had laid it out incorrectly, including the placement and description for bulk mailing.

When I confronted the woman about not
telling me, her response was denial at first. Then
she said she had assumed I knew all about printing
flyers.

Not giving colleagues and co-workers information,
whether it is requested or not, when the information could
enhance their knowledge and skills is definitely a form of
sabotage. One of the most common reasons why women
withhold information from other women is that they want
to appear to know more and be more valuable than others
in the workplace.

Compare Theresa's report about some of the women
with whom she works, including a nurse manager in the
operating room at her hospital. According to Theresa,

There is one woman, who works in orthopedics,
whom everyone calls the Ortho Queen. She holds all
the information dealing with cases, or with what's
coming up, because she is afraid that someone will
become better than she is. In my department, we
identified five women she has driven out because
they refused to work with her. She undermines them,
ridicules them in front of surgeons and staff, and
refuses to share anything. When she is on duty, things
don't run smoothly.

The departments in our hospital are all very
territorial. Few talk to each other. We are bringing in
experts who work on team building to help us break
the gridlock. My predecessor was a "mother superior"
type. She ran the place, and no one dared to cross her.

My goal is to do team building and put shared
governance in place. The end result is that we should
be able to talk to each other. With shared governance,

we are now in charge of budgeting and staffing. Nurses select their assignments, and it's very scary for them, because they have never had to do it before. I have been with the hospital for five years, and I'm just beginning to see some changes.

What You Give Is Not What You Get

Jennifer was a sales representative for a pharmaceutical company. The company had recently brought in 27 new sales reps, 25 of whom were women. Jennifer had been with the company for several years. When asked to assist in a training class, she gladly gave her time. She remembered what it had been like when she started in the field. She would have welcomed input from others who had been out there and were successful. Jennifer freely gave her expertise, but what she got in return was not what she had expected. Her words,

> I spent a week out of my territory, to assist 25 female and two male reps in training. When the evaluations came through, I was stunned.
>
> I had worked up several sales scenarios, using different phraseologies appropriate for doctors, nurses, and receptionists. Role playing was developed, so that they could see how to gain additional information and strategies for closing their sales. When the evaluations came in later, the class assistant told me that this was the class from hell—they gave everybody a hard time.
>
> In the class, there were four women who stayed together all the time, like a clique. They made negative comments on just about everything. On the

final evaluations, two women wrote that I was too abrupt, too blunt, and too aggressive. They also threw in that I had wasted their time, and they felt that I was there to pursue my own goals instead of theirs.

I didn't really have to participate in the training, but there was a lot of pressure from colleagues of mine, who felt I could help these women achieve their goals. But their objective seemed to be to put me down and devalue my assistance. I have heard of similar experiences from other reps, so I feel that my reactions were more typical than not.

Competition

Diane, an admissions coordinator for a hospital in California, felt that she was in competition with a colleague, the director of a medical-surgical nursing department,

> It started a several years ago, when everyone was getting nervous about the direction of health care. There were four directors of nursing, and it seemed that two of us were in competition. If I came up with an idea or made a decision, my colleague would counter it, sometimes even telling me never to do something again. After meetings, I found out later, the other three directors would discuss the way I had acted or discuss how my facial expressions were, or even my state of mind: "She seemed to be far away," or "She wasn't responding."

Some of these things may seem minuscule, but when someone is being undermined, the work is often done in bits and pieces—a gradual nudging over, until suddenly the victim is off course.

Leaving Is Not Rejection

When a woman makes a decision to leave a position, the people she leaves behind may feel betrayed. Roz, now a sales representative with a pharmaceuticals company, had been a manager in women's health care. When she turned in her resignation, her boss made her last few weeks miserable. She added,

> All the time I had worked there, she had been very complimentary. We had done several great things together, and I had expanded the position I held. I was quite optimistic about the women's health program, and I knew that with her guidance and management it would continue to grow.
>
> When I turned in my resignation, I gave her two weeks' notice. I thought she would be pleased that I was achieving one of my goals. Instead, she began to throw obstacles in my way that prevented an easy transition out. I feel that she felt threatened. As I got closer to my final days, she kept backing away from me. I think she felt that I had betrayed her.
>
> I told her that I wasn't leaving because I wasn't happy. I had always wanted to work in the pharmaceuticals area, and the opportunity had finally opened for me. She would not talk to me the rest of the time I was there. I had several weeks of vacation coming, and she attempted to reduce the amount allocated. I then had to go to Human Resources to reinstate it. Normally, an exit interview is done, but not in my case. She also refused to give me a copy of my final evaluation.
>
> She refused to see me when I tried to make an appointment to sit down with her. The purpose was to go over some aspects of my job, so that she would

have all the necessary information when she decided to fill the position. Instead, she insisted that everything be put in writing.

Disappearing Money

Money is definitely a factor in sabotaging behavior; several of the respondents to our survey stated that they had lost funds when they were undermined. Ellen has been practicing dentistry since 1985 in the Midwest. She had an office manager who "borrowed" money. Her words,

> My office manager worked poorly, hid things, and borrowed money without asking or telling me. When it was discovered that $10,000 was missing, I confronted her and then fired her. I ended up writing it off on my corporate tax return, and she declared bankruptcy.

Women who were not doctors also stated that they had lost money through loss of a job—being fired, or missing a promotion. Ellen also is quick to add that she has had good experiences with other women in her office. She had two managers for over ten years (both left when they married), and she has assistants who have been with her for several years. One, who had been with her since the opening of her office, died recently.

Margaret has practiced internal medicine for thirteen years in Houston. She too had a problem with an office manager who wrote checks, paid bills, and falsified accounts. Margaret discovered the employee's theft early on as she shared her situation,

> The woman I hired was the ex-wife of a doctor. She was using drugs. After I discovered the embezzlement, I spoke to her ex-husband. He told me

that he also thought she had embezzled from him, but it's very difficult to prove when the embezzler is your wife, and he certainly couldn't take her to court.

I knew something was wrong after the first month she was here. She paid the bills and used my stamp to falsify checks and accounts. At the time she was fired, $18,000 had been taken. I elected to prosecute, and the court put her on probation and ordered her to reimburse me at the rate of $45 per month.

Note that both Ellen and Margaret confronted their employees. It will take Margaret a long, long time to recover her funds, but she is committed to following through and letting others know, so they can avoid the same situation.

Women in Charge

Control, or lack of it, is an important issue for a lot of people. Peggy, a partner in a family dental practice in Connecticut, was a student when she encountered a woman who needed to be in control. This woman specialized in giving female dentistry students a hard time,

I had completed my four years of dental school and had just begun additional specialty training. It is similar to a combination of an internship and residency program for a medical doctor and includes a great deal of supervision. The official rule is we don't write up cases and recommendations, but the unwritten rule is that we do. If the recommendations are reasonable, the staff looks the other way and even follows our recommendations before the supervisor has the opportunity to sign his or her approval.

There was one supervisory dentist who was resembled Nurse Ratchet in *One Flew Over the*

Cuckoo's Nest. She was miserable to all women students. I had a patient in acute pain and I needed to get some medicine to him. She would not honor my recommendations or listen to me. I had my work and recommendations cosigned by another dentist, but she snatched them up without looking at them. Then she demanded that I get them cosigned. When I brought it to her attention that they had already been cosigned, she just stomped off in a huff.

Robyn has a family practice in New Mexico. She recalls a nurse who didn't like her,

When I first got out of my residency, I worked in the emergency room in Santa Fe. There was another female physician who had a good reputation and was well liked. With a woman doctor already ahead of me, I felt that my transition would be much easier.

I was wrong. The head nurse decided she didn't like me. She told the other nurses not to help me. When I had a patient who needed stitches or something cleaned out, the nurses would disappear. I would end up doing everything myself. I wouldn't have known I was the head nurse's victim if one of the nurses who liked me hadn't pulled me aside and told me that the head nurse had instructed them not to help me.

That nurse had been around for more than 25 years. Eventually, I concentrated on growing a family practice, and I moved on. She's probably still there.

Horizon Violence and Oppression

Many professionals believe that hospitals pit nurse against nurse by establishing such systems as primary nursing, shared governance, and career ladders. In the nineties, hospitals reduced the RN population, replacing them with LPNs (Licensed Practical Nurses) and CNAs (Certified Nursing Assistants). Highly trained RNs, regardless of professional level were delivering lunches and emptying bedpans and trash. As the Millennium birthed, these same hospitals were scrambling for the RNs they laid-off.

When nurses were put in charge of their own budgeting and staffing, it was believed that it would have a positive effect, a good thing. Unfortunately, when budgets shrank, nurses ended up grumbling among themselves about overtime and work loads. Career ladders are associated with teamwork. Many felt that when one team gets a reward, it's usually at the expense of another.

In 2001, I was contacted by Herb Dunn, a practicing RN since 1980 and based in a New Jersey Magnet hospital. He asked permission to use the *Are You Sabotage Savvy?Quiz©* I developed for identifying sabotage and conflict that he found published in one of my books as his thesis questionnaire (the quiz is in the previous chapter). Telling him yes, with a string attached—I would like to see the results and data of the survey when completed, he proceeded with his study, which would serve as his final paper for his Masters in Nursing Administration.[1]

Upon completion, he reconnected and shared his info and that he had been invited to present his findings to the 2002 annual meeting for the Association of Operating Room Nurses. When I asked him what surprises surfaced, he said,

> I expected to find that horizontal violence existed
> among operating room nurses. The surprise that
> popped up was that there was a direct relationship
> between sabotage and work satisfaction. Work

satisfaction *actually increased* when there was a higher level of reported sabotage among nurses.

This is not good news. Dunn found that nurses would actually rationalize/justify their actions. In fact, the attitude was, "We must like what we do (sabotage and conflict); otherwise, why would we still be doing it to each other and why would we still be here?" Probing Dunn further, I asked what suggestions he would make,

> My experience is that Administrators don't want any more change. I feel that they are too focused on the money side, budgeting, and not on the personnel and communications side. That needs to be changed. Co-workers need to be educated about horizontal violence and oppression so they understand what is going on.

According to Dunn, he believes, as most health care professionals do, more staff is needed. It's not so much that the staff wants more money. What is desired is autonomy and respect—much higher levels, especially from physicians. Education is valued in health care—usually, the more you have/seek, the more respect is derived from others . . . and self.

Within the nursing profession, it's not uncommon for a beginning nurse—the student, to hear early on that only half will make it. Truth be told, that's high. But my question is—why drop that on a bunch of eager women and men who view nursing as a long term career, and why so early in the game? Do other health care support professionals hear the same thing? I suspect so. Every profession has a measured percentage that don't complete the course of study, whatever it is, but why rub anyone's nose in the possibility/probability early on? Isn't this the time to be enthusiastic, encouraging?

It's not likely that physicians or dentists hear that half of them will drop out. It's most likely assumed that they will succeed in their pursuit of their MD or DDS. No, I suspect that the women and men who enter the halls of medicine and dentistry today are far more likely to be greeted as a "doctor" even though they have years to go before the title is legitimately bestowed on them.

When individuals in a group feel oppressed and suffer a lack of or decline in self-esteem, they are more likely to undermine one another and create conflict. Either to draw attention to themselves or some type of situation they feel needs to be addressed. The problem here is that is rarely in a direct manner or straightforward.

Nurses, in particular, are an oppressed group. Although they flock together, they don't stick together. In using the *Managing Conflicts Style Questionnaire©* tool introduced in Chapter 9, most health care professionals will report that their primary style in dealing with conflict is that of being collaborative. Taint so, it's usually their secondary style that determines how they will respond to a conflict.

The last thing that hospitals should be doing is pitting nurses against each other, or any group for that matter; when it occurs, co-workers end up lashing out at each other—the phrase horizontal violence sticks. Because of horizontal violence, there are times when a patient's life may be in jeopardy. In a situation where a patient is hemorrhaging, the floor is short staffed, a nurse needs help, and the only person who is available isn't among her "friends," the odds that the other nurse will help in a timely manner are greatly reduced. Scary—scary for the patient and family, and scary for staff and management.

Verbal Abuse ... Alive and Deadly

Several years ago, I received a letter from Luther Christman, PhD, RN regarding a reference I made in my first book on women in health care about symbolic cannibalism among nurses. As Dean Emeritus of Rush University College of Nursing, he felt that there were several reasons for it. He wrote,

> Bickering and backbiting begin in the beginning— education and service. Both are strongly separated from each other. There's a lack of real career commitment—most nurses have a series of part time jobs instead of a true career. More education is needed, the majority of practicing nurses don't have a BSN. With powerlessness, other bad behaviors are bred.
>
> Nurses display tribal-like behavior that is evidenced in the almost 100 national nursing organizations that atomizes loyalty to the profession and to each other. There is a lack of racial and gender diversification in the primary women's professions.

Luther Christman has seen it all. He was the first to be honored as a "History Maker in Nursing" by the Center for the Advancement of Nursing Practice in 1992. He feels that the remnants of the Nightingale model has been an impediment to progress for nurses in general and that there is a "glass ceiling" for men in the professions that have a high incidence of female employment.

In the early eighties, S. B. Freidman did a study focusing on relationships between nurses and physicians. She concluded that nurses were subjected to condescension, temper tantrums, scapegoating, and public humiliation at the rate of six occurrences per month per nurse. In 1987,

Helen Cox, the Associate Dean of Continuing Nursing Education at Texas Tech University Health Science Center for the School of Nursing in Lubbock, Texas, released her findings on verbal abuse among nursing personnel.

The purpose of her study was to identify the frequencies, sources, nature of impact, and possible solutions for verbal abuse. According to the study, these kinds of conflicts between nurses and their peers and between nurses and both top level administrators and nursing administrators contributed more to nurses burning out and leaving the profession that any other factors. She found that 82 percent of staff nurses reported experiencing verbal abuse. The perpetrators of the abuse in order of rank were: physicians, patients, families of patients, and immediate supervisors.

Verbal abuse, whatever the cause, has a negative effect on everyone. Verbal abuse has been linked to feelings of powerlessness, incompetence, and low self-esteem and self-worth. In a follow-up to Cox's work, Kathryn Braun, Donna Crisde, Dwayne Walker and Gail Tiwa-nak of the Queens Medical Center in Honolulu, Hawaii, decided to survey all registered nurses employed by the hospital in mid-1989 using Cox's original survey questionnaire. Nurses again reported six or more abusive situations a month, with 80 percent of the staff reporting abuse from patients, 78 percent from a physician, 60 percent from a patient's family, 52 percent from staff nurses, 24 percent from immediate supervisors, 21 percent from subordinates, and 6 percent from administration.

Suzanne Zigrossi, who heads the Women's and Children's Center at Baptist Hospital in Miami, Florida, found in a study that the predominant abuser was the patient, followed by the patient's family, physicians, peers and then supervisors—a slight variation from what Cox found. Types of behaviors included anger, disapproval, belittling comments, obscene language (usually from patients), name calling, rudeness, unreasonable demands, physical threats, sarcasm, sexual suggestions, condescending behavior, and ridicule.

Are Nurses Battered?

A common reaction to abusive behavior is reduced self-esteem and self-worth. If nurses, 93-97 percent (depending on who you talk to) of whom are women, report they experience verbal abuse six times a month, it is not surprising if low self-esteem results. Many of the women interviewed for this book compared the experience to that of a battered woman.

In 1979, Lenore Walker published her ground-breaking book *The Battered Woman*. In it, she said the typical battered woman has a poor self-image and low self-esteem. Battered women base their feelings of self-worth on their perceived capacity to be good wives and homemakers. If they have successful careers outside the home, they are secondary. If you take Walker's description of a battered woman and change just a few words, it fits the feelings of many women in the nursing profession.

> The typical *abused nurse* (battered woman) has a poor self-image and low self-esteem, basing her feelings of self-worth on her perceived capacity to be a good *nurse* (wife and homemaker), whether or not she has successful *career* (life) within her *workplace* (home).

Words Are Harmful

Many said that one form of sabotage particularly painful to them is gossip, especially malicious gossip. Naomi, director of a women's health floor in a hospital with 500 beds, looks back at the time when she was clinical nurse specialist in obstetrics. She remembers the gossip factor all too well. She feels that there is no worse gossip than what is heard on an OB floor. Her input,

> A lot of gossip was around sexuality and sex. Some of the jokes were funny. I wasn't married, nor was I dating at the time. I'm straight and had never done anything to indicate otherwise, but I was the butt of jokes on my floor. I remember one time a nurse came up to me and said, 'Naomi, you're just like the slogan for 7-Up: you never had it, and you never will.' And then she started laughing out loud in front of ten other women in our department. I was so angry and stunned, all I could do was cry.

When people aren't busy, they have more time for whatever it is they want to talk about. Naomi suggested that this could be a factor with OB nurses: there are times when they are intensely busy, and times when babies aren't being born. Idle time is perfect for gossip.

Sue Anne agrees with Naomi. She works as a clinical educator in surgery and is aware of the closeness of the operating-room personnel. When we asked if she had any preference in terms of working with men or women, she had none. But then she added that women gossip and tear each other apart. It infuriates her,

> I work in several different operating rooms. Each is a close-knit group of women, most of whom, I found, don't want to confront a situation, especially if it's ugly. When someone is angry, the prevailing style is not to go directly to that person and try to resolve it. Rather, it's to talk to someone else, which eventually has the whole unit buzzing about whatever it is that

happened. It's heard at second, third, fourth, fifth, and tenth hand and blown all out of proportion. If I have done something, I want to hear about it now, not six months down the road.

The *It* Girl

Kimberly is now the office manager in a dental practice in the South that specializes in orthodontics. She had several comments about the time when she worked for another practice. Her words,

> I did primarily clerical work at a general dental practice with four doctors. It was small quarters, and each week we would have a meeting. I hadn't been there too long, but it seemed to me that each time we got together, a person would be picked on. Initially, I didn't pay much attention. They were nice to me, but after a while I became the current *It*.
>
> The manager, and a couple of other people who were her close friends, selected someone early in the week. Throughout the week, they treated her coldly and with indifference, even making the job a little harder on her. They would start to let personal comments slip out, which would eventually lead up to the meeting on Friday—the grand finale.
>
> By the time we got to the meeting, the manager would say something like, 'We need to discuss the problems we are having with Joanne,' or 'Let's identify some problems that Joanne is having.' Then everyone would be free to make comments. I'll never forget the time it was my turn to be *It*. Someone made comments about my hair and how I really needed a perm. Then another woman in the group acknowledged the first commentator, saying that I did

need to do something about my hair. Someone even offered to pay for the perm!

I remember one time when another assistant was *It*. She had been there longer than I had, and the group started to talk and say things about her being slow and not moving fast enough, and about her starting to gain weight. She'd had it, and she was ready for them. She pulled out her resignation, already typed, and dropped it on the table. Then she walked out.

Kimberly also left that workplace eventually. Leaving is always an option—usually not the first choice, but one that should be considered early in a deteriorating situation. The prospect of leaving should not be used as a threat to the saboteurs, at least not initially. Rather, it should serve as a personal option, to be put into play if the situation doesn't change.

Summing Up

Are there shortages in the workplace, the workforce? Yes, always in some area at one time or another. For years, I've said that I wish I had $10 for every nurse and health care provider who had left their respective profession saying that they had had it—no longer would they be subject to rotten and toxic behavior of their co-workers . . of their management. I would be independently wealthy.

Organizations are spending hundreds of thousands of dollars on marketing, sign-on bonuses and recruiting. How many truly do a realistic, probing exit interview to determine "why" someone quits? Is it because there is a better deal across town, another location? Is it because they feel that the new workplace they are going to is better? Are they being offered the opportunity for more training? Mentoring? Why? It would make far more sense to create a statistical model of why nurses (or other specific health care providers) quit so that problems, issues and bad behaviors can be dealt with.

Deteriorating situations exude negativity—contagious negativity. It's quite easy to absorb negative energy from others, as well as yourself. Guaranteed, negativity is always on the lookout for a new home. Once negativity has infected a deteriorating situation, its impact seeps into every corner of the workplace, adding to the toxicity.

No organization is immune from conflict, or even sabotage. Because it exists, it should not be a license or assumption that it be allowed (sometimes even encouraged by management's ignorance or benign neglect) to fester, to grow, to eventually take over an entire organization. If it does, forget about workplace shortages, extinction is on the way.

> ## ZAP Tip
> *Better and wiser to keep the excellent employee than to lose them to a competitor or other industry because management failed to deal with the real cause of departure.*

Part II:

Thriving in the Workplace

Each day, you get to choose your interactions with your co-workers and managers—be present or distant; and each day—be encouraging or negative.

To create a thriving workplace, you have choices— which are yours?

Shift Happens— Change is the Work

7

C**hange** is the culprit to all the conflict reported in health care, at least, that's what the majority of managers said—it was the leading reason why conflict had increased. Change created by and from downsizings, mergers, too much turnover, and confusion. Not so for staff—their #1 complaint was that management didn't communicate effectively and that goals and purposes of any proposed change were jumbled when they did get "explained".

In my workshops, I always toss the participants this caveat—many times, their managers hear confusing and unclear messages from their own administrators—what they are passing on, in an attempt to communicate, may be misleading, unclear because that's the way they got it.

Even if you're on the right track, you'll get run over if you just sit there.

—Will Rogers

Change is the Work

Tim Porter-O'Grady, EdD, PhD, FAAN has been involved with health care for three decades. Positions have ranged from staff nurse to both a hospital and health service executive, as well as speaker and consultant. He's authored several books including *The Nurse Managers Problem Solver* and co-authored *Leading the Revolution in Health Care*. He knows that the aggressive change in health care is frustrating for many and contributes to increased conflict. His words,

> Twenty years ago, the average patient stay was 5.7 days; today, the average stay is 4.5 hours. In the old days, nurses were trained to take care of fewer patients over a longer period of time; today they take care of more patients over a drastically reduced period of time. The end result is frustration, feeling over-whelmed, even guilt that they can't take care of the patient the way they think they should. It impacts all disciplines. Health care providers must get over it and change their mindsets.

He views conflict at three levels. At the first level, it's usually between work and the ability to do it—are there the competency skills and time to take care of the patient? The second level is woven with change—the employee can't count on things to remain stable long enough—change happens over and over, so skills become obsolete. The result is the employee feels threatened and highly frustrated. The third level deals with relationships—colleagues change, the employee is changing and the result is conflict with each other. It becomes difficult to find a common ground. Porter-O'Grady continues,

> The health care workplace needs manager leaders who are in tune and aware of what is changing and its impact. They can't lie and say it will get better, that it will pass. They have to tell them what they know, what they don't know (it's like standing on the balcony vs. getting on the floor with them so they can see the direction that the staff does) and that they won't desert them. Staff watches management. Are they congruent with their message? After all, if they are up in the balcony, how can they really see what's going on?—management has got to be the director of the parade! If they don't, how can any change or new direction be translated to a language that the staff understands?

Porter O'Grady firmly believes that managers must learn how to manage change. It's the new constant. They need to understand the challenge of change and embrace it as a part of the normal workplace, not a broken one. In doing so, everyone—staff and management—must obtain, develop and learn the skill sets that relate to conflict management.

Do You Resist Change?

Let's face it, the great majority of your workplace doesn't enthusiastically love the idea of another change—is it for real, or just another fad that's being passed around? Take a few minutes and find out where you are on the quick quiz that follows.

Do you resist change because . . .

1. . . . you like things the way they are?
2. . . . you don't want to look foolish if I make a mistake?
3. . . . chaos reigns when change occurs?
4. . . . you feel out of control?
5. . . . change comes too fast?
6. . . . everything feels like it is in limbo?
7. . . . no one wants your input?
8. . . . change always brings on more work?
9. . . . communications nose-dive within your team (or department)?
10. . . . too much change is implemented at one time?
11. . . . you're afraid you won't have the needed skills?
12. . . . positive results are expected too soon?
13. . . . management can't make up it's mind what it wants to change?
14. . . . you feel your job will be in jeopardy?
15. . . . not enough time will be given to accomplish the change goal?
16. . . . management doesn't know what it is doing?
17. . . . a realistic transition period will not be allocated?
18. . . . the change proposed is just another management fad?
19. . . . you don't really trust management (or co-workers) to pull it off?
20. . . . the goals, purpose and directions are not clearly defined?

If you responded "yes, that's me" to 3 or more statements, you most likely dig in your heels at the hint of a "new" change suggestion.

Source: The Briles Group, Inc., Aurora CO © 2002 All Rights Reserved

Figure 7.1

Walking on Eggshells

The women interviewed for this book say that change is everywhere in health care—change coupled with fear. For example, I spoke with Melissa twice. A follow-up call was made two months after her initial interview. I asked if there had been any changes since I had last talked with her at the hospital where she worked. She added,

> In the last two months, we are all walking on eggshells. At every meeting we have, a recurrent theme, "We just don't know what's going to happen" surfaces. People speculate how much we'll have to trim, and what's going to be affected by financial cutbacks, even though we are in a shortage. We are very fearful.

Many women felt that the continued projections of shortages would be hard on staff, especially nursing. Rita, one of the women surgeons, sees desperate behavior among doctors and administrators. Her words,

> Everyone feels very threatened and is panicking. People feel that they are losing control and are snapping at anyone who gets in their way. They are less patient with everybody and everything.

A great many of the women felt that their hospitals existed only for profit and had forgotten about taking care of people. Margaret, an internist, feels that hospitals have lost sight of their mission. She adds,

> They have become greedy. I can remember a time when they used to have nonprofit hospitals, whose mission was primarily to take care of people. Today, hospitals have lost their vision of what they are

supposed to be doing. I see them doing all this fancy marketing, and charging huge prices. I'm really not thrilled with the hospitals. They have caused a lot of their own problems.

Too Many Layers

Throughout the nineties, the transition to outpatient care was aggressive. The general consensus among those interviewed was that health care will have to move toward prevention and farther away from treating sickness. They felt that money should be focused on women and children, where prevention would be most effective. Many felt that there was too much money being spent on high technology, and that financial and technology-related abuse was pervasive. It was commonly heard that there were too many chiefs, and some thought their organizations were just too big as they continued to gobble up other hospitals forming huge systems.

Maureen has worked for thirty years. Presently, she's a senior nurse manager in a large nonprofit hospital in oncology. She believes her hospital is no different from any other in trying to reduce costs. Her thoughts,

> We were recently asked to look at ways to cut back. The head of dietary said she could cut back on some cheap people, those who deliver the trays. What happens then is that the nurses are expected to deliver trays.
>
> I believe that people forget that hospitals are like a mobile in a baby's crib. If you remove one of those pieces, the rest of the mobile slants to one side. That's what I see happening in the hospitals. I believe the pieces that have to be removed are some of the layers that are higher up in the hospital.

Maureen would begin at the departmental level, from the department head on up. In her hospital, the president doesn't even maintain an on-site office. She shares,

> When the president comes to our hospital, he needs someone to show him around. On-site officers are the CEO and the COO, who report to the president. Under them are a series of vice presidents. At one site alone, we have 10 vice presidents. Over me is the vice president of nursing. Under her are four directors. Under them are the nurse managers. Under the nurse managers are clinical nurse coordinators, and then staff nurses.
>
> Can you imagine? You've got to go from the nurse to the nurse coordinator to the nurse manager to the director to the vice president of nursing to the COO to the CEO and then to the president. No wonder we are in hell. When you think about the information flow—they are always centralizing or decentralizing— they don't know where they are, they don't know what they are doing or what anyone else does. It's amazing we can function at all.

When Maureen started at the hospital in 1964, there was an administrator. There was also one person in finance, and there was a director who reported to him. That changed as times got better and more money was produced. She continues,

> As times got better, things got more complicated. We added a vice president for marketing, a vice president for finance, a vice president for services, a vice president for nursing, a vice president for purchasing, and a vice president for communications. We started

adding so many vice presidents that it was hard to keep track. And under each vice president there was a departmental director.

I personally believe that incompetence starts at the vice presidential level. They are so tied into money that they do stupid things. Last year, all the vice presidents went to a resort to talk about cutting budgets. Their spouses accompanied them. When they came back, their credibility took a hit. After all, how can you go to this posh place and spend big dollars and then come back and recommend cutting someone's position?

Equipment Costs Big Bucks

There are too many inequities in the system. In the past, physicians have demanded expensive equipment for very select and rare procedures. Equipment can cost hundreds of thousands of dollars, even millions. Most insurance companies aren't paying the "going rate" billed for and actually can take a loss on a procedure. Nevertheless, in their drive for power and their desire to keep up with the Joneses, some doctors pressure hospitals to carry financial burdens that make little sense, economically or otherwise.

Diane, an admissions coordinator, is glad to be out of nursing management. She believes that general nursing is pretty streamlined but that there is fat in other departments. According to Diane,

> Nursing is pretty lean. I suspect it will be made leaner. In other departments, there are a lot of management people; there could be some streamlining done there. In nursing, we have

always bit the bullet and found out later that other departments haven't reduced their personnel.

Tracking Means Survival and Thrival!

Since the late eighties, I have worked with over 500 women's health care centers. Few are stand alone, the great majority internally located in a hospital. Many of the women who are directors of these centers are geniuses in their marketing strategies and programming. Some have taken over existing programs. Others have created programs and events from scratch.

They have brought their vision and their touch to the workplace and have made a significant difference to the women in their outreach areas. To continue offering their vision and their voices, they have developed methods of measuring their own effectiveness. Unfortunately, they are in such a minority. I can count on my fingers the number that have implemented some method of measuring how their programs affect the women in their communities and what their participants contribute to hospital revenues.

In other words, women's centers must view themselves as businesses, with standard profit-and-loss statements. It's the bottom line that counts.

Are Physicians Out of Sync?

In locations where there are multiple types of visible inequities, it's easy to welcome change. Many women in nursing express heightened fear and stress in the workplace. Most of this stress seems to have resulted from physicians' fear of the coming changes in health care. Mary Ellen, a nurse manager, feels resentment toward the power of the physicians. She tells,

I don't know a nurse manager here who hasn't had a problem with a physician in the last couple of months. It seems that any little thing will set them off. They complain about the most ridiculous things you can imagine.

Many of us believe that the physicians have been on the gravy train for a long time. In some places, they have actually bankrupted the system. We also believe that they are taking advantage of consumers. There is inequity in reimbursements, in terms of who works hard to provide care for patients.

I personally believe that it has been this self-centered approach in medicine that has literally corrupted our system. I feel it has to change, but I fear that it won't change in the right direction.

Mary Ellen believes that the physicians will be the last ones to suffer, because they still have power and prestige, and they control the purse strings.

When it comes to who does the most work, some patients seem to agree with Mary Ellen, according to three studies. The studies show that when nurses are allowed to do their jobs properly, patients benefit. In the late eighties, George Washington University did a study that showed the death rates in various intensive-care units were best predicted by just one factor: the level of nursing care. In the nineties, a national study commissioned by Nurses of America, a consortium of nursing organizations, found that nurses far outshine other medical personnel in patients' minds: 77 percent of the respondents said that nurses played a constructive role in health care, compared with only 42 percent saying the same about doctors. And a study from Strong Memorial Hospital, in New York showed that patients had a three times greater risk of dying or being readmitted into intensive care when doctors ignored nurses' suggestions.

ZAP Tip

For women's centers and programs,
one of the most critical tasks in changing
times is to create measurement systems that will
validate their position in hospitals.
According to Richard Ireland, publisher of **The**
Ireland Report on Succeeding in Women's
Health *(www.snowmassinstitute.com), the lack*
of tracking looms as a threat to many well-
intentioned programs whose main downfall is
the inability to prove their worth to the
institutions they serve. In addition, it's critical
to know what types of revenue they're
generating including downstream revenue
that comes from eventual referrals.

When it comes to the purse strings, however, the women physicians didn't agree with Mary Ellen. But why should they? Few of them are really in the powerful positions that their male colleagues have enjoyed for decades.

Margaret, a family-practice physician, feels that many doctors get a bad rap, and that many of them aren't in medicine for the money. Rather, they are there to help people. Her thoughts,

I hear lots of anger and depression, but I don't hear many ideas. Many of the doctors feel unappreciated.

They feel like everyone is after them, that no one appreciates the work that is done. Despite what many say, most of us are not in medicine for the money.

Margaret believes that any type of change in the health care delivery system could be a disaster for doctors in general. She feels that doctors should not be construed as the culprits. There are others—namely hospitals and attorneys who have mucked up the waters. She adds,

There are numerous articles and programs that talk about the moneys that doctors make and that doctors should be regulated because they make too much.. Granted, some make a lot. In my field, it's not true. My reaction to that is, when they regulate lawyers, they can regulate doctors.

From Change Resister to Change Enthusiast

In 1981, I published my first book, *The Woman's Guide to Financial Savvy*. Because I thought it would be the only book that I would ever produce, I really didn't pay much attention to the process. After all, why bother when it's a one-time shot? Well, the one-time shot turned into multibooks with no end in sight today. *Zapping Conflict in the Health Care Workplace* is my 23rd book. And the process that takes any work to publication has changed significantly since 1981.

I started to tune into the changes in the book business when I began work on my second book, *Money Phases*. New technology was rapidly coming on the scene. In 1979, when my agent sent the manuscript of *The Woman's Guide to Financial Savvy* to publishers, the concept of word processing was unheard of by most. It would be a few years before the computers made by the upstart kid—Apple—broke into the headlines and the workplace.

When I started to work on the second book in 1982, I heard about these new "gadgets" that were replacing the typewriter. I resisted trying one—the computer—because it wasn't cheap. Contrary to popular belief, most authors don't make a lot of money—the average income from selling books is less than $10,000 a year. I reasoned that a new computer would never pay for itself. My secretary Louie disagreed—she wanted one!

After all, my typewriter was good enough. And mine was impressive for its time. It had the capability of remembering 50 pages of material. In the early '80s, it was IBM's state-of-the art for small businesses. Granted, they were not used for writing books at that time. They were primarily for storing letters to be sent to my clients.

In the old days, from 1979 to 1986, I wrote my articles and books on a typewriter and retyped each page as changes were made. I recognized there must be a better way. So I persevered through five stages of change before finally accepting this new "gadget."

Shifting to New Technology

While in the process of producing book number two, I experienced the first two stages: resistance and great skepticism. I knew there was another way to do it, but believed that the old way—the typewriter—was good enough. And I wasn't convinced the new equipment could speed up a writer's work.

Yet, it only takes an author a short time to seek a better way than rewriting an entire manuscript, every time a paragraph needs to be moved or a few more typos are uncovered. In fact, back in the Stone Age of the '80s, it was quite common to turn in manuscripts with typos and crossed out sentences and paragraphs. We authors knew the publisher's typesetter would "clean it up." Today, clean manuscripts from author to publisher are the rule!

Louie was persistent, and I gave in—we decided to rent a computer for a month ... just to give it a trial run. While Louie embraced the genius of it, I still *resisted*. I was both *skeptical* and *hesitant*, still viewing it as a new-fangled device. But, since she was the one transferring my spoken words to paper, I let her have her way. It soon became obvious that the computer enhanced her speed and efficiency levels significantly.

I then moved into the third stage of change—*adaptation*. My attitude became, "Well, we'll keep it, but we won't get rid of the typewriters—we had three. After all, we could always use a typewriter if we needed to do something in a hurry. I certainly didn't know how to operate this new gadget. To me, "booting up" was what a woman did with her winter footwear. I didn't have a clue that it meant turning on the computer and opening a file.

In 1986, Louie went on a well-earned holiday and left me with written and detailed instructions on how to turn on the computer and access files I might need during her absence. At that time, I had begun research for the book that was published the following year, *Woman to Woman,* and was also working on my doctorate degree.

My agent had asked me to make a few changes in the book proposal and return a clean copy to him in New York. The change seemed simple—converting some single-spaced text to double spacing. So, tapping into the magic of technology, I booted-up the computer, opened the appropriate file, and proceeded to give it the commands to change from single to double spacing using Louie's instructions. But in the process, I deleted the entire manuscript! To say that this was not a good day for me is an understatement!

For three days, the techie experts tried to retrieve the lost material—and were unsuccessful. My emotions ran the gamut—from disbelief, to denial, then anger. Because of Louie's absence, I had no choice but to do it over—on a computer! I reluctantly sat down and recreated what had been lost. What do you know? I really liked using the marvelous new gadget. The computer had the ability to erase, delete, edit, and move phrases, sentences, and paragraphs around with a tap of a key. It was unbelievable to me; my "gadget," was a writer's dream.

By the end of the day, I went from *adaptation* to the fourth stage, *shifting*. I began to wonder what else could I do with the computer and word processing programs. What kind of overhead pages for workshops could it produce? What about creating cartoons to use during lectures? How about pasting graphs into articles? I was sold. In a nano-second, the fifth stage called *cohesiveness* hit. Within the month, five Apple Macintoshes found new homes in my office.

I was hooked, almost becoming evangelistic is my pronouncements of what my "Macs" could do. Today, 20 plus years later, I am still in awe of these machines. And in the process, I had become a *change enthusiast* for anyone who was contemplating a computer for home or office use.

Computers, do we need them?—Yes, I openly and loudly say I couldn't *imagine* not using a computer. I could not produce the volume of written material I do if these machines weren't an integral part of my office team. Those original three Apples have been upgraded, replaced, and added to. What happened to our state-of-the-art $3,500 IBM Memory Typewriter? I gave it away!

Resisting Resistance

Some people take forever to move beyond *resistance*. They will do whatever they can to ward off changes when the only reality is change. In working through to the fourth stage, *shifting,* many still feel uneasy or uncomfortable. Sometimes the "good old days" seem simpler. They may be, but know that we can't turn back, we can only go forward.

When people arrive at the final stage of *cohesiveness,* they've accepted the change and can work with it comfortably, whatever "it" is. They think back and fail to remember what it was really like before the change . . . with a greater sense of confidence and control.

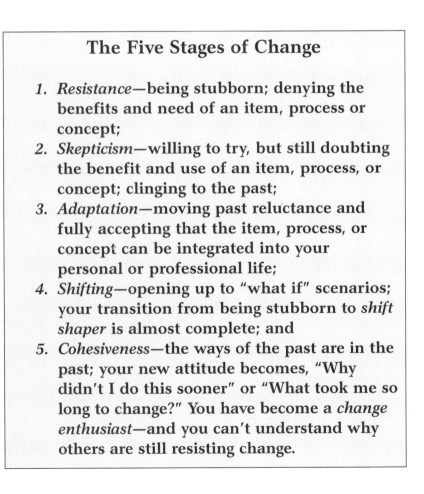

The Five Stages of Change

1. *Resistance*—being stubborn; denying the benefits and need of an item, process or concept;
2. *Skepticism*—willing to try, but still doubting the benefit and use of an item, process, or concept; clinging to the past;
3. *Adaptation*—moving past reluctance and fully accepting that the item, process, or concept can be integrated into your personal or professional life;
4. *Shifting*—opening up to "what if" scenarios; your transition from being stubborn to *shift shaper* is almost complete; and
5. *Cohesiveness*—the ways of the past are in the past; your new attitude becomes, "Why didn't I do this sooner" or "What took me so long to change?" You have become a *change enthusiast*—and you can't understand why others are still resisting change.

The Way of the VCR

Usually, people react to change in one of three ways: *reactive*, *non-active*, and *proactive*. Think of these actions as if people were VCRs. Those who are *reactive* jump out of the way, as if a car suddenly crossed the path. . They would push the "pause" button on the VCR. They'd rather not get involved. Uncertainty or lack of confidence tells them they'd be safer to step aside and see what evolves. In time, they may find that the change was exactly what they wanted, but they are too late to get on the bandwagon. They sat on the "pause" button too long.

People who are *non-active* stand still. They are paralyzed. They would push the "stop" button on the VCR. In some cases when they just want to back-peddle, they act as if they pushed the "rewind" button. Simply put, the non-active reaction means they are stuck. While in this state, it is easy to be run over, ignored, or viewed as invisible.

People who take a *proactive* position in life, however, will most likely win the race. They set the VCR at "play." They don't spend much time pausing or stopping; they get involved, ask questions, create their own future, and have a great time doing it.

Consider how you operate the VCR of your life when it comes to change. Do you push "pause", "stop" or "play"? Just realize that, if you choose to be proactive about change, you will adapt to new situations more quickly ... and with a lot less stress.

Most people are just about as happy as they make up their minds to be.

Abraham Lincoln

Personal Action Plan for
Thriving with Change

Ask . . .

1. What is the *Change* being proposed or implemented?
2. How BIG does the proposed *Change* feel?
3. In an ideal environment, does the proposed *Change* match your vision for the organization (or relationship)?
4. What factors of the *Change* can you control?
5. What elements of the *Change* can you influence or negotiate?
6. What factors of the *Change* can't you control?
7. How do you think the *Change* will impact you?
8. What do you think the final result of the *Change* will be?
9. What skills and strengths do you presently have that will be used during the *Change?*
10. What skills do you think you need to master the *Change?*
11. What attitude adjustments do you need to use during the *Change?*
12. How much time do you need (or are allowed) to implement the *Change?*
13. What roadblocks do you anticipate that could prevent you from completing the *Change?*
14. What incentive is there for making the *Change?*
15. How will you identify, reward and celebrate the completion of the *Change?*

Source: The Briles Group, Inc., Aurora CO © 2002 All Rights Reserved

Figure 7.2

Change, Change, Change

To survive and grow in a changing environment, whether professional or personal, takes a personal action plan. Change doesn't wait until you are ready to deal with it. It just happens, and quickly. The sooner you acknowledge it, the sooner you'll be able to become an active participant in whatever the change is.

As change evolves, it's important to position yourself. Begin by making a commitment to continual improvement and to learning new things. Start a program that either enhances the current skills you have or expands them, and let them take you into another field.

There is no question that jobs are being eliminated as you read this. Windows close, but new doors open. Thousands and even millions of new products, jobs, and companies are created because of change. Inpatient care has shifted to outpatient care. In the past, insurance companies, the government, and even the medical community resisted home care (or at least paying for it), but that is changing, too.

Dramatic shifts in attitudes have emerged since the nineties. New professions opened, expanding opportunities for nurses, technicians, doctors, dentists, and consultants have been created. No longer will around-the-clock patient care be the norm; rather, patients and clients need to hear all their instructions clearly in ten to twenty minutes max. This means that greater communication skills are urgently needed by care providers. From that mere fact, gadgets and gimmicks will be produced and marketed to the home-care industry—items to trigger memory, facilitate care, and make life easier.

Becoming A Change Enthusiast

As a speaker, trainer, and consultant in health care, there is no question that change is everywhere. And, it will continue for several years to come. In my workshops, I sometimes ask the participants to list the areas of change that they have experienced or observed.

Some create an incredible list; others appear or act brain dead. "What change?" they ask. If "What change?" is your mantra, guaranteed, your tenure will indeed be short. You might as well write your termination notice today. Change is not invisible—it's everywhere.

Surviving and growing in a changing environment— whether it's personal or professional—takes a commitment from you. For most people, the old saying, "One for the money, two for the show, three to get ready...," is never completed with the final phase "four to go." Most get stuck on getting ready; no one gets stuck on going. If these people operated like a VCR, they would perpetually stay on "stop". Rarely does change wait until you are ready to deal with it. It just happens, and moves along quickly, causing others to reach for the "pause" button. The sooner you acknowledge change and get on board, the sooner you press "play" and become a player.

While simply acknowledging the presence of change is not exactly proactive, anticipating the parameters of future change is very proactive. Begin your productive co-existence with change by making a commitment for ongoing self-improvement. Learn new things. Embrace a personal program that either enhances your current skills or expands them sufficiently to take you into another field.

Welcome Destruction!

Few enthusiastically jump in and wallow in change. The norm is to avoid it. For most change and shifting gears is scary business. Your fear factors rise. Denial matches fear's level. It's easy to become paralyzed. Welcome to changeophobia.

Change is usually messy. It's destructive. Things get broken along the way—old beliefs, habits, traditions. Naysayers will issue warnings—take it slow or stop it. You tiptoe around, avoid them or try to be nice. After all, no one really wants someone to be hurt in the change process.

It doesn't matter, toes will be bruised. If you, and your organization, are unwilling to break a few things along the change path, heavy baggage accumulates. Bad habits stay intact. By being careful and protecting the sacred cows, you sabotage the "could be" generation of events—your future. A caterpillar must shed its cocoon to become a butterfly. You and your organization must shed many of the old ways and habits to spread wings and fly.

Try It 21 Times

Studies have shown that to learn new behavior, an activity needs to be reinforced approximately 21 times. One of my favorite cartoon characters is *Cathy*, created by Cathy Guisewite. In one of the strips, Cathy has embarked on a new exercise program. She gleefully proclaims to the reader that it will only take 21 days of repetition to get in the swing of the new habit. After 21 days, she will be a changed woman. But by the end of the strip, she's asking herself "What is 21 days?" Her answer: "It is 20 days, 23 hours and 59 minutes longer than the time needed to get uncomfortable with a bad habit."

Few enthusiastically jump in and wallow in change. Habits, be they bad or good, are difficult to break. Most people believe that shifting gears is scary business. Fear factors rise with change. Denial matches the level of that fear and it's easy to become paralyzed. When you feel that change is escalating, try some of these tips as an offset to the fear and uncertainty that usually surfaces when change is in process:

✓ Find a place and time to relax, by yourself. Breathe. Meditate. Stretch.

✓ Take walks in your neighborhood frequently. Better yet, find out where Nature Trails and Open Space Parks are located in your community. Try exploring a new trail every time you go out.

✓ Eat a balanced diet and include foods that add nutrients, not take them away (like coffee and alcohol do).

✓ Get plenty of sleep. Soak in a hot bath or get a massage before bedtime to soothe your nerves. A good sleep is the greatest source to give you energy for dealing with change.

✓ Join a support group or take a class that interests you. These activities can create a regular structure of activities that provide a sense of stability as change rages around you.

✓ Learn how to vent in healthy ways. Take time to express your emotions freely with your spouse, your friends, and a counselor. You might even turn to journal writing where you can be especially free to say what you feel.

✓ Don't get caught up in the BMW cycle—no bitching, moaning or whining is allowed.

✓ Work out faithfully at a gym or swimming pool or on your bicycle. Releasing stress during exercise gives you more energy when you have to deal with a changing situation.

✓ Create a special ritual for yourself ... use a special place where you go regularly ... a sanctuary ... an activity you look forward to every day. Some choose reading; some time with "no noise"; some even choose a special show to watch; some want a little excitement where others want total calm. Whatever it is, it becomes your reward.

Whether change is forced on you or not, draw on your own courage and confidence. You will need it. Many types of jobs have been and will be eliminated as you read this. Windows close, but new doors open. Thousands—yes, even millions—of new products, opportunities, services, jobs and/or companies are created because of change.

Embracing change and being a *change enthusiast* enables you to take advantage of any opportunity that may catch your eye—opportunities you had not previously envisioned or contemplated. In other words, you won't be left behind. Get ready for change.

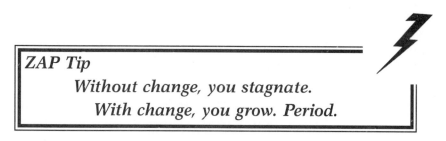

ZAP Tip
Without change, you stagnate.
With change, you grow. Period.

Summing Up

Reengineering, TQM, horizontal structures, redesigning, virtual teams—welcome to the wide world of buzzwords and management's latest, and greatest pet fads. Think back...what was your workplace like five years ago? Three? How about last year? Stable...Calm...Tranquil? Definitely not. No one in today's workplace has been untouched by the amount of significant change woven in every organization, at every level. Most people will say that their workloads and stress levels have increased over the past three years. Attribute it to change.

The evolving health care field must reinvent itself. It is, and will continue to be, one of the most important sectors of the economy. Embracing change enables you to take advantage of any opportunity that comes your way, so you won't be left behind.

Years ago, Helen Keller wrote,

> Security is mostly superstition. It does not exist in nature, nor do children of men (and women) as a whole, experience it. Avoiding danger is no safer in the long run than outright exposure. Life is either a daring adventure or nothing.

Change is here to stay—it's inevitable. And, the only thing that will change in the change process, is that it will accelerate—its rate will continue to increase. Think exponentially, not incrementally. Because of technology and communication capabilities, any changes in the future will will take place at a faster, even explosive pace.

Get over things are not going to be the way they use to be—shift happens. In order to exist and grow in today's world, you need to accept the fact that change surrounds you. If you will allow it, change will deliver phenomenal opportunities. The elimination of old habits and comfort zones will be celebrated. Thriving with change will become your work. And that's exciting.

8   Speak Up, Speak Out or Speak Not

Most people think of power as having money. For some, that may be true. In reality, power comes in other forms. One of the most powerful tools you will acquire comes from communicating: being able to speak loudly and clearly so that what you meant to convey is understood, and having the verbal savvy to articulate your words in the right context. *When dealing with and confronting conflict or a saboteur or conflict creator, communicating effectively is essential.*

In the staff/employee responses to the survey, the #1 reason for the increase in conflict was that management was unclear with communicating goals and objectives—68 percent of the respondents reported it was the major problem in their workplaces; only 19 percent of the management group felt it was. I would agree with the staff, communication (or lack of it) is at the top of the list. Without a clear, concise and consistent communication system, the workplace easily slips into chaos—an active ingredient in the conflict recipe.

ZAP Tip

The lack of communications skills labels people as being less confident and less qualified to do a job.

Managers and administrators need to wake up and learn the art of effective communicating. This doesn't mean the staff has perfected it—contraire! Staff muddles their communicating methods too. One of the most important things a manager and leader can do within their departments and workplaces is to set up an effective, smart communication system with staff—one that is understood and participated in by all members of the department (including themselves).

Creating Communicating Smarts

When it comes to any communication, there are responsibilities for both the speaker and receiver/listener.

As the speaker or initiator of a conversation, yours include four components:

- Speak loudly enough to enable the listener to hear whatever the message is.
- Speak clearly so that the listener understands what you mean.
- Use terms and words that will be of interest to the listener. When possible, use their jargon, their word

phrases, and examples that can be easily identified and related to.

- Be specific, call for action. Don't just fill the air with words; be prepared to ask for help, deliver a plan, and so on.

For the listener/receiver of the message, the four responsibilities include,

- Hearing the message generated by the speaker in an unobstructed manner. Outside noise and interference (phones ringing, others interrupting, etc.) lead to hit and miss hearing.
- Understanding what the message is. If unsure, clarity should be sought. Ask for it.
- Appreciate the fact that the speaker has attempted or conveyed the message in a manner that can be absorbed. This doesn't mean the listener must necessarily agree with what the message is, but acknowledges that it is coming across in a communication style and language that is understood.
- Participate acts on the request. This means the listener may not agree with the request and may choose not to comply with it, or even put it off.

It is imperative to understand that most communication is nonverbal, with the majority coming from gestures, tones, and body language. This means that, as a speaker, the last thing you want to do is to speak or present in a straight-faced, dull, monotone, statue like delivery. Guaranteed, within seconds, at the most minutes, your listeners will be looking over shoulders, at walls, at other people, at their hands, or through their notes or doing anything else that are deemed an alternative to listening to you.

> ## ZAP Tip
> *Communication is much more than just words. Tone, inflection, and facial expression account for approximately 93 percent of your message—words, a mere 7 percent on first contact. The key components of nonverbal communication include body posture, eye contact, distance and physical contact, vocal tone, inflection, volume, gestures, facial expression, even clothing and accessories.*

What Kind of Listener Are You?

When conducting interviews for *Zapping Conflict in the Health Care Workplace*, I work harder to limit my comments. I listen and wait, hoping to hear a nuance or one of those "gems" to which I can say, "Aha!" or "She did what?" Listening is hard work. Do you know what kind of listener you are?

- When someone is talking with you, do you doodle, take phone calls, or rearrange your desk?
- Have people ever said that you don't pay attention when they are talking to you?
- When you meet people, do you ever look over their shoulder for someone else when you or they are talking?
- Do you interrupt people before they finish their sentence or thought?
- Do you find yourself thinking about other items that need to be dealt with while another person is talking?

- Do you have a policy that allows or encourages others to interrupt you when you are talking?

If you answered yes to any of the above questions, you are a one-way communicator and most probably, a poor receiver/listener. In communicating, it is critical to let others know how you best receive information so they can adapt to you. On the other hand, you need to know how they best receive so you can adapt your style to match theirs. In the end, you both win.

> **As a listener, you listen with your ears and eyes. You listen with the sensing of those around you. It is not difficult to pick up whether others are agreeing or disagreeing with, enjoying or not enjoying, what is being presented.**

No one is born or, for that matter, wakes up suddenly and decrees they know how to communicate. Communication is a learned behavior. The first component in becoming a terrific communicator is to learn how to be a terrific listener. And with that comes an understanding that men and women, cultures, generations, etc. have different communication styles.

Technology Speaks . . . Do You Hear?

Technology is wonderful—the advances within the health care community are incredible. Imagine having open-heart surgery, an organ transplant or a dental implant using the techniques that were common 15 years ago. I doubt that you would be at the head of the line for choosing to do it the "old" way.

The way we communicate has also been impacted by technology too. Information can be distributed the old fashion way—by mouth, letter, memo, phone . . . and then there's the new way—the Internet and email. The great majority of households have Internet access; over 90 percent of businesses and organizations use it; and the great majority of patients use it.

The Internet is a fountain of information (most terrific, some rumored and wrong)—and a source that is routinely used to gather information about anything related to an illness, procedure or even information about a connected organization, association or career. Presto—it's all there with a few strokes on the keyboard.

> **Ironically, when I ask audience members of health care audiences if they are proficient with personal computers and the workings of the Internet, less than ten percent respond that they are. It's time to dust off the keyboards and hire any kid over eight to be a tutor. A whole new world opens up, one that every health care provider should have some familiarity with.**

It's not uncommon for a patient to arrive at a doctor's and have a printout of everything related to his or her disease in a file with them. It's also not uncommon for the same patient to be more current in what's going on and recommended treatments than the health care providers are. Many medical and dental practices are setting up email hours to communicate online with their patients. Hospitals are sure to follow. Clear and quick communications delivered via email can certainly reduce conflicts with patient and provider.

When one of my close friends was diagnosed with colon cancer, the first place I went to was the Internet. Within seconds, I had access to a huge amount of information that would have normally taken me days and weeks to acquire.

PowerPoint Rangers

Technology has also invaded the meeting planning industry. As a speaker, I'm always asked what audio-visual support I need. When I do a plenary or general session at a conference, I rarely use anything to support my presentation outside of a microphone. Too many times, I've sat through general sessions where the presenter shows slide after slide—most of which I can't read. At one recent presentation, the speaker before me went through three reels of slides—they didn't need a speaker—all she did was read her slides. I had also brought slides to support my presentation. I immediately told the tech to bring up the lights and the only visual would be me. I want to see the audience—it's part of communicating effectively.

When I do training workshops, I use a variety of support—overheads, interactive quizzes, games, and activities—and I sometimes use PowerPoint if the room can remain light. Why? Simply this—PowerPoint usually requires a darkened room. Darkened rooms encourage the senses to back off. If attendees are to be present, the senses should be activated. If we are all in a darkened room, I miss out on their facial expressions and they miss out on mine.

I know, I know—I too have been taken by all the flash. We have all been in an audience and watched spectacular presentations using PowerPoint and reels of coordinated slide carousels, and think, "Wow, if only I could do that!" Now, most of us can. But, and it's a big but, just because something is available, doesn't mean we have to use it! The explosion of exciting new A/V technology has made a wide range of special effects generally available to presenters. Most deplore the current trend toward replacing solid presentation content with flashy audio/video effects.

In an article in *The Wall Street Journal* "The Pentagon Declares War on Electronic Slide Shows That Make Briefings a Pain" (4-26-00), General Hugh Shelton, chairman of the Joint Chiefs of Staff, reported that he had issued an order to all U.S. military bases worldwide which translates as, "Enough with the bells and whistles—get to the point." Army Secretary Louis Calderna suggests that the Pentagon's PowerPoint presentations are alienating lawmakers when he said, "People are not listening to us because they are spending so much time trying to understand these incredibly complex slides." And Navy Secretary Richard Danzig added his two cents when he announced that he was no longer willing to sit through slide shows, saying they were necessary only if the audience was "functionally illiterate."[1]

That's exactly the problem. Misuse of technology can turn speakers into mere readers of captions for slides just as the speaker referred to above. The conference could have saved thousands of dollars by not hiring the speaker and just renting a slide show. A recent survey of Captains at Fort Benning, GA cited "the ubiquity of the PowerPoint Army" as a prime reason why the Army is losing too many bright young officers. "The idea behind most of these briefings," it said, "is for us to sit through 100 slides with our eyes glazed over." The term *PowerPoint Ranger* has even become a derogatory term, describing a desk-bound bureaucrat more adept at making slides than tossing grenades.

The downside of all the presentation-enhancing technology can be summed up by what many managers confide,

Our CEO (or Director, Vice President, Chair, etc.) used to be a really great presenter before he had

PowerPoint. Now he relies on it so much that he is less effective at motivating our employees.

That's exactly the problem. Misuse of technology can turn speakers and presenters into mere readers of captions for slides. Personal communication is lost. As a dynamic and effective communicator, you need to echo the General's words, "Enough with the bells and whistles—get to the point."

Communicating Should Be a First Language

Madison is a radiation technician on the East Coast. There are five other techs in the department beside her; two who speak a foreign language. She reports,

> When we have department meetings, a lot of the times I feel my concerns and the things that I would like to see done are never understood or heard. I don't believe the other two are tuned into the communication differences between those of us who don't understand their native tongue.
>
> There are too many times when I don't think they hear a thing I say and I don't understand what they are saying. It may be on purpose.

Holly, a director of community relations of a large hospital, faces a different type of communications problem. She reports that working within her organization is comparable to walking on eggshells. Communication is poor to nil. She finds that communication between administration and staff is so bad that someday soon all the small fires will explode and grow out of control. Her words,

> My staff is fantastic. They work long and hard hours; they increase the volume of contacts and routinely

exceed goals set by senior administration. The problem is that the administration doesn't recognize the staff. At least, they don't recognize the staff the way they would like to be recognized.

Administration seems to be stuck in a time warp. When employees reach specific goals, its style for rewarding them is to buy them lunches every two or three months. In the summer, there's a picnic; and in December there is a Christmas party. One time, the staff got a sweatshirt, another, they got a watch. But that's not what the staff wants.

What they say is, "Keep your money, keep all your toys and trinkets; just talk to us. Listen to us. If you want to recognize us above and beyond, either say so with a bonus—money even a few dollars, or simply say, 'Thank you, you did a great job.'

Now, the staff is not asking for a lot of money; they could use the bonuses. What they don't want is to have money wasted on lunches, especially when lunch is presented as more of a spur-of-the-moment thought. One time, I didn't know they were going to give a 'reward luncheon.' A majority of us were in the cafeteria and lunch was actually delivered to the tables where we were sitting. We'd already paid for our own.

It's not uncommon to hear a phrase such as "I was zinged" or "I was zapped" by someone. Typically the issue wasn't non-communication, but rather misconstrued communication. Melanie is a nurse manager in a large hospital in California. There are three other managers who work in the emergency department. All report to one director. It is not uncommon for a manager to compile various problems and wrong doings—the gnats of the workplace—put them into her complaint bag, and take them to the monthly meetings. She says,

> It is routine for one of the managers to gather up various problem situations, most of them quite minor, such as "Suzie was 10 minutes late to work," and bring them to our monthly manager/director meetings. All the problems would be unloaded at that time, and as a result the director began to believe that we couldn't handle anything on our floors.
>
> The other nurse manager and I would respond to her that it would be much more helpful to resolve whatever the problem is by bringing it to us immediately, or at least by the next day when it involves another shift. Why hold it off for several weeks and put us on the spot as if we were incompetent?
>
> It wasn't uncommon for me and the other nurse manager to zap her back with a laundry list of problems. Finally, after attending a program where we heard you speak, we decided to bring it to a head and explain how it felt to be zinged. Initially, the manager denied it. But we were prepared; we cited various examples. We finally all agreed that we did have communication problems, and have agreed to keep talking to try to resolve it. So, it's a first step.

Removing the Zaps and Zings

Melanie indicates that talking it out is a first step, and she is correct. She and the other manager waited over a year before they finally confronted the third manager on her methodology of identifying and presenting problems. During that time, on-going conflicts were everywhere. Many problems were construed as minor ones that should have been dealt with immediately, before they had the opportunity to mushroom. If minor issues of the workplace are not dealt with, they become erupting volcanoes.

> **When one individual zaps another, whether it is a staff employee or someone in management, it definitely leaves a bad taste. A common—and in some places, expected—reaction is to zap back. The zinging and zapping become a vicious cycle, and if not nipped in the budding stages, are likely to infest the workplace, turning it toxic. Morale and cooperation plummet. It sometimes is difficult to tell who is doing what to whom.**

Another factor that is insidious within the workplace is gossip, the number one way to undermine another. Both men and women gossip, but women tend to be more probing and to obtain more personal information that can be spread about.

As the health services administrator at a jail on the West Coast, Deb feels that workplace gossip is counterproductive and extremely negative. She constantly counsels her staff not to feed into it. In keeping ongoing communications on line, Deb has supported an open door policy. She has found that innocent, casual statements have been misinterpreted and circulated among those in her workplace.

In the past, it wasn't uncommon for me to respond to anyone who came to my office door to come on in and sit down. When they started to talk about their family and what they do on their days off, I would listen and make casual comments. The next thing I knew, everyone in the jail knows what I like to do, where I live, and what my hobbies are. I learned that it is very easy to be misquoted.

I've learned to document everything I say. Before I call people into my office, I write it out. I then say only what is on the piece of paper. After I tell them whatever it is I need to tell them, I have them sign the paper when I finish, so there is some basis for agreement upon what was said—and what wasn't said.

Unfortunately, most people are on automatic when they communicate. Sometimes the brain is not put in gear before the mouth opens. Speech patterns are learned early on and engaged with little thought. Childhood speech characteristics are deeply imprinted by the time a woman reaches adulthood. A native speech pattern, whether it is stuttering, having your speech littered with "umms" and "ahs," or even slurring words, can damage your credibility, your ability to get a point across and to confront a saboteur or a conflict creator in your midst.

ZAP Tip
When gossip is circulating, rarely is the benefit of doubt given—people love to think the worst, not the best—which is usually the mission of gossip . . . and the gossip.

Apologizing, Hedging & Qualifying
Another factor that appears to have a greater drawback for women than for men is the use of *polite* speech. On one

side, it shows a high regard and respect for another. That's not bad. Some cultures covet this behavior. But there are times when too polite speech lacks the necessary assertiveness or forcefulness.

In almost every book on communication, there is mention of women's use of *tag* questions or qualifiers. Whether women use them more than men is not clear. There is a debate. The important fact is for you to be aware if you use speech mannerisms that can be misinterpreted. Typical *tag* questions include,

"This needs to be completed by four o'clock. Is that OK with you?"

"We need to be at the meeting at 10 AM tomorrow. Is that a problem for you?"

Where the first sentence is declarative, the second sentence—the *tag*—can be interpreted as a window for choice. The receiver of the remark may say, "No, it's not OK with me." "Yes, it's a problem."

Other factors of nonassertive speech patterns that can get you into trouble include the use of *qualifiers*. Qualifiers are often interpreted as a form of discounting what is being said. Qualifiers are hedges—words or phrases that make you sound uncertain,

"You know," "Sorta," "I guess," "I suppose."

When you are uncertain, *qualifiers* are perfectly legitimate. But as fillers or hedges, they *lessen your power* when communicating with another. Examples of beginning-sentence phrases are,

"I'm not sure that this is a good idea, but..."

"You may think this is dumb (stupid, silly, idiotic), but ..."

Women also get into trouble when they use too many adverbs or adjectives. The result is that their speech is sometimes trivialized. Such as,

"It's so lovely and wonderful to be here today.

"I think this is so very wonderful, exciting, and fabulous. I know it's going to be beyond belief."

Sometimes, women feel inhibited to ask for something boldly. So as not to appear so bold it is common to soften a statement. Let's say you want to go to lunch. Instead of saying, "Let's go to lunch," to a co-worker, you might say,

"Gosh, I'm famished, and I've been so busy: would you like...Oh, you're probably really busy too, and don't have time to take a break ... Or do you think you'd like to get a bite to eat with me??????"

ZAP Tip
Women need to learn goal-oriented language in order to relate their messages more effectively.

Because many women are process-oriented in their relationships, they are that way with answers and explanations as well. When someone asks you something, it's not uncommon to tell the reasons in detail of how you arrived at your answer. Some people love to hear all the details; others don't. They'd rather you focus on the bottom-line impact.

When people apologize, it is usually an expression of regret at having done something wrong to another. Unfortunately, women are harder and more judgmental of themselves when it comes to accepting or taking on blame. Men tend to apologize only when it is expected or when it can't be avoided. In fact, sometimes men never say, "I'm sorry." Instead, they make another statement with the, "I'm sorry" implied, as in "I screwed up."

One of the reasons men avoid apologizing is that it tends to put them in an inferior position. Since women are often people pleasers, being apologetic doesn't make them feel put down. According to Deborah Tannen, Ph.D. and author of *You Just Don't Understand,*

> There are many ways that women talk that
> make sense and are effective in conversation
> with other women. When in conversation with
> men, they appear powerless and self-depreciating.
> One such pattern is that women seem to apologize all
> the time.[2]

One thing to keep in mind is that it is not necessary to apologize over a situation over which you have no control. If a land mine is exposed (or explodes), it's sufficient to state whatever the problem is (minus any apologies), followed by recommended solutions to fix it. What Tannen implies is that when the issue is between women, it's OK to apologize; in fact, it can be advantageous in creating a bond and even encouraging intimacy. For men, though, apologizing may be construed as a weakness.

Another common speech faux pas is inviting disagreement. When you have a strong opinion about a situation, or you require someone's participation, it doesn't make sense to preface your statement or request with a disclaimer:

"I may be wrong, but..."

"You may not like what I'm going to say, but..."

Not only do such statements lessen your speech and presence power; they also invite your listeners to move into a defensive posture, and disagree with you before you have a chance even to make a statement. *Saboteurs and conflict creators who are being confronted look for windows to disagree or counter what you are attempting to get across.* Being friendly can do wonders in the right place at the right time, but it also can be a distraction. Don't chitchat excessively.

What to Avoid When Miss Manners Isn't There

Unassertive-type mannerisms can get women into trouble. As a rule, women are more inclined to create eye contact with the person they are talking to. That's the good news; don't avoid it. Good eye contact is a communications gesture that should be mastered early on. With it, you are more likely to be taken seriously. If you constantly hop around with your eyes, rarely connecting with the person you are talking to, your remarks can easily be interpreted as meaning you're not serious, or you're nervous. A subtle message can be sent that your concern, opinion, or statement is not important. When you don't make eye contact with another you are attempting to confront, you can signal fear or submissiveness or even invite interruption.

In addition to using speech patterns that are unassertive, women are far more likely to smile inappropriately, especially during times of conflict, than are men. It is not uncommon for both men and women to interpret a smile during a stressful or conflicting time that all is OK, you're OK, and the issue is not as big a deal as you feel it is. It is also not uncommon, during stressful and painful times, for women to laugh or, worse, giggle. One of the best things that a woman can do is learn to keep a straight face, especially when it comes to dealing with a saboteur. Your goal is to get your point across—that the behavior directed toward you (or another) is not OK.

Normally, when listeners nod their head up and down, most people assume that they agree with the speaker. Not necessarily so. Women appear to be more inclined to nod their heads during a conversation than do men—even when they don't agree with or understand what's being said. It's more of a mannerism of taking information in.

Since conflict knows no gender, it can be generated from a woman or a man; the *Communications Savvy Quiz* below is designed to bring up your awareness on gender differences in communicating. Answer true or false to see how well you understand women and men.

Your New Guideposts

No one communication style is the best. Contrary to your own belief, you may think that your style is the preferred way. Wrong. Depending upon the situation and the circumstance, other styles may be preferable. Learn to respect the strengths and weaknesses of each. There are parts from each style that might assist you in communicating better with another.

Communication Savvy Quiz©

1. Men tell more jokes than women do.
2. Women avoid verbal confrontation more than men do.
3. Women speak more politely than men do.
4. Women tell fewer stories than men do.
5. Men look at women more frequently when talking with them than women look at men.
6. Men talk about their feelings more often than women do.
7. Men would prefer to talk about things rather than people.
8. Men talk more on the phone than women do.
9. Men accept words at their face value more often than women do.
10. Women brag about their successes more often than men do.
11. Gaining respect is more important to women than to men.
12. Men gossip more than women do.
13. Women smile more than men do in conversation.
14. Women and men use the same set of words.
15. Men are likely to repeat requests more often than women are.
16. Men interrupt others more than women.
17. Men's faces are more expressive when they speak than are women's.
18. Women make decisions quicker than men do.
19. Men tend to be more apologetic than women are.
20. When a woman is in conversation with another, she tends to nod her head in approval of the speaker.
21. Men use vocal put-downs with others more often than women do.

Quiz Answers

1. True	8. False	15. False
2. True	9. True	16. True
3. True	10. False	17. False
4. False	11. False	18. False
5. False	12. False	19. False
6. False	13. True	20. False
7. True	14. False	21. True

A score of 19-21 is excellent; 16-18 is good; 13-15 is fair; 14 or less is big trouble. If you score less than 15, it's critical that you go back to basic Communications 101. Ask a close friend to give you honest feedback about your speaking and listening styles. You need help.

———

Source: The Briles Group, Inc. © 2002 Aurora CO. All Rights Reserved

Exhibit 8.1

Being Assertive Wards Off Saboteurs and Conflict Creators

As the century turns, many women are still expected to stay with the more traditional feminine style-soft and sub-missive communication style. A stereotype holdover. In reality, women should tap into the method that works best for them, which could be a variety. Consider the classic *Gone with the Wind.* In it, Scarlett O'Hara displayed every tendency imaginable. At times, she was soft. She could be manipulative. And she could run over anyone as if she were a Mack truck.

Miss Scarlett was as competitive as any men that she encountered. She was assertive, innovative, creative, pushy, and at times, vindictive in order to get what she wanted—just as some of the men were. In other words, Scarlett did what she had to do to get what she wanted. The men were no different. One of the Momisms you probably heard growing up was, "Your turn will come." Scarlett didn't believe that her turn would come. She had to create the path to get there and make it her turn. She took it. So should you.

The women and men you communicate with, whether it's a friendly and non-adversarial or it's a confronting and adversarial situation, will communicate with and to you in different styles.

- some are direct in their communications—the bottom liners, they want minimal information, just get to the point
- some are data gathers—the more information they get, the better
- some react and speak intuitively and emotionally—they follow their gut reactions and hunches
- some are more interested in keeping the peace—they never raise their voices and try to get all sides heard
- some communicate in multiple channels—they jump around and have difficulty focusing on any one topic or person at a time
- some are silent, almost passive—they take it in, but have difficulty articulating what they want or what their concerns are.

Your ability to be assertive is the basis of clear and honest communication between you and another. Most communications and behaviors fall into four categories: assertive, passive/submissive (nonassertive), confusing and aggressive.

Aggressive behaviors can be divided into direct and indirect.

Women who are nonassertive are most likely reluctant or unable to confidently say and express what they feel, believe, or think. When you cross the line from assertiveness—confidently expressing yourself—to outright aggression, you enter troubled waters. There's a big difference. Granted, you are able to express yourself, but the method in which it's done often involves intimidation, degradation, or even demeaning another.

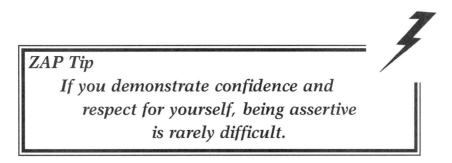

ZAP Tip

If you demonstrate confidence and respect for yourself, being assertive is rarely difficult.

When you have low confidence and feel that your opinions or beliefs are of little or no value, you often find yourself as a "doormat." Others may view you as someone they can easily work over and push around. If you appear or act with low confidence or passiveness, your behavior is easily interpreted as being a "wimp." You are fair game for the saboteurs and conflict creators of the world.

Do you recognize what type behavior you use and how you communicate? Are you assertive, passive, confusing, or aggressive? Recognition is a big step toward making your communication style a more appropriate and accurate display of what you want and how you feel. There are four parts to effective and assertive communication especially when your objective is to change a behavior or an outcome:

- A nonjudgmental description of what you want changed
- A disclosure of how you feel
- A clear description of the impact and effect of the other person's behavior on you
- A description of what behavior you desire

This approach works whether you are a beginner or feel that your skills are quite good. Every master always goes back for retooling. When you speak clearly and succinctly, you are far more likely to gain the admiration and respect of others. You are also less likely to be a target of a saboteur and when you are, you have the tools to articulate clearly what you expect in the future. But that's not a 100 percent guarantee; there are always those who will respond to your assertiveness with put downs or other demands. Those who do are usually insecure and are attempting to put you in your place—so that they can maintain theirs.

When you are communicating a problem, make sure you communicate the real issue and the factors within the problem; and make sure you communicate to the right person. One of my personal mottoes is "Don't take no from someone who does not have the authority to say yes." If you are communicating a specific issue that you desire to be changed, make sure you communicate it to the person who has the capability of making the changes. Depending on the degree of conflict or sabotage you are dealing with, the identified saboteur or conflict creator is the person to be confronted and communicated with.

Eliminating the Conspiracy of Silence

When respondents to the survey were asked to identify factors helping to eliminate some of the traps of the workplace, the need to speak up and speak out and communicate more effectively was the most frequent response. To be believable in any work environment, the silence trap of not dealing directly with an issue (versus the preferred indirect method of grumbling and complaining to colleagues about whatever the problem is) must be eliminated.

ZAP Tip

This is where the men and women are separated. Men are far more inclined to speak up, confront the issue or blow it off; it's not worth their time. Women are less likely to speak up, confront it, don't blow it off and allow whatever it is to fester or resurface in other areas. Women also assume (or possibly hope) that someone else will step forward and speak up and front for them. That's not the way the world works, at least not today.

If you don't speak up and speak out, you are liable to be stymied by others who do. A very vocal minority ends up speaking for everyone, making decisions that affect the silent majority, and often not to the majority's liking.

Speaker, Trainer and Consultant Venner M. Farley, the former Dean of Health Professionals at Golden West College, in Huntington Beach, California, leads programs to help nurses speak up when hospital conditions are unfair. When a physician asked her if she was one of those nursing teachers who attempt to make students think like doctors, her response was "No. Actually, I expect much more of them than that."

Enough Was Enough

Several years ago, I spoke at a women physicians' conference in Vail, Colorado. The other key speaker was neurosurgeon Frances Conley. The previous year, she had gone public about the sexual harassment that she had been subjected to over the years at Stanford University's Medical School and Hospital. She made national headlines when she resigned and spelled out her reasons in op-ed pages across the country.

Reverberations echoed throughout the country. At every level of the medical community, a torrent of similar stories from women was unleashed. Conley felt that speaking out has to be viewed as a crusade to reawaken others' thinking. The need to do this is rooted in a sexist society. Conley told me about a letter she received from another woman after she went public with her statements and accusations. A portion of it said,

> Men learn from early childhood that they are
> superior to women. They, the men, cultivate methods
> for keeping women in their place throughout their
> lives, and the behavior becomes automatic for them.
> Society teaches women the same thing that men are
> better than we are, and we believe it.

Conley added that since women also believe that men are superior, society considers women expendable. She notes that when women hit the 40-45-age bracket, they become not only expendable in the United States but also invisible.

Before meeting Conley, I had seen her on a televised panel with three other professionals: former Congresswoman Pat Shroeder of Colorado; Bernadine Healey, former head of the National Institutes of Health; and a male cardiologist from New York, whose name I have repressed because I was so appalled by his remarks. The overall discussion was about earmarking of National Institutes of Health funds for research on women. The three women all supported more funds for research on women's health, since major health studies have usually included majority or exclusive populations of men, and few have included or been dedicated to women.

The cardiologist felt that there was no reason to allocate additional funds for research on women. His rationale? "There are lots of problems that males have that have not been researched adequately, including impotence in males over 60." His exact words were, "Impotence is a huge problem for men." I just about fell off the couch laughing. And of course, he was right! —Pfizer has made a fortune from Viagra™. My only disappointment was that the three women weren't laughing along with me.

Management Doesn't Get It

Georgia, a former accountant, is now a nurse manager who says her medical director is impaired by substance abuse, and the hospital will take no action. Her words,

> A number of the nurses have witnessed and documented his drug and alcohol use. Nothing is ever done about it. The medical staff doesn't do an investigation, although they have the power. Their approval of the use of drugs is their non-action.
> I called my boss one day to intervene because the medical director smelled so strongly of alcohol. She

did come in and confront him and then told us to mind our own business.

I've worked closely with my staff over the years to teach them techniques for dealing with conflicts. When we confront a situation that we know is dangerous, especially together, upper management consistently backs down.

We have an OB on the staff that has been here for ten years. On several occasions he has come in drunk to deliver babies and been put to bed by the nursing staff. Nothing has ever happened. This is a small community. The last few years, maternity cases are down and the hospital has hired a consultant. We have done more advertising, programs have been revamped, and the facility has been redecorated; yet maternity cases continue to decline. It's not that women are having fewer babies; there are actually more. They just don't come here.

Georgia is caught in a Catch-22 dilemma. Doctors do bring in revenues by their affiliations with hospitals. When they have privileges at more than one hospital, they can direct patient loads and enhance a hospital's status. Power talks, hospitals listen. But, all that is needed to derail a hospital is a few malpractice cases. Word spreads in a community, especially a small one. Money talks, hospitals sometimes listen.

Instead of addressing the problem directly, managers hired marketing consultants to tell them how to bring in more business. If a doctor can't be detoxified, his privileges should be terminated. Most intelligent people know it, including the patients. Management needs to get it—the nurses know why cases are down, a consultant wasn't needed.

Send More Men

Claudia has been a staff nurse for many years. She agrees that speaking out is necessary, but she also says that if you don't follow through, speaking out doesn't work. She also believes that as more men enter nursing, nurses will move from complaining to formulating an action plan. Her take,

> I've been around enough nurses to know that they complain, but they don't take an active role in the solution. I feel that when there are male nurses, it's good for us. They are inclined to say, 'We have been talking about this long enough. Just do it.'

Sue Anne, a clinical educator in surgery, agrees that there is a new breed entering the profession. She adds,

> My facility does a three-year diploma course. I see older staff undermining the new nurses. Many of them hold little bits of information over their heads, not giving them the full picture of a specific problem or procedure that would make it so much easier. The newer generation of nurses has learned how to ask the right questions and how to confront those who are withholding information.

Sue Anne is on the mark when she talks about education. It has to be a factor. Coupled with public awareness, it will raise the consciousness level for speaking out.

Summing Up

What is the bottom line when it comes to communication? First, moving beyond miscommunication, non-communication and wrong communication is critical. Second, by not communicating a problem when it occurs, your silence says it's OK to continue doing whatever the activity is. And third, neither men nor women are the "better" communicators. Both women and men must learn to be more flexible in their styles of speaking as well as in their interpretation and understanding of speaking. It is absurd to pretend or ignore the fact that there are communication differences between genders as well as cultures, races and ages.

> **It is always ideal when others speak out at the same time, but that is rare. And going solo is lonely. Friends and co-workers, who you thought were with you, mysteriously disappear and withdraw their support. By their actions, they are saying that they don't want to speak out, at least not to anyone who can make a difference.**

There are two sides to communication: the speaking and the receiving. As the receiver or listener, it is your responsibility to clear up any potential misunderstandings. The speaker knows what she or he wants to communicate—what he or she means. If you are unclear as to what is said or meant, you must clear it up. Try,

"I'm sorry. I'm not sure what you meant. Is it _____? If not, would you be more clear?"

By encouraging others to do the same, you will significantly reduce problems in communications in both your workplace and personal life. By expanding your communication skills, you enhance any confrontation you may encounter or initiate with a saboteur or conflict creator in your future.

Women need to speak out sooner, instead of maintaining their silence. One of the reasons you remain silent is that you are embarrassed by what has happened. Some may squirm and be uncomfortable. Too bad. It is the same type of behavior that happens within dysfunctional families. Talking about it, even though you are embarrassed, is best. Bring it out in front, and let others discuss it with you.

Bringing "it" out into the open and talking about it is an appropriate response to a dysfunctional workplace, too. There is another parallel: in a relationship that has gone sour, there comes a time when it needs to end. At work, too, if you are going to speak up and speak out, you have to be prepared to leave. Don't put energy into rearranging the deck chairs on the Titanic—people have to be willing to vote with their feet.

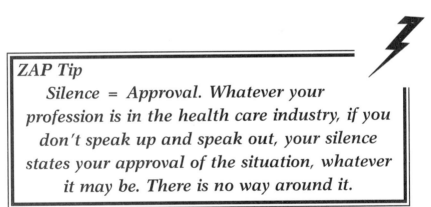

ZAP Tip

Silence = Approval. Whatever your profession is in the health care industry, if you don't speak up and speak out, your silence states your approval of the situation, whatever it may be. There is no way around it.

By encouraging others to speak up and out, you will significantly reduce miscommunications, non-communications, and wrong communications in both your workplace and your personal life. A total win for all.

9

The Art of Carefronting

Conflict and confrontation should go hand in hand, and many women realize that they ought to confront, yet they often don't. So why do women so rarely engage in direct confrontation? The answer is found in an old dictum/Momism: "Nice girls don't complain" and "Nice/good girls don't fight."

Anger and Conflict—Misconceptions

Many believe that the sign of a poor manager is the development of conflict. Some believe that a conflict signals low concern or support on the part of management. And, most believe that anger is destructive, while others believe that if you leave a conflict alone, it will go away. There is also the belief that all conflicts must be resolved, no matter what; smile, shake hands, and let bygones be bygones. Phooey.

All these beliefs are misguided and usually wrong. Conflict arises in the workplace because people have different goals and objectives. Their perceptions vary. They hear differently. Culture, race, and gender all play a part. There is also general "noise"—news, events, fear, and concerns—that creates conflict. Most conflicts are believed to be rooted in some specific action or context. In reality, however, they are usually caused by communication failures or breakdowns, specifically in listening.

There are times, of course, when conflict results from deliberate provocation. When you can identify a situation in which another is purposely trying to hurt you, my advice is to get out. You are not going to change this person, and you will not have time to go through the series of processes that might enlighten her. Most of the time, though, a conflict creator is out to enhance his or her own reputation, and you just happened to be in the way.

Because women are inclined to have "confrontophobia," what seems to be a primary conflict may actually be an accumulation of half-remembered and relatively minor items, which can magnify a problem the size of a gnat into a problem the size of an elephant.

Traits of Conflict

There are several traits and characteristics of conflict. As a conflict escalates, concern for self increases in a parallel manner. When there is conflict, the desire to win increases with the rise in self-interest. Saving face takes on an increased importance.

Managing techniques for conflict vary. What works at a low level of conflict can be ineffective and counterproductive at an intense or high level of conflict. People can use different styles of conflict within a conflict.

When dealing with someone you are going to confront,

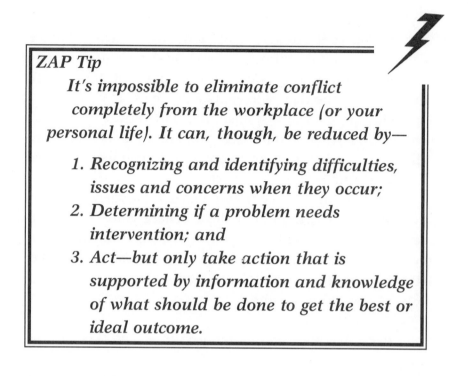

ZAP Tip

It's impossible to eliminate conflict completely from the workplace (or your personal life). It can, though, be reduced by—

1. *Recognizing and identifying difficulties, issues and concerns when they occur;*
2. *Determining if a problem needs intervention; and*
3. *Act—but only take action that is supported by information and knowledge of what should be done to get the best or ideal outcome.*

personally or professionally, it makes sense to identify what her strengths and weaknesses are by understanding her preferred style of handling conflict. It means you have to step back, change hats, and put yourself in her place by anticipating her responses or reactions when you confront her.

The Key Styles of Managing Conflict

Sometimes a particular conflict-managing style will work best in a specific situation. Ideally, you should be able to recognize which conflict styles are emerging when you are dealing with someone, as well as the style or styles with which you are responding. As you become more skilled in dealing with conflicts, you will be able to choose the conflict-managing style that is most appropriate.

One of the first steps is to discover what your preferred

style of managing conflict is, and Exhibit 9.1 will help you do that. Figure 9.1 displays five modes of managing conflict—competing, collaborating, accommodating, avoiding, and compromising—along two axes, one that represents assertiveness and one that represents willingness to cooperate.

Below, circle the response that best reflects your feelings/actions when you imagine you are under stress. After all, when conflict is at your doorstep, do you feel calm and happy? It's an odd duck who does.

Complete the survey in two ways. First, answer as you normally would; then do a shift. Where you see the personal pronouns relating to you, revise and substitute *she, her, he,* or *him.* For example: "When *she has* (you have) strong feelings in a conflict, *she* (you) would _____ ."
Now answer as you think the person you need to confront would answer.

After you complete the exercise the second time around substituting *she* for *you,* you should have a strong indication of what "her" style of dealing with conflict is. The result is that you are now in the driver's seat. You have the opportunity to take the lead and adjust your style to match hers. When this happens, she will be better able to "hear" what you have to say. A compromise that allows for a win-win result, versus lose-lose or lose (you)-win (her), is more likely to be achieved.

Conflict Managing Styles Questionnaire©

1. **When you feel strongly about a conflict, you would:**
   ___ A. Enjoy the excitement and feel a sense of accomplishment.
   ___ B. View the conflict as a venture and a challenge.
   ___ C. Be concerned about how others are impacted.
   ___ D. Be dismayed because someone could be harmed.
   ___ E. Become persuaded there is little to nothing you can do to resolve it.

2. **Ideally, what's the best result you expect from a conflict?**
   ___ A. It will encourage others to look at the issues and face facts.
   ___ B. It will eliminate extremes in positions and enable a middle ground to surface.
   ___ C. It will clear the air, increasing commitment and results.
   ___ D. It will clarify the absurdity of a situation and draw co-workers closer together.
   ___ E. It will reduce complacency and apathy and identify who is to blame.

3. **When you have the final word in a conflict situation, you would:**
   ___ A. Let everyone know what your view is.
   ___ B. Attempt to negotiate the best settlement for all concerned.
   ___ C. Encourage others to share their opinions and suggest that a position be found that both sides might try.
   ___ D. Provide support to whatever the group decides.
   ___ E. Remove yourself from the process, citing rules if they apply.

Conflict Managing Styles Questionnaire© (continued)

4. **If anyone is irrational, illogical or unreasonable, you would:**
   _____ A. Be blunt and say that you don't like it.
   _____ B. Drop hints that you're not pleased; but avoid direct confrontation.
   _____ C. Identify the conflict and suggest that you both probe possible solutions.
   _____ D. Not say anything.
   _____ E. Keep away from the person.

5. **If you disagree with co-workers, you:**
   _____ A. Hang firm and justify your position.
   _____ B. Appeal to the logic and goodwill of the group in the hope of persuading most that your way or idea is the best.
   _____ C. Identify and review areas of agreement and disagreement, then look for options that reflect everyone's views.
   _____ D. Give in, go with the group to keep the peace.
   _____ E. Withdraw from discussing the project and don't commit to any decision reached.

6. **When you find yourself disagreeing with other members about a project, you:**
   _____ A. Stand by your convictions and defend your position.
   _____ B. Appeal to the logic of the group in the hope of convincing at least a majority that you are right.
   _____ C. Explore points of agreement and disagreement, then search for alternatives that take everyone's view into account.
   _____ D. Go along with the group.
   _____ E. Do not participate in the discussion and don't feel bound by any decision reached.

7. **When someone takes an opposite position to the rest of the team, you would:**
   _____ A. Tell the others in the group who the roadblock is and encourage them to move on without him or her if necessary.
   _____ B. Encourage them to communicate their objections so that a trade-off can be reached.
   _____ C. Learn why they view the issue differently so the others can re-evaluate their own positions.
   _____ D. Recommend the problem area be set aside and discuss other areas that are in agreement.
   _____ E. Keep quiet because it is best not to get involved.

8. **When conflict surfaces in your team, you:**
   _____ A. Press forward for a quick decision so that the task is completed.
   _____ B. Attempt to shift the dispute toward a middle ground.
   _____ C. Analyze the problem with the group so that it can be discussed.
   _____ D. Relieve the tension with a good story.
   _____ E. If the conflict doesn't involve you, steer clear of it.

9. **In handling conflict between co-workers, you would:**
   _____ A. Anticipate areas of opposition and prepare replies to perceived objections prior to open conflicts.
   _____ B. Encourage co-workers to identify possible areas that may meet objections.
   _____ C. Recognize that conflict does not mean disaster and encourage them to identify shared concerns and/or goals.

Conflict Managing Styles Questionnaire© (continued)

     ____ D. Promote unanimity on the basis that the conflict can lead to the demise of friendly relations and friendships.

     ____ E. Find someone who is neutral to arbitrate the matter.

10. **In your opinion, why would one group fail to work with another?**

     ____ A. Lack of a clearly stated position, unstructured or failure to back up and support the group's position.

     ____ B. Tendency to force leaders to abide by the group's decision, as opposed to promoting flexibility, which could facilitate compromise.

     ____ C. Tendency of groups to be myopic and view negotiations with a win/lose perspective

     ____ D. Lack of motivation to work peacefully with the other group.

     ____ E. Leaders place emphasis on maintaining their own power versus addressing the issues involved.

Total the number of A's, B's, etc. and insert below:

A _____ B _____ C _____ D _____ E _____
Competing   Compromising   Collaborating   Accommodating   Avoiding

_____

Source: The Briles Group, Inc.© 2002 Aurora, CO All Rights Reserved.

Exhibit 9.1

    To score the survey, total the number of A's, B's, C's, D's, and E's from questions one through ten. Most health care professions will say that they are highly collaborative (C responses)—yet they don't act so collaborative when conflict surfaces. That's because when conflict happens, your most likely response will be in the back-up—#2 mode.

It's as though you save your real strength if all else fails. The problem, though, is that you may not have the opportunity to be collaborative; there isn't time for "back-up."

Use the conflict-handling grid below to identify your or another's method of using conflict. There are five styles: *competitive, collaborative, avoiding, accommodating,* and *compromising.* Look at the dimension of the grid that is labeled unassertive-assertive. You know when you are unassertive; it means that you want to pull back from a conflict; you will do anything to avoid a confrontation, to make it go away. If you are assertive, you will be more aggressive and active in dealing with it.

Five Modes of Managing Conflict

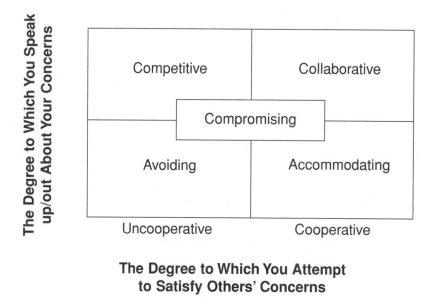

The Degree to Which You Speak up/out About Your Concerns

Competitive	Collaborative
Compromising	
Avoiding	Accommodating

Uncooperative   Cooperative

The Degree to Which You Attempt to Satisfy Others' Concerns

Source: *The Five Conflict-Handling Modes.* (Adapted from the Thomas-Kilmann Conflict MODE Instrument, developed by Kenneth W Thomas and Ralph H. Kilmann in 1972. (MODE is an acronym for "management of differences exercise.")

Figure 9.1

ZAP Tip

*Complete the Questionnaire a second time, this time substituting the pronouns **she** (he), and so on, for **you**. You will then have a strong indication of what your opponent's conflict-managing style is. This puts you in the driver's seat, allowing you the opportunity to take the lead and adjust your style to match hers. When this happens, she will be better able to hear what you have to say, and a solution is more likely to be achieved.*

I have never met a person who said she did not know whether she was assertive or unassertive. If you speak up for what you believe in or what you perceive as justified, you are on the assertive side. If you believe that others routinely take advantage of you and that your voice isn't heard, you lean toward being nonassertive or unassertive.

Now look at the uncooperative-cooperative dimension—the degree to which you attempt to satisfy someone's concerns. If you are a cooperative person, you know that you will do what you can to work along with another, even when you don't agree with her. If you are the opposite, or uncooperative, your choice is either to avoid any dealings with her or to attempt to resolve the issue your way.

Again, step back. If things don't go your way, have you ever felt or said, "I'm out of here."? Or do you say, "Hold on; let's continue to work and see if we can get a resolution."? The first is uncooperative, the second, cooperative.

By putting the two dimensions of the grid together, you will end up with a matrix of five different styles of dealing with conflict. The compromising style will be in the center. It represents the balance of being cooperative and uncooperative, assertive and unassertive.

Meet the Styles

This section looks at each of the following styles more closely—competitive, collaborative, accommodating, avoiding, and compromising. As you look more closely at the different styles and read the following descriptions, you'll recognize one or another that is the normal or usual way in which you deal with conflict.

Think about individuals you work with. You should be able to identify their more dominant style by asking yourself, "Is she cooperative or uncooperative, assertive or unassertive." Each of the five styles has unique characteristics.

The Competitive Style

Competitive women and men are very assertive. Getting their way is often at the top of their list and cooperating with others secondary. They approach any conflict in a direct and forceful way. A competitive woman's attitude could be "I don't care what other people think; it's my way or none." Women whose dominant style is competitive are more interested in satisfying their own concerns, often at the expense of others and they will do it by pulling rank, being forceful, and/or arguing.

The competitive style is a good one to have in your corner when you are in a position of power. It can, though, alienate people. If you are someone of little power (or you are wrong or you have no support) in a disagreement with a co-worker, manager, or supervisor and you use a competitive style, you may find yourself without a job. A competitive style doesn't work without power contacts and/or support behind you.

Competitive styles work when you:

- Create win-lose situations
- Use rivalry
- Use power plays to get what you want
- Force submission
- Feel the issue is very important and you have a big stake in getting your way
- Have the power to make the decision, and it appears that is the best way to act
- Must make a decision quickly, and you have the power to make it
- Feel you have no other options
- Feel you have nothing to lose
- Are in an emergency situation where immediate, decisive action is necessary
- Can't get a group to agree or feel you are at an impasse, and someone must make the group move ahead
- Have to make an unpopular decision, but action is required now, and you have the power to make that choice

Your primary objective when you enforce a competitive style is not popularity. You may pick up supporters and admirers along the way if your solutions work. A competitive style is used to get your way for something that is important to you. When you feel that you are confident that you have to move quickly or act immediately and you will succeed, using a competitive style does not necessarily mean that you are a bully or pushy.

The Collaborative Style

People who are collaborators are actively involved in working out any conflict. If your style is one of collaboration, you vocally assert what you want. At the same time, you also cooperate with others.

Being collaborative takes time. It is not an instant "my way," as someone with a competitive style would demonstrate. Collaboration takes longer because you first have to identify the issues and concerns. Then, each party must be willing to listen to the other's needs and concerns as well as other issues. If you have the time to process within the collaborative style, it's more probable that a win-win scenario will evolve.

A collaborative style may initially surface when parties say that their goals are the same. As the surface is probed, other issues emerge which can lead to confusion about the overall goal. The collaborative style works very well when the parties involved have different underlying needs.

When a collaborative approach is used, it often encourages each person coming to the table to identify her needs and wants. A key factor to a successful collaboration involves taking the necessary time to identify the needs and interests of the parties involved. The issues are understood, and it is far easier to seek alternatives and compromises that will work for all. The collaborative approach works when you:

- Are in a problem-solving position
- Confront differences by sharing ideas and information
- Search for integrated solutions
- Find situations where all can win
- See problems and conflicts as challenges
- Know that the issues are very important to both or all parties involved

- Have a close, continuing, or interdependent relationship with the other party
- Have time to deal with the problem
- Know that you and the other person are aware of the problem and are clear about what you want
- Are confident that the other party is willing to put some thought and work into finding a solution with you
- And the other party has the skills to articulate your concerns and listen to what others have to say
- And the other party has a similar amount of power in a conflict, or is willing to put aside any power differences in order to work together as equals in arriving at a solution

If the parties involved in a conflict will not agree to any of these elements, a collaborative style won't work. Because collaboration involves more time and commitment, it's more complicated. Used successfully; it can be the most satisfying resolution for everyone involved, especially if there is a serious conflict.

The Accommodating Style

The person who uses the accommodating style is one who likes to help or lend a hand, and often is someone who easily conforms. It's a style that works on a cooperative basis with another when asserting one's own claim for power. The accommodating style works well when the end result is not a key factor or concern for you. When you have assessed a situation and decided that it's a no-win for you, it makes sense to be accommodating. You might as well go along with whatever the other person wants. As an accommodator, you cede your own concern in order to satisfy another's, by sympathizing with another or otherwise giving in.

When you invoke an accommodating style, it means that you are willing to set aside your own concern; you feel that you do not have a lot invested in the situation or the outcome. But if you feel that in the end, you would be giving up something that is vital or key to you, or would not feel good about giving it up, then the accommodating style is not going to be an appropriate fit. It is a perfect style to use when you feel that you are not losing too much by your giving up or backing off. The accommodating style is also effective when your immediate strategy is to smooth things over and then bring the issue or subject up at a later time. This is viewed as a deferral, not an avoidance technique.

The accommodating style has some similarities to another style—avoidance. It may be used to delay a final resolution to a particular issue or problem. There is a difference. In avoidance, you back out or away from something; in accommodating, you are cooperative. You are willing to acknowledge the situation and agree to do whatever the other person wants to do. When avoidance is enforced, your position is that you do not do anything that will enhance the other's desires, and a decision is arrived at more or less by default.

Situations in which the accommodating style seems most appropriate include:

- Giving way
- Being submissive and compliant
- When you don't really care what happens in the end
- When you want to keep peace and maintain harmony
- When you feel like maintaining the relationship and don't want to get the other person angry
- When you recognize that the outcome is more important to the other person than it is to you

- When you recognize that you are wrong
- When you have minimal or no power
- When you have no chance of winning
- When you think the other person might learn from the situation if you go along with her, even though you do not agree or think she is making a mistake
- When you want a better position to be heard
- When you want to learn more
- When you want to show that you are a team player
- When you want to collect "chits" for later issues
- Minimizing a loss when you are outmatched and know that you are losing
- When issues are not as important to you as to others

When an environment is negative or hostile, harmony can often be restored by initiating an accommodating style in dealing with a conflict. By giving in, agreeing, or sacrificing your concerns and yielding to what the other person wants, you may be able to smooth over a bad situation. The resulting period of calm allows you to gain time. In the end, it enables you to work out a resolution that you would prefer.

The Avoiding Style

The fourth major style is avoidance. It occurs when you don't assert yourself, you don't cooperate, or you avoid the conflict entirely. The avoiding style is initiated when you feel that you are in a no-win situation, that you don't want to be a bother, or that the whole problem or issue is irrelevant. It is also used when you feel the other person has more power or is right or when, for whatever reason you don't want to stick your neck out and take a position.

Your posture is more of sidestepping and ignoring the

issue, delaying any input or decisions. It may also be that you don't have the time or choose not to deal with the issue now. Avoidance can work temporarily when you are dealing with someone who is difficult and you are not required to work together.

When you don't have to make a decision immediately or are unsure about what to do, the avoiding style may do the trick. Instead of getting stressed out trying to push for a resolution, you have extra time. In reality, you have made a choice not to make a decision. The Catch 22 is that if you don't come back at a later date to deal with the issue, others may view you as irresponsible or a procrastinator.

Avoidance also works when you have not been able to gather enough information to allow yourself to make a decision or recommendation. It gives you the ability to be late with your input. If deferral is your objective, be aware that eventually you may have to come back and deal with the issue. The avoiding style works well when:

- You want to ignore a conflict or hope it will go away
- You prefer to put the problems under consideration on hold
- Slowing procedures can help stifle a conflict
- Secrecy is desired to avoid confrontation
- You feel an appeal to bureaucratic rules can aid in conflict resolution
- Tensions are too high and you feel the need to cool down or back off
- The issue is not very important or is trivial to you
- You are having a bad day and there is a high probability that you will get upset and not deal logically or rationally with the situation
- It's improbable that you will win, or you know that you can't

232 / Zapping Conflict in the Health Care Workplace

- You want or need more time, either to gather information or to get help
- The situation is complex and difficult to change
- You feel any time spent on the issue will be wasted
- You have little power to resolve the situation or get a resolution that is beneficial
- You feel that you aren't qualified to resolve the situation and others can do better
- The timing is bad; bringing the conflict out into the open might make it worse
- You want to let people cool down

Many think that when people use avoidance to deal with conflict, they are being evasive or running away from the issue. There are times when an evasive or delaying tactic is appropriate and can be constructive. And some conflicts do resolve themselves when given breathing room.

The Compromising Style

In the center of the conflict management matrix is the compromising or sharing approach. In other words, you end up giving up a little bit of what you want to get the rest of what you want. The other parties involved in the conflict do the same. A compromising solution is reached when exchanges, concessions, and bargaining are used to reach a conclusion that rarely satisfies everyone's concerns or objectives 100 percent. The solution will, though, meet the majority of each party's concerns and objectives.

One of the differences between collaboration and compromise is that in collaboration you search for underlying needs and interests. In compromise, both sides end up giving up part of their needs and/or interests before a resolution is reached.

A compromise approach is often used when each party

wants the same thing but is not willing to give up certain things to get it. Let's say two of you have families and you both want to take the first two weeks of July off. You each have the same objective, yet only one can have vacation during that period. It's clear that one of you is going to have to work unless the company decides to close its doors for a very long Independence Day recognition.

The compromise will more likely be that one will take the long vacation this year and the other will take it next year. Who gets it first could be determined by the flip of a coin, seniority, work output, and so on. Whatever the solution, no one is going to be 100 percent satisfied, because neither of you got what you totally wanted.

In collaborating, you focus on resolving various issues and needs. In a compromise, the conflict situation is a given. What you are dealing with is a way to influence or alter the conflict to a give and-take exchange. Often the goal in collaboration is a long-term win-win solution. In a compromise, the outcome may more likely be short-term and expedient.

At the end of a compromise, the normal response from the parties involved is, "I'm OK; I can live with the results." The emphasis is not on winning but on "We can't both get what we want, so let's see what we can work out to satisfy our most important needs."

Ways in which a compromising style works best are:

- Negotiation
- Looking for deals and trade-offs
- Finding satisfactory or acceptable solutions
- When you have power equal to that of your opponent, and you are committed to mutually exclusive goals
- When you want to achieve a resolution quickly

- Saving money
- When you are willing to settle for a temporary resolution to a complex issue
- When you will benefit from a short-term gain
- As a backup when collaboration or competition is unsuccessful
- When the goals are not important to you and you are willing to modify your own
- When it makes the relationship or agreement work, and it's better than nothing

The compromising style can be valuable at the beginning, when you know you don't have the power to get what you want. This way, you get part of what you want, and the other party gets part of what she wants. You may come back to the table at a later date if the issue resurfaces.

In order to be successful in compromising, you need to clarify your needs and wants, as well as those of the other parties involved. Then, determine what areas you agree on. Once there is some agreement, a compromise settlement can be worked out. Listening is a critical part of the art of compromise.

Be willing to make suggestions and listen to what the other party says; she in turn should be willing to do the same. Be prepared to give some things up-make offers and exchanges. It is imperative that you identify areas that are uncompromisable—those that you are not willing to budge on. The end result is that both of you should have some satisfaction with the outcome.

Which Style Is You?

Remember, no one style works best in every situation. You need to be able to recognize what styles are surfacing when you are dealing with another party, as well as the styles with which you are responding. As you become more skilled in dealing with conflicts, you will be able to consciously choose the most appropriate style to use at a given time.

Look at the extremes. If you prefer working only within the competitive or avoiding style, you place yourself in a win-lose or lose-lose situation. Strict style preferences limit you. It's natural to prefer certain styles over others. One of the first steps is to assess your dominant style preference in approaching conflict (by completing the *Managing Conflict Styles Questionnaire©*).

Dominant and Secondary Modes

If you work only within the competitive or the avoiding mode, you limit yourself to a win-lose or a lose-lose scenario. It's natural to prefer a certain mode over others, and this one is your dominant mode. But you may also have two equally characteristic modes, such as avoiding and accommodating. This combination would indicate that you will do a lot to prevent any type of conflict. As mentioned above, when you have two equally characteristic modes, you are *bimodal*. If you have three, you are *trimodal*.

Exhibit 9.1 gave you an individual profile of how you respond to conflict. Now that you have read the descriptions of the five modes of managing conflict, stop and think for a moment. Which mode best describes you? Is there one that stands out, or do you feel that you use several equally? When you tallied your responses, did your profile match the way you perceive yourself?

Turn the Tables

Now, switch. You need to confront someone. You have already identified what you believe the problem to be. The

Sample Scenarios of Conflict Managing Styles

Style	When It Works	When It Doesn't
Competitive	When you have the Power	When others don't respect your abilities or power
Collaborative	When you have time; when you have a good relationship	When there is a lack of trust; when time is short
Accommodating	When the other person needs status	When you need a real solution
Avoiding	When you must have the other person's participation	When you have a lot to lose; When the other person is right
Compromising	When both parties are right; when you want to keep the relationship going	When only one party is right; when you have little to give

next step is to identify the dominant and backup conflict styles of the person you are confronting. You now know how you and the other party normally operate in a conflict. There are times where it may make sense to use one style over another. On the previous page are sample scenarios that work and don't work with each style.

The bottom line is that most conflicts need to be confronted for a resolution. Very few resolve themselves or go away with no action. Conflicts are similar to aging. Both are inescapable.

The worksheet on the next page is to used to see how you measure up. Most health care professionals want to use the collaborative style—it would their "prefer using" mode. Identify what style you use the most, which you dislike and use the least.

The Face-Off

In addition to determining your conflict management style and that of the person you will confront, there are a few other techniques to use. The first is to identify a neutral area in which you can talk. Your office or "her" office is the wrong turf; neither can be considered neutral. So are any public areas in which anyone can watch and listen. Get a cup of coffee or tea and take a walk or find a quiet, isolated place where you can sit down one on one.

Before any confrontation, you need to set some rules for yourself—for your own behavior. First, calm down. If you don't step back and take a moment to compose yourself, you'll make the best speech you will ever regret. Second, take the time to assess what's happened. View it from two sides: your perspective—what the impact has been on you and possibly on others—and hers—what do you think her perspective is? Last, take a deep breath. You need fresh oxygen in your system.

Self-Assessment of Using Conflict Styles

Conflict Style	*Prefer Using*	*Use Most*	*Dislike Using*	*Use Least*
Competing (do it my way)				
Compromising (give up something and get something in return)				
Collaborative (take time to work something out that we both like)				
Accommodating (let others have their way)				
Avoiding (do almost anything to stay away from conflicts)				

Exhibit 9.1

ZAP Tip

This is not the time to lose control.
It is normal to feel upset, angry, betrayed—
whatever you are feeling, your feelings
are your feelings. But yelling, screaming,
hitting, etc. doesn't resolve it—escalation of
the conflict becomes the prize. When
you lose control, the other side wins.

A key skill is your ability to listen. Too many times, the mouth is put in gear before the brain has a chance to warm up. She who listens usually ends up in control. Don't wait for the other person to come to you. Ideally, you initiate the confrontation. As you listen, you will need to formulate the feedback you will give. Be willing to acknowledge that a behavior or action of yours may have been a factor in whatever the problem is.

It's not uncommon to hold back, waiting for someone else to deal with the problem. They wait for someone who finally has the courage to speak up. Talking with another person face to face is usually the best way to confront a problem. That way, she can see your body language and you hers. You can observe whether she is listening. Some face-to-face confrontations require nerves of steel. You must be composed and have your facts together. Otherwise, emotions can erupt, and you end up either attacking or retreating. At this point the conflict only grows.

If meeting face to face is impossible, writing becomes

your second best choice. But, it has drawbacks. You can't be sure that she will read your letter (or e-mail). Writing does, though, give you an opportunity to set out the facts, as you understand them and to let the other party know how you have been affected by her action.

Before you send any letters, have a confidante read over your words to eliminate undue sharpness or overemotional responses. This is a time to explain, rationally how you perceive the facts. If you wait too long to confront, it also can be a disadvantage. The other party may be clueless as to what she did, or why you are upset about it.

The least preferred way to confront is over the phone. This has several disadvantages. First of all, less than 10 percent of communication comes through words that are spoken. The majority comes through seeing, feeling, and interpreting—through gestures, body language, and voice tone. Most is unspoken. You visually see and react to what the other person is saying. Phone calls eliminate this aspect of communication.

Second, if you attempt to confront her on the phone, you can't be sure that she is listening to what you say. In fact, she could put you on hold, walk away, or even hang up before you are aware the line has been disconnected. Even if you both remain on the line, you are unable to see her face, her eyes, and her body expressions. Nor can she see yours. She is unable to visibly see your anger or your hurt. She may hear it through your tone.

Deal with the situation when it arises and work toward destroying sabotaging behavior as a model. By acting affirmatively and immediately you are also putting others on notice that you aren't willing to tolerate it. This means speaking diplomatically to the person about the problem in ways that produce solutions, not battlegrounds.

> ## ZAP Tip
>
> *When you observe conflict creating
> behavior, whether directed at you or somewhere
> else, be conscious of it. Be aware that it
> contributes to destructive role modeling.
> Ask yourself, "Is this really a conflict? Or am
> I merely letting my low self-esteem perceive a
> slight where it may not actually exist?"
> If you determine that it is true conflict and
> a problem, take overt action—immediately.*

Suppose you become aware that another woman has been backstabbing or gossiping about you. Consider approaching her and saying that you are aware of what has been happening; that you are hurt, disappointed, and angry; that you would like to change the situation; and would like to work with her to effect a solution. This enables her to feel receptive, not defensive, about the situation, and she may be more inclined to seek a positive way to change. If she claims no knowledge of the behavior you describe, then explain exactly what happened.

Tell her what actions were done and how they had a negative impact on you. Such a process should help raise the woman's level of awareness. And your diplomacy may be a critical factor in the behavioral change you are seeking. She may truly be unconscious of what she is doing; she may be acting out of fear or an inner desire to get ahead, and may be sabotaging you in order to achieve that goal without realizing the impact of her actions on you and others.

It is important to let the other person know you are aware he or she is acting in this unconscious, destructive way. By making him or her conscious, you hope he or she will be more aware in the future, and will want to change. Use remarks such as the following to make this point:

> Maybe you don't realize that what you have been saying about me might hurt me. But it does. I hope that now that I have told you this, you will be more aware when you are talking to anyone about me. I would trust that you would ask yourself, "Can this possibly affect anyone negatively?" Or, "Even if it is positive, should I be the one to be talking about this?"

The key to success in using such an approach, however, is in not causing the other person to become defensive. Avoid saying, "You did this," or "You did that which comes across like an accusation. Preface your comments with an "I" statement, in which you express your own feelings and indicate how you felt in response to what you perceive someone did. An "I" statement softens the impact of your claims about another's behavior. It emphasizes your feelings about the situation rather than what the person did.

You do not cause the person to become defensive. The simplest example I can think of is if you walk up to somebody and say, "You did something," that person is immediately going to think, "Oh, oh, what did I do?" But if I come up to you and say, "I am really hurt by what you have done," or "I am really hurt by something you said," it lessens the impact of the statement a little bit, because I am saying I am hurt. I'm not saying, "You screwed up." It is an "I" statement. I am stating my feelings.

Hidden Factors

Communicating how you feel, what you feel and why you feel the way you do can be challenging. You may think you are incredibly clear and precise—the listener will most likely be putting a "spin" on it. It's important to look for clues and cues—some come across loud and clear, others are disguised in body language, posturing, tone and words.

ZAP Tip
Changes rarely happen overnight.
It will probably take a few confrontations
for her to stop whatever she is doing to you or
to others. Confronting is not easy—it is
painful and very uncomfortable. But,
each time you do it, it becomes less stressful.

- *Pay attention to your gut feelings and what you perceive is going on.* If you feel internally that there is distrust, negativity or distancing, there most likely is.
- *Look for discrepancies in what the other person is saying, what kind of tone is being used in communicating and his or her body language.* If she is all smiles, yet arms are crossed, her body is turned away, and speaks sharply, the smile doesn't match the rest of her.
- *Tap into someone you trust for feedback.* Sometimes you may over react or misinterpret what you see or hear.
- *Share your perceptions with the other person.* This

doesn't mean you are on the attack, rather that you feel that the other person is open to talking/ listening and wants to make the workplace better.

On the next page are sample scenarios. In your workplace, you will experience a variety of situations that warrant and demand your attention. It is amazing the amount of unspoken, but communicated meanings and intent, that add to the level of conflict within your workplace. Look for hidden meanings—don't manufacture them—but if there is any uncertainty, get clarification.

The Art of Carefronting®

When I do training sessions and workshops on conflict, I routinely bring laminated cards for all the participants with the Carefronting dialogue. Participants who have name badges often hole punch them and add them to back of their badge—when they come across a situation that needs addressing, out come the cards.

Confronting another isn't always easy. But, it must be done. Otherwise, you create a movie dialogue in your head, spend hours (sometimes days/weeks/months) on whatever the issue/problem is, most likely grumble about it with co-workers who all will agree the person is a real jerk . . . and nothing is done to get resolution. With Carefronting©, you are an adult.

Carefront® another in a neutral environment—go for a walk, get a cup of tea (avoid doing this in front of others); make sure you write out a list/agenda of what it is you want to talk about (it's common to attempt to distract you and get you off track, this helps you to stay on target); determine ahead of time which battles you want to take on (and if you don't, drop it now); and listen. My personal keeper here is— she or he who knows how to listen usually succeeds.

Hidden Meanings

What is Said	What You Hear	What You Say to Probe to Bring Out Meanings
"It's your assignment."	*I'm ticked that you get the key jobs and credit—you won't get any support from me.*	I'm swamped and could use some input. Would you like to be involved? With your help, we might be able to improve it.
"I wasn't involved on this job."	*Thank God—what a Disaster. At least I was smart enough to stay away. If you want someone who does quality work, call. Otherwise, keep using this fool.*	Hmmm, sounds like you have some concerns. Is there anything you can tell me about it?—I'd like to hear what you have to say.
"Do it your way."	*Damn, I can't be involved. Since the door is shut, I'm not going to waste my time and put energy into it. Don't ask me for help, even though I have some great ideas.*	Sounds like you might have some ideas—what do you suggest I do to enhance the idea?

Carefronting® Dialogue

When you _____ (What was the action that was done?)

I felt _____ (What was your reaction—were you angry, upset, feeling betrayed?)

Because _____ (What does it look, sound, or feel like—does it look like the person never credits anyone on the team, or does it sound like she purposely spreads rumors?)

Was it your intent to _____ ? (Repeat what the action was....then STOP!!!—do not respond until there is a response from the other side.)

In the future _____ (What behavior do you want to see? Say what you want.)

If there isn't a change, _____ (What's the consequence—will you include everyone on the email distribution list so credit is appropriately given?)

_____

Source: The Briles Group, Inc., ©2002 Aurora CO All Rights Reserved

Exhibit 9.3

Don't Rearrange the Deck Chairs on the Titanic

What if this non-threatening, diplomatic approach to resolve the problem doesn't work? Depending on your position in the organization and whether the person causing the problem is a co-worker or an employer, there are two options.

First, if a co-worker, do everything you can to resolve it directly with her or him, and then talk about taking it to a higher level; say you feel you have to see a supervisor about the problem if you can't work it out between yourselves. If your suggestion does not motivate the other person to change, then it might be appropriate to seek assistance from someone in a higher position.

So, approach him or her and invite him or her to coffee, lunch or to a walk, and then finally, just appeal—

> I don't know what else to do. I have tried everything to contact you about this problem that I feel we are having together. Do you have any suggestions for what I might do?

If that absolutely fails, then the only thing left to do is to say,

> Look, I really don't want to have to go to the supervisor, but this is affecting my work tremendously. I had hoped to work it out with you, but we don't seem to be getting anywhere. I don't want to bring in so and so. Would you prefer that I do, or do you have any suggestions on how we might work it out?"

The other option, finally, is to leave the organization, which may be necessary if the person causing the problem is above you. If a supervisor has been made aware of the problem and continues to act in a way that hurts you, it may not be possible to change the situation. Going higher in the organization might make it more difficult for you under other circumstances if the higher-level manager supports your supervisor.

The working environment could become even worse if you complain and your supervisor knows that you have. If you choose to dig in your heels and stay despite being the target of sabotage, you are likely to get more upset and hostile. This can lead you to react vengefully yourself, which can result in worse problems, such as being fired and getting a bad recommendation. If you recognize that the situation won't get any better and you leave, the odds are that you can find a new and much better working environment.

If you leave because of an uncomfortable situation, it's crucial that you leave gracefully. Keep the doors open for the future, because you may find you are involved in working with someone who previously treated you unethically; or that that person perhaps is in power over something you want. If you've burned your bridges behind you by staging a nasty or public confrontation, you may undercut your opportunities in the future. If you've been as diplomatic as possible under the circumstances, future possibilities are left open.

People and circumstances change, and you may want to establish contact again. As long as you leave smoothly, you can. Otherwise, it may be difficult, if not impossible. At all costs, avoid parting shots. It makes good business sense to avoid making enemies and to leave the doors open for future business together. It's like playing a game. You may wallop your opponent; but at the end, you shake hands and make up. Then you're ready to play again.

By metaphorically shaking hands when you leave a job, you keep the doors open and the bridges up. Then, there is always that opening to do business again when the opportunity arises. It may feel good to get out the explosion of anger and resentment, but in the long run, you pay.

When you can identify a situation in which you strongly believe that another person is purposely trying to harm you physically, psychologically, or professionally, my advice is to get out. If you want to practice confronting, go ahead. But, be forewarned. It is improbable that you will have the time to go through a series of processes that might enlighten the other party.

You are better off gathering up your marbles and finding another field to play in. Don't expect to change her ways. Working in a toxic environment will eventually make you sick. There is another job out there; start looking now. In most cases, the only regret you'll have is that you didn't leave sooner.

ZAP Tip

When a workplace turns sour, it is reasonable to seek employment somewhere else. Usually men are the first to go. Women hang in, feeling that the job/work/boss, etc. needs them.

If workplace (or friendships-relationships) are not positive, ask yourself why are you still in them. Health care in the decade of the 2000s offers plenty of opportunities to move about.

Staying put because you "need the money" doesn't fly—money is being offered across town. Open your eyes, your ears and start networking. It's a good thing.

Summing Up

Conflicts and confrontations involve a tap dance—a series of moves and countermoves by each person. Some dances end shortly, while others add new movements. Conquering confrontophobia will enable you to deal with conflict, miscommunication, power plays, and sabotage.

With the subsiding and elimination of confrontophobia, you will add a powerful skill to your tool kit for the workplace. Confronting someone takes responsibility. It also holds the other person accountable for whatever her actions are. If you do not confront the person who creates offending behavior or actions, your silence condones it. It says that it is OK to continue to do whatever that person has done—not only to you, but to others.

When you know a confrontation is coming, step back and look at the dominant conflict-managing style of your opponent. Your effectiveness in negotiating a resolution will be enhanced.

As you learn more about yourself and the people you work with, you will be able to act with more power and confidence. Mastering conflict and confrontation will be part of your formula. Doing it in a carefronting manner creates a positive workplace.

10 Not Everyone's Friend Material

A crucial step toward empowerment in the workplace is to develop and cultivate healthy relationships with other women. Women have entered the work force in unprecedented numbers. Contrary to popular belief and to some articles in the media, few women are really leaving. The Small Business Administration estimates that there are in excess of five million women-owned businesses today. This means that, no matter where you work, the odds are you will be working with other women.

In health care, the great majority of employees are women, and with over one-third of our 2002 survey respondents stating a preference not to work with other women, there are going to be problems. When women work together, there appear to be two camps—the good one and the bad one. The women who are in the good camp are more likely to be open about their positions, supportive of other women, and caring. They are confident about their skills and assertive, and they advocate advancing other women. The other camp, the bad one, is viewed as the troublemaker.

The women within the bad camp tend to be more distant and uninvolved with group activities, are perceived to be at the heart of most rumors, and view other women not as their competitors but as their rivals. They are the type that is more likely to take credit for someone else's work, as well as not to acknowledge or applaud the work of others. These women are the saboteurs in your midst and conflict creators.

ZAP Tip

It's amazing—the tongue only weighs a
few ounces . . . and so few can hold it.
Don't get caught up in the rumor mill.
Delete rumor creators, rumor carriers and
gossips from your circle of "friends."

There are three primary relationships in which women work with other women. One is on the colleague to co-worker level—nursing, dental hygienists and assistants, drug sales, or marketing. The second will be between someone who is in management and a worker or employee. The third involves an employer or employee connection (a woman doctor or dentist working with a nurse or dental assistant).

When women work with other women, confusing friendships with friendliness can and does create mayhem. Women too easily cross the line. There are work friendships that should remain within the work-related environment. Going out with other female nurses, co-workers, and doctors for a drink or playing in the summer softball or volleyball league continues the "work" flavoring. The crossover to family and more personal activities complicates the picture.

Female work friendships can be as complicated and, in some cases, as painful as workplace romances. Work friendships can create immense conflicts between work and personal life. This doesn't mean that all female relationships should be scrapped and not extended to your personal "other" life. It does mean that you need to be careful that friendships are privileges and are built and earned over time. Few people meet and instantly fall in love. The great majority of positive, caring, and growing relationships have substantial investments of time in them.

In direct or indirect employee-employer or colleague-co-worker relationships, it's time to ask some serious questions. There are always the "right" or "Politically Correct" responses, but those are rarely your gut-level reactions to real-world situations. The *Friendship-Savvy Quiz©* asks ten questions, to be answered *yes or no* with your gut reaction, not necessarily the one you know would be politically correct or expected in dealing with women in your workplace.

ZAP Tip

One of the Momisms of life is to be friends with everyone. Mom is wrong— the correct Momism is "Not everyone is friend material—there are plenty of jerks and jerkettes out there. Be cautious when sharing personal information."

Answering *yes* to any of the questions indicates that your personal expectations of others can be a damper on your own work, as well as on that of others. Women need to recognize that healthy relationships are a necessity—and that friendships, real friendships, are a luxury.

Friendship-Savvy Quiz©

1. Would you feel uncomfortable if you needed to criticize her work?
2. Would you allow her extra time to complete tasks or projects?
3. Would you feel hurt or be angry if she took another position without telling you about it first?
4. Would you feel left out if she transferred to another department or moved to another city?
5. Would you feel excluded if she went to lunch with another coworker and didn't invite you?
6. Would you feel overlooked or forgotten if she forgot your birthday?
7. Would you feel bad or uncomfortable if she criticized your work?
8. Would you feel betrayed if she told another a personal story or revealed anything that you considered intimate?
9. Would you feel uncomfortable competing for a position or promotion with her?
10. Would you cover for her if you knew she was having personal problems?

Source: The Briles Group, Inc. ©2002 Aurora CO. All Rights Reserved.

Exhibit 10.1

How Do Women Build Positive Relationships?

In the case histories that follow, you will see how women working together are learning to speak up, compete, confront, and collaborate—actions that are the building blocks of healthy relationships.

As a supervisor, Cam sees a difference in how male and female doctors work with their colleagues, as well as with their patients. Cam sentiments are echoed by others; there is far more collaboration among women doctors. She shares her experience,

> Overall, I believe women doctors collaborate with their patients and the nurses. There are, of course, always exceptions. One female doctor has learned what she needs to do to get what she needs or wants. We don't have a lot of female doctors, but the ones we have appear to be kinder to their patients. They talk and listen to them. I don't believe that there is the arrogance among female doctors that male doctors routinely display. It seems like more of a collaborative effort, as far as working with the nurses is concerned. The women doctors really talk a problem over to find a solution.

· As an office manger in a dental practice with four dentists, Kimberly witnessed changes as soon as women dentists began to join the staff. Before that, she didn't see a lot of doctor-patient interaction. For her, the women have changed it. Her words,

> The female dentists tend to refer their patients for additional information, have more follow-up, and tend to be more open about the whole concept of providing dental care information to their patients.

They also want to teach them to be more aware and to be a part of making decisions in their own care. In the past, the male doctors just have not done that.

In the intensive-care unit, Marilyn has seen dramatic changes in the interaction of women doctors and nurses over the past decade. She echoes Kimberly's experience in the dental office,

> Women doctors are great. First of all, they are much more down to earth, less godlike, and they work very hard. They are bright and have a good relationship with the nursing staff. In our unit, they collaborate on the different issues involving patients. The male doctors are still handing down edicts.
>
> The male doctors threw temper tantrums, blamed nurses, and wrote derogatory comments to them on order sheets. One even wrote a letter to the nursing vice president, complaining about a nurse who consulted with him about a patient and then reported their joint observations and conclusions in the progress notes on the patient's chart. The doctor was incensed that she had done so without his permission.

Dorothy sums up her own reaction to women doctors: it's just easier. As a nursing supervisor, she has had the opportunity to work with them and evaluate the doctor-nurse working relationship. She shares,

> There is a much more relaxed relationship—more of a camaraderie with the women, versus working with the male doctors. With a man, you have to approach him correctly and make it look like 'it's' his idea, whatever it is, even though you planted it in the first

place. With the women doctors, it's totally different. You just state the way you think it ought to be, and they just say yes or no. We don't have the confrontations and conflicts that we routinely have with the male doctors.

It has been several years since Ursula worked in a clinical situation. Today, she is a quality-assurance manager, and she has little opportunity to interact with physicians on a day-to-day basis, but she reports that she has noticed a difference since there have been more women doctors working in the hospital. She observes,

Today I see the women doctors and the nurses being friendlier to one another. They call each other by their first names, which the male doctors do not encourage. Male doctors still want to be waited on. From what I see, there haven't been a lot of changes with the male doctor-nurse relationship.

Some of the women doctors who were interviewed indicated that not everything was perfect in their working relationships with nurses. As an RN for several years and now an emergency-room doctor, Kim sees a lot of friction between female physicians and nurses. Her opinion,

Most recently, I've seen envy of some of the nurses toward the female health care workers. I believe it comes from their non-understanding of why another female in the hospital has more power than they do.
   The public also makes wrong assumptions. They expect to see women as nurses or lab technicians, but not doctors. It's not that they dislike it. Rather, they just don't recognize that we are there.

Geography plays a role in attitudes. From the southern states, many interviewed reported that the expectations for the women (doctors and staff) split down the gender lines. In the South, it's not uncommon for patients to expect a woman doctor to act like a nurse—to be softer and caring, not to give orders or tell them what they have to do. It's also probable that many of the patients don't move about much—they stay within a tight radius of where they grew-up, live and work. They get their information from TV— many of these people firmly believe that you don't take orders from women.

One of the women doctors I spoke with practices in the Carolinas. She commented on male and female differences,

> Overall, I don't see the nurses here cooperating as well with the women doctors as they do with the men. I believe that a lot of the nurses view themselves as women doctors' rivals, not as our helpers or assistants. They are far more inclined to help the men.

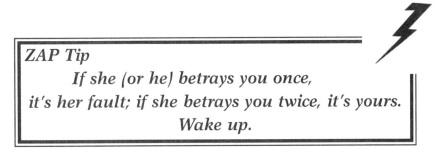

ZAP Tip
If she (or he) betrays you once,
it's her fault; if she betrays you twice, it's yours.
Wake up.

As an administrator, Gloria hears a lot of the hospital scuttlebutt. She is interested in the changes that the female physicians have brought to her workplace. She has noticed there is a difference in the newer physicians and how they interact with the staff. Her experience,

The older female physicians had to fight to get through school. I've noticed that their attitude with the staff is more likely to be 'I'm the doctor, and you're the nurse.' The younger and newer physicians are a little bit more relaxed. They view their work with the nursing staff as using a more team-oriented approach. I feel the younger generation of doctors will change our workplace for the better.

Many who were nurses went back to school and became physicians. Donna, a nursing supervisor, talked about one of her hospital's physicians, who used to be an RN,

There had been reports that she was more demanding of the nurses. Many had labeled her a bitch. The reality is that she is a little bit more demanding of them because she knows what the work expectations are and she knows what sluffing looks like. After all, she has been in their shoes. Since she's only been out of medical school for a few years, she watches herself, because she doesn't want to screw up. The bottom line is that she wants things done correctly.

Donna added that she doesn't see women speaking out against men when they screw up; they are more likely to speak up when another woman does. She also noticed some discrepancies in which doctors are called in an emergency— far likelier to be a woman than a man. She continued,

Many times, the male doctors don't want to work off-hours. They would rather sit home and watch the football game. The nurses would then call the female doctors. They (the female doctors) really got blasted with emergency situations.

I've also noted that the women doctors are not as quick to jump on the nurses or reprimand them for not coming to their rescue and helping them out as would the male doctors. Patient wise, women patients love the female physicians. They feel that they understand what they need.

Finally, Donna concurs with other women who were interviewed in her observation that women doctors listen more effectively than their male counterparts,

I find it very refreshing to have female physicians in our practice. They bring a whole different twist to how we interact with our patients. These ladies don't make any bones about a situation. If they don't think something is right, they are more inclined to say, "Cut the bullcrap." They talk to the nurses as human beings, and they understand some of the frustrations we experience with patients as people, not just as bodies with an illness. The women will call a jerk a jerk.

Robyn has been in general dentistry practice for many years. Several of her patients are hygienists and assistants. Her take on male-female differences includes,

I believe a lot of older women prefer working for a man. Part of it is age. I know for me it's much easier to work with people my age or younger than to work with people who are older.

When I worked for a male dentist as an employee dentist, the dental assistant and staff, all women, would work for him but not for me. I remember asking one of the assistants to do something for me.

She just left the room. I believe it's a generational thing. Older women prefer working for a man, and his age doesn't matter. They feel much more comfortable.

They used to get really ticked off when my patients called me by my first name. It's never been a big deal to me to be called Doctor, but to them it was very important. The woman who is now my partner is nine years older than I am. She believes that patients should call her Doctor. Mine call me Robyn.

Building Respect

The newest generation of female doctors is far more positive about their support staffs than the women physicians and dentists who completed their training more than ten years ago. Peggy is representative of many of the women doctors we interviewed. She recalls being a resident and doing a surgical rotation with another woman in a community hospital. Some nights were hard, but at times she was actually able to get five to six straight hours of sleep. Shannon, her fellow resident, wasn't so successful. She revealed,

> Shannon is a wonderful person. But she knows how to annoy nurses better than anyone I know. She started on the rotation a few weeks after I did, and she came to me after a few days. She said she was getting stupid phone calls every half-hour, and it was a pain in the ass. I had to bite my tongue, because she didn't see that she was pissing off the nurses, and they were getting back at her. The first rule I learned is keep the nurses on your side. They are the ones who really have the power around here. Once you piss them off, you're in trouble.

Doctors like Peggy view nurses and assistants as an intricate part of the team. The best way to work with nurses is to respect them as individuals and for the talent they bring. Through the years, Peggy has observed male interns, residents, and specialists handing down orders. Their style is more dictatorial. Unfortunately, she says, some of the women doctors behave the same way the men do. She continues,

> I have a great deal of respect for nurses. At times, though, I believe the women doctors and nurses get into a type of competition. I've also been on the receiving end, when nurses sometimes had a problem accepting orders from me. It's only from the female nurses that I have had problems, when I've given orders and they haven't wanted to take them. When I observed their interactions with the male interns and residents, I didn't see the problems that I had over the same issue.

What Peggy understands is that there are times when there will be competition between women in the workplace. Peggy feels that when the competitive spirit rears its head, the best way to resolve the problem is to defuse it. Her way is to actively work with the nurses and reinforce the fact that they are on her team. Her solution,

> When I did my first internship, it was in a neonatal nursery. I'd never even been in a neonatal nursery before, much less worked in one. There were nurses who had worked there for twelve years. The reality was they could run that nursery just fine without me. I would have been an idiot to think that I always knew what was best. Anytime that orders needed to be written, I got into the habit of sitting down

with whoever the nurse was and saying, "What do you think?"

Doctors who don't think they can learn from nurses are crazy. I think most nurses are dynamite. I can't tell how many times I've had my tail saved by good nurses over the years.

Let's say I have a patient with diabetes. I'm so focused on her diabetes that I welcome the nurses' input. One nurse may say that this patient could really do well with this instead of that. Another may think of comfort measures that I'm overlooking. Nurses also really know what to look for, and they catch which drugs interact with one another and which don't. I see having great interaction with nurses as part of good basic patient care.

Peggy's rules for dealing and working with nurses are designed to build positive relationships. But the building is not something that is done overnight. It takes time, even years. When individuals are treated with respect—be they co-worker, manager or patient, and honoring their diversity, not purposely getting others angry, and living and working with integrity, we can make our workplaces far more pleasant.

If We Are Friends, Can We Compete?

Picture this—imagine that you are at work, having lunch. Your floor has been buzzing with the news that a position is opening up for a clinical specialist. You pick up your tray and join five of your colleagues, and they too have heard the news.

Amanda mentions her qualifications, and all of you agree that she is a perfect candidate. Then Sherri says that she too is planning to submit her resume. Amanda is quiet for a moment, and then she begins to talk about the pitfalls of the position, and about courses she, Amanda, should have taken to expand her present skills. Sherri makes the same types of comments about herself. So far, so good—what looked like a tense situation appears to have smoothed itself out. Everyone finishes lunch and goes back to work.

When the position is filled, neither Amanda nor Sherri gets it. Annette, another friend who was at lunch that day, gets the promotion. Hearing the other two talk about the job and the qualifications, she decided to submit her resume.

Now—here's the question . . .If you were Amanda or Sherri, how would you feel? What would your reaction have been if Annette had also said she was interested in the job? You might not have been enthusiastic about someone else's putting her hat in the ring, but at least you would have known who the competition was, and you would have been able to assess her strengths and weaknesses. But the odds are quite high that your friendship with her would have been strained, even terminated. Why? It's another Momism—among women, friends don't compete, at least not in the old-fashioned way.

In another scenario, Ellen and Patricia are two friends considering the same job. When Ellen says she is interested, Patricia may decide not to submit her resume. Patricia may feel that it wouldn't be fair to Ellen, even if Patricia's qualifications are better. But if Ellen gets the position, Patricia may feel resentful if her friend doesn't acknowledge that one reason why she got the job is that Patricia didn't compete with her.

If and when you do compete with another, there are two unwritten rules for dealing with the outcome: whoever ends up winning should be congratulated, and then both of you must move on.

> ## ZAP Tip
> *A woman competing with other women may be blocked by old messages about being nice. There is nothing wrong with being nice while being in competition, but mixed messages may be sent and received as fear of losing surfaces: "If I'm too nice, I can't really compete. If I don't compete, I can't win. Therefore, I lose."*
> *Men have a different perspective. They are more inclined to skip being nice and to view losing as part of the school of hard knocks: that's life—get over it.*

Not being the victor can give you an opportunity to do some reflecting. If you lost a promotion, did your rival have qualifications that you didn't have? If you still aspire to the promotion, are there coalitions you can form that will ease your way the next time you're at bat?

Competition is not going to go away, and there are things you can do when you are in competition. Acknowledge that competition in the open.. Bring it out in the open. If a new position is available or an opening exists, encourage others in your group to seek it openly. If you see anyone undermining anyone else, making derogatory comments about her abilities or skills, with the intent to influence or color a decision maker's opinion, speak up and speak out.

Missing out on a coveted opportunity, a promotion, or an award is disappointing and maybe painful, and it's natural inclination to want to withdraw when you don't receive it. But don't! Stay in circulation. People are going to be watching how you handle the situation.

Look First, Then Blow Your Own Horn

Phyllis, a nurse from Florida, recently applied for a supervisory position. Her approach was open competition. She let the other women she worked with know that she was applying for the job, and she even encouraged others to apply.

Not only did Phyllis land the job, she had the support of the other nurses. Word spread about her open dialogue and her encouragement of others.

But people can be suspicious, and there are times when it does not make sense to trumpet your intentions to one and all. If a position is opening up in your immediate environment, or if one is announced within the overall system of your workplace, everybody who has tapped into the grapevine is going to know, and the application process will be open to everyone.

Let's say you work at Women's Hospital, and you've heard through a friend that a position is opening up at her hospital, Good Samaritan. It sounds like your dream job. If you apply and get the job, it will not mean that you have sabotaged, undermined, or betrayed your colleagues. They may be somewhat surprised to learn that you were seeking employment somewhere else, but once they get over your impending departure, they may even ask you to keep your ears and eyes open for them. It is unlikely that you will be viewed as being in the "out group" until you leave your present position.

When you are seeking new employment outside your present organization, do not broadcast this information. After all, if you don't get the new job, your current supervisor may punish you for attempting to leave. And while you are waiting to hear whether you got the new job, management may hear about your desire to jump ship and may escort you out immediately.

ZAP Tip

Women competing with other women should "deep six" many of the messages they heard as girls. There is nothing wrong with wanting to win; there is nothing wrong with stating your intention to go for a position, an award, or whatever is out there for you; and there is nothing wrong with competing for a position with a friend or colleague.
What's wrong is the way many women have gone about it. Declare yourself and bring the rules out in the open. If a colleague or friend is going for a position and you too would like, declare it and openly compete. If you win and get the position, that isn't a betrayal of another woman or yourself. Rather, it's an opportunity for both of you.

Summing Up

When it comes to women working with women, they definitely can be more open, honest, and supportive with each other. At the same time, they can compete and be assertive without viewing all other women as rivals.

When women are confident about who they are and what they are, they won't have a problem with other women stretching, reaching, and growing. Welcome it. It will be women, not men, who redefine what it means for women to work with women.

11

Red Ink Behavior— The Curse of the Workplace

icture this—Brenda has been late for her shift at least once a week for the past six months; Patricia knows just about everything about a patient's family that anyone could imagine and she gleans the information in chatty phone calls with them; Dennis doesn't respond to any issue until it moves into chaos; Caroline consistently withholds information from her coworkers; Martha is cryptic in her communications, leaving her coworkers and managers to "guess" what she really means; Tom waits to the last minute to do any project then gets others to drop whatever they are doing to assist him; and Bertha is just cynical about every new idea that is presented at a staff meeting. Does any of this sound familiar? Welcome to *Red Ink Behaviors*.

One of the most eye-opening activities we do in the two-day intensive program, *The Judith Briles Health Care Man-*

agement-Leadership Forum, deals with *Red Ink Behaviors. Red Ink Behaviors* are the working manners, habits and styles that can directly and negatively impact the bottom line. I'm talking about money—lots of it. Sometimes these behaviors are unconscious, people are truly not aware of what they are doing and what the impact is on others, their department and the organization. Most times, though, the creator is aware of the behaviors that irritate others and how they disrupt the "normal" flow of the workplace. In either case, productivity suffers. With it, you lose money—it takes more time to complete tasks, meaning overtime or even the hiring of additional personnel.

Most organizations are not aware of are the cost—what does a chatty phone call cost an employer? An employee who thrives in chaos, while those around him don't? Or the withholding of information that could smooth out a project's process or enable a coworker to work more efficiently? The answer is simple—money. And it is money that today's health care management teams are in search of. Can a manager do a reasonable guesstimate of what bad behaviors cost? You bet. In fact, a manager must. As an employee, it's a smart thing to do as well.

Why?—simply this. One of the biggest complaints I hear when I work with organizations is that moneys that had previously been dedicated to fund and sponsor educational activities have been slashed or eliminated. And, it's this very reduction of education that's among the top five reasons conflict has increased in the health care workplace. So, when you identify behaviors that reduce productivity and morale—change them, including *your own.*

The net result will find that you have less moneys going toward replacement and overtime costs. I've seen groups reduce these behaviors and discover that the need for overtime is reduced—in some cases, the need for personnel. That means money can be redirected to educational activities, or something else that is desired. It becomes a win-win.

Although the health care sector will continue to grow in relation to overall national revenue and expenses, many facilities will still feel strapped for cash. Zillions of dollars come in, more zillions go out. A savvy manager needs to know all the avenues of disbursement—both in hard dollars and soft. Hard dollars you write checks for; soft dollars are stolen away from you in the form of lost time and efficiencies that eat away at productivity.

The Domino Factor

Let's say that Bert or Bertha has once again taken credit for the work that you have spent grueling hours over, to the extreme annoyance of your family and friends . . . and you are a man. Or, let's say that Bert or Bertha has once again taken credit for the work that you have spent grueling hours over, to the extreme annoyance of your family and friends . . . and you are a woman.

Same culprits, different recipient of the treatment. As a man, how will you most likely react? As a woman, how will you most likely react? Is there a difference in reactions and/or outcomes? Yes, there is.

The challenge for women in the workplace (and for managers who manage them and co-workers) is that there is a difference in how men and women respond to the rotten players in their offices and work environments. Rotten players are riddled with *Red Ink Behaviors.* Men are more inclined to quickly evaluate what ole Bert and Bertha have done—they either confront the offender or decide that it's not worth their time and drop the situation.

Women react differently. Far fewer women take the

man's approach—directly confront or to drop it. Women are more inclined to side-step the conflict creator . . . and then tell their workplace friends, co-workers, anybody else who's in listening range about what ole Bert and Bertha have pulled this time; they will share how upset they are and how it hurts or impacts them. Their listeners are sympathetic—empathetic. After all, they most likely have borne the brunt of bad behavior as well. It's the *Domino Factor*—everyone gets caught up in it.

The Cost to the Employer

Productivity, or the reduction in it, rears its head. So does turnover. This is where the male/female differences are measurable. Women report that when conflict and saboteurs lurk in their workplaces, it takes them two to four times as long to complete a task.

As an employer or manager, it's not difficult to figure out what the bad apples cost you and your department and organization. Get your calculator out. When good people leave—which is a direct result of keeping marginal employees like Bert and Bertha—you now must replace them, possibly paying finder's fees and/or signing bonuses. You may have to pay higher wages. You may even have to get more than one person to replace the good person who finally threw in the towel.

In a recent interview with a manager in a hospital on the East Coast, she complained about a problem nurse—a woman whose behavior had led to three nurses quitting and going to a competing hospital within the past year. To replace the three nurses, she had to budget $250,000 (roughly one and one-half an annual salary). In addition, complaints bounced around the unit she worked in that work wasn't getting completed . . . the *Domino Factor* was in motion. Most likely, that one marginal nurse had cost her unit in excess of $500,000 in lost productivity. Add that to the replacement cost of the estimated $250,000 and you have a tidy sum!

What to Do

As a manager, you need to tune in to the different styles of handling conflict. You also need to acknowledge that it exists, determine its roots and work on resolution. If you don't, it festers, plain and simple. Not all conflict is bad—but when it escalates to include others, then it costs money—lots of it.

As an employee, it's important to look in the mirror and determine how you handle conflict. Do you identify the source, get your facts, confront it and work for resolution; or, do you bite your tongue, only to share it with others (never the conflict-creator) or act on it at a later time in a revenge mode?

Wakeup and Smell the Coffee . . .

Are there tell-tale signs of disruptive and unproductive behavior? Yes. I've spoken to countless managers and employees who complain and grumble about staff and coworkers. Some have openly said that they are aware of employees who have quit and gone to work somewhere else. The primary reasons? Their workplace environment is the pits—it's toxic. Poor and abrasive managers or bullying and non-collaborative coworkers top the list. I call it the Toxic Workplace Syndrome, a chronic disorder that costs money—overtime, replacement costs including signing bonuses, orientation, possible moving reimbursements, etc. Our studies have shown that 45% have left employment due to abusive and subversive behaviors.

So, open your eyes and ears. Tap into your experience. Ask yourself—

Is Red Ink Behavior in Your Midst?©

1. If there is overtime, is it excessive and why is it needed?
2. Is productivity lower in your department or office than in others that are similar?
3. Is work just not getting done?
4. Are you getting complaints or hearing others continually complain about others?
5. Is the *Domino Factor* in play?
6. Is there someone who everyone avoids dealing with?
7. Are deadlines repeatedly missed?
8. Is absenteeism high?
9. Is there a high level of tardiness (coming to work as well as returning from breaks)?
10. Do people ask to transfer to another department or quit—and tell the exit interviewer the reason they are leaving is for a "better" opportunity or being closer to home?
11. Do you feel that your workplace is the pits?

Source: The Judith Briles Health Care Management Leadership Forum ©2003 Aurora CO. All Rights Reserved.

Exhibit 11.1

A yes to any of the above means you need to probe. Money is going down the drain.

Red Ink Behaviors in Your Midst

Years ago when I was working on my first book about sabotage in the workplace, Jean Hollands, the CEO of the Growth & Leadership Center in Mountain View, California shared a list of behaviors she had identified as *Red Ink Behaviors*. Below is a partial list that has been modified and added to over the years that can lead to *Red Ink Behaviors*. This list is fine-tuned on an ongoing basis. Identify areas that you can identify with both staff and administration. Which ones, and combinations, could be lethal for your department or office?

- *Anger*—always has a chip on the shoulder, has a short fuse in dealing with situations or seems hostile.
- *Arrogance*—is better than anyone and/or above it all.
- *Attacks*—blows up at the slightest situation, often turning a very small mole hill into a mountain.
- *Authenticity*—doesn't walk their talk or talk their walk.
- *Awareness*—is clueless to how their behavior impacts others
- *Barriers*—is evasive and keeps others at bay.
- *Bullying*—belittles and cuts others down.
- *Collaboration*—cooperation isn't in their vocabulary.
- *Communication*—doesn't.
- *Complains*—takes the opposing side in most discussions.
- *Confidence*—lacks self-esteem and confidence and doing/completing projects and tasks.
- *Conflict*—ignites and adds to it.
- *Controlling*—almost impossible not to meddle or be involved.
- *Covertness*—routinely displays activities and behavior in a shadow format or behind the scenes.
- *Credit*—claims accomplishments of others as well as discounts their contributions.
- *Criticizes*—without any sensitivity to others.
- *Defensive*—has a chip on their shoulder and appears that they are ready to attack.
- *Domino Factor*—doesn't confront and shares everything to everyone, over and over.

- *Empathy*—does not demonstrate concern or care for coworkers.
- *Feedback*—reacts negatively to others giving it.
- *Fire hoses*—routinely negates new ideas and creativity generated by others.
- *Flexibility*—resists change and doesn't adapt well to procedural changes.
- *Gossip*—is a messenger of personal news about coworkers.
- *High Maintenance*—managers spend lots of time dealing, talking, thinking about.
- *Humor*—lacks a sense of one.
- *Inflames*—adds fuel to difficult situations.
- *Inspiration*—incapable of encouraging and cheering others on.
- *Isolates*—keeps others out of the information loop.
- *Listening*—is a selective, only hearing what appeals to them.
- *Mentoring*—doesn't receive nor give; difficult creating coaching relationships.
- *Perspective*—doesn't read or interpret others well.
- *Power*—routinely discounts or ignores another's power.
- *Priority*—unable to distinguish what's important, and what's not.
- *Proactive*—doesn't initiate things, waits to react.
- *Procrastinates*—waits until the last minute to do anything.
- *Reactionary*—rarely is proactive; waits for something to happen.
- *Realigns*—workplace friendships and relationships don't stick.
- *Reality Check*—doesn't check back with others, often stubborn in beliefs and not open to others' viewpoints and opinions.

- *Reluctant*—rarely reaches out to assist, teach, coach, or to share info.
- *Repair Ability*—can't mend difficult situations
- *Resists*—routinely digs in heels to doing things their way.
- *Rigid*—resists all, wants to keep the status quo.
- *Sabotage*—undermines others activities.
- *Sarcastic*—cuts others down and creates distrust.
- *Stress*—a stress creator and carrier
- *Team Player*—lacks both social and workplace skills to be involved as a member.
- *Tolerance*—non-accepting of others.
- *Trust*—lacks faith in others as well as the ability to create confidence from them.
- *Uncooperative*—isn't team player, isolated and cares little about others or getting something done in a timely manner.
- *Un-empowered*—feels hopeless and out of control.
- *Vision*—has little and rarely thinks beyond today; lacks the big picture.
- *Withholds Information*—uses as a power play.

Identifying the Players and Numbers

I've included two tables we use in the *Judith Briles Health Care Management Leadership Forum.* The first reflects the high cost of doing nothing—keeping marginal employees. Marginal employees usually display multiple *Red Ink Behaviors*—the result is that they don't work at capacity. The end result is they get a bonus for not performing—a heck of a deal!

The High Cost of Doing Nothing . . . Keeping Marginal Employees

Table 11.1 uses salaries ranging from $50,000 to $100,000 a year (1). Productivity ranges from 85 percent to 55 percent

The High Cost of Doing Nothing... Keeping Marginal Employees

Salary	At 85% of Productivity, a Marginal Employee is really being paid:	At 80% of Productivity, a Marginal Employee is really being paid:	At 75% of Productivity, a Marginal Employee is really being paid:	At 70% of Productivity, a Marginal Employee is really being paid:	At 65% of Productivity, a Marginal Employee is really being paid:	At 60% of Productivity, a Marginal Employee is really being paid:	At 55% of Productivity, a Marginal Employee is really being paid:
$50,000	$57,500	$60,000	$62,500	$65,000	$67,500	$70,000	$72,500
$55,000	$63,250	$66,000	$68,750	$71,500	$74,250	$77,000	$79,750
$60,000	$69,000	$72,000	$75,000	$78,000	$81,000	$84,000	$87,000
$65,000	$74,750	$78,000	$81,250	$84,500	$87,750	$91,000	$94,250
$75,000	$86,250	$90,000	$93,750	$97,500	$101,250	$105,000	$108,750
$80,000	$92,000	$96,000	$100,000	$104,000	$108,000	$112,000	$116,000
$85,000	$97,750	$102,000	$106,250	$110,500	$114,750	$119,000	$123,250
$90,000	$103,500	$108,000	$112,500	$117,000	$121,500	$126,000	$130,500
$95,000	$109,250	$114,000	$118,750	$123,500	$128,250	$133,000	$137,750
$100,000	$115,000	$120,000	$125,000	$130,000	$135,000	$140,000	$145,000

At 75% of production and an annual salary of $50,000, you're throwing away...

$240	*every week...*
$1,042	*every month...*
$3,125	*every quarter...*
$12,500	*in ONE YEAR...*

Table 11.1

and reflects what the employee is truly being paid (2). Some-one who gets $50,000 a year and is really working at an 80 percent productivity level is actually making $60,000 (3). Let's say you are making $50,000 a year and work at full pro-ductivity and are a great team member; your coworker drags her feet and grumbles lots and works at the 80 percent level. She makes $10,000 more! Good deal for her . . . not so hot for you!

Staff Turnover Costs

The second table reflects replacement—what are the costs when someone quits and has to be replaced? You can sub-stitute in the employment category the appropriate type of employment as well as the appropriate salary range. We've created three categories—low end salary of $40,000; average salary of $50,000; and a high-end salary of $60,000 (1).

Assumptions are that the total population is 900 with a turnover rate of 15 percent (2). To replace an employee, most human resource professionals factor in one to one and a half times the annual salary. This includes search fees, if needed, orientation, retraining, bonus, temporary help costs, etc. The target turnover reduction rate is expressed in a range from 14 percent to 9 percent (3).

In reviewing Table 11.2, let's look at the average salary of $50,000 (4). With 900 employees and a turnover or churn rate of 15 percent, it means that 135 employees must be replaced annually (5). At 100 percent of their $50,000 salary, the cost to the employer is $6,750,000 (135 x $50,000) (6); at 150 percent, the replacement cost is $10,125,000 (7).

If the employer was successful in reducing turnover from 15 percent to 9 percent, the money saved is significant. Instead of replacing 135 employees, only 81 are replaced—we like to say that 54 employees have been saved (8)! At the

Staff Turnover Costs

The Judith Briles Health Care Management Leadership Forum

Hi-End Salary of: $60,000

Staff #	Turnover Rate	Target Turnover Rate:	Yields: Staff Lost	Rate Reduction of:	Yields Staff Lost	# Staff Saved:	At 100% of Salary, Current Replacement Cost Is:	At 150% of Salary, Current Replacement Cost Is:	At 100% of Salary, Target Replacement Cost Is:	At 150% of Salary, Target Replacement Cost Is:	At 100% of Salary, Savings Realized is:	At 150% of Salary, Savings Realized is:
900	15%	14%	126.0	1%	135.0	9	$8,100,000	$12,150,000	$7,560,000	$11,340,000	$540,000	$810,000
900	15%	13%	117.0	2%	135.0	18	$8,100,000	$12,150,000	$7,020,000	$10,530,000	$1,080,000	$1,620,000
900	15%	12%	108.0	3%	135.0	27	$8,100,000	$12,150,000	$6,480,000	$9,720,000	$1,620,000	$2,430,000
900	15%	11%	99.0	4%	135.0	36	$8,100,000	$12,150,000	$5,940,000	$8,910,000	$2,160,000	$3,240,000
900	15%	10%	90.0	5%	135.0	45	$8,100,000	$12,150,000	$5,400,000	$8,100,000	$2,700,000	$4,050,000
900	15%	9%	81.0	6%	135.0	54	$8,100,000	$12,150,000	$4,860,000	$7,290,000	$3,240,000	$4,860,000

Average Salary of: $50,000

Staff #	Turnover Rate	Target Turnover Rate:	Yields: Staff Lost	Rate Reduction of:	Yields Staff Lost	# Staff Saved:	At 100% of Salary, Current Replacement Cost Is:	At 150% of Salary, Current Replacement Cost Is:	At 100% of Salary, Target Replacement Cost Is:	At 150% of Salary, Target Replacement Cost Is:	At 100% of Salary, Savings Realized is:	At 150% of Salary, Savings Realized is:
900	15%	14%	126.0	1%	135.0	9	$6,750,000	$10,125,000	$6,300,000	$9,450,000	$450,000	$675,000
900	15%	13%	117.0	2%	135.0	18	$6,750,000	$10,125,000	$5,850,000	$8,775,000	$900,000	$1,350,000
900	15%	12%	108.0	3%	135.0	27	$6,750,000	$10,125,000	$5,400,000	$8,100,000	$1,350,000	$2,025,000
900	15%	11%	99.0	4%	135.0	36	$6,750,000	$10,125,000	$4,950,000	$7,425,000	$1,800,000	$2,700,000
900	15%	10%	90.0	5%	135.0	45	$6,750,000	$10,125,000	$4,500,000	$6,750,000	$2,250,000	$3,375,000
900	15%	9%	81.0	6%	135.0	54	$6,750,000	$10,125,000	$4,050,000	$6,075,000	$2,700,000	$4,050,000

Lo-End Salary of: $40,000

Staff #	Turnover Rate	Target Turnover Rate	Yields: Staff Lost	Rate Reduction of:	Yields Staff # Lost	# Staff Saved:	At 100% of Salary, Current Replacement Cost is:	At 150% of Salary, Current Replacement Cost is:	At 100% of Salary, Target Replacement Cost is:	At 150% of Salary, Target Replacement Cost is:	At 100% of Salary, Savings Realized is:	At 150% of Salary, Savings Realized is:
900	15%	14%	126.0	1%	135.0	9	$5,400,000	$8,100,000	$5,040,000	$7,560,000	$360,000	$540,000
900	15%	13%	117.0	2%	135.0	18	$5,400,000	$8,100,000	$4,680,000	$7,020,000	$720,000	$1,080,000
900	15%	12%	108.0	3%	135.0	27	$5,400,000	$8,100,000	$4,320,000	$6,480,000	$1,080,000	$1,620,000
900	15%	11%	99.0	4%	135.0	36	$5,400,000	$8,100,000	$3,960,000	$5,940,000	$1,440,000	$2,160,000
900	15%	10%	90.0	5%	135.0	45	$5,400,000	$8,100,000	$3,600,000	$5,400,000	$1,800,000	$2,700,000
900	15%	9%	81.0	6%	135.0	54	$5,400,000	$8,100,000	$3,240,000	$4,860,000	$2,160,000	$3,240,000

Table 11.2

100 percent gross replacement level, the amount is $4,050,000 and 150 percent, $6,075,000 (9)—**a savings ranging from $2,700,000 to $4,050,000** (10). Now we are talking big money, meaningful money. Money that could be used for a variety of purposes. Purposes that create a better workplace—a workplace of choice and of choice employees.

Get Your Calculator Out . . .

At this point, it's your turn. I mentioned a few behaviors and styles that could constitute *Red Ink Behavior*—working with a chaos creator; tardiness; withholding information; being cynical and cryptic in communicating; and too chatty phone calls and/or inter-office or department dialogues. Add to the list below things that you are aware of that are costing you (and your department) time and money. And, look in the mirror; are you the creator of any?

Who Creates It?	What Is It?	How Much Time is Lost?
_____	_____	_____
_____	_____	_____
_____	_____	_____
_____	_____	_____
_____	_____	_____

Of the ones you have listed, which ones do you feel are the most costly? Why?

Now you are ready to take it to the next level. You need to identify the numbers.

If you are a *manager*, everyone who works for you gets paid. Every department has some percentage of turnover— some high, some low. Turnover comes from a variety of areas. Write the number of employees in your department, the average annual turnover and the average moneys you are paying. Include overtime, benefits and any bonuses.

Department _____

Number of Employees _____

Average Annual Compensation _____

Annual Turnover _____

Percent of Turnover to the # of Staff _____

Replacement Costs at 100% _____

Replacement Costs at 150% _____

If you are an *employee*, you get paid as others do. You may not know what your co-workers get, although most employees are aware of hourly ranges—i.e., $24 to $32 an hour. For annual compensation, double the hourly rate and multiply by 1000—$48,000 to $64,000. Don't forget overtime and benefits. Interesting, employees rarely consider benefits—from the employer contribution to Social Security, retirement accounts, education grants and the like as part of compensation. It is.

If you work in a department with 12 or 47 employees and two leave during the year, you have the turnover number. Divide the number who left by the total number of a full department. If two left, then it's 2 divided by 12 = 16.7% or 2 divided by 47 = 4.3%.

Department _____

Number of Employees _____

Average Annual Compensation _____

Annual Turnover _____

Percent of Turnover to the # of Staff _____

Replacement Costs at 100% _____

Replacement Costs at 150% _____

Feeling a tad baffled? Let me work one through for you. Let's say you manage or work in the OR and there are 52 nurses with an average income of $62,000. During the past year, nine have quit. Your numbers look like this—

Department	OR
Number of Staff	52
Average Annual Compensation	$62,000
Annual Turnover	9
% of Turnover to the # of Employees	9 ÷ 52 = 17.3%
Replacement Costs at 100%	$62,000 × 9 = $558,000
Replacement Costs at 150%	$93,000 × 9 = $837,000

Take it a step further, using the Tables I've provided as a model and determine what moneys would be saved if you reduced turnover from 17.3 percent to 10 percent. How much money is saved by reducing your turnover rate? Lots.

The Spill-Over Factor

In workplaces, employees report that it takes two to four times as long to complete tasks when conflict creators, saboteurs and ongoing conflict are in action. The same goes for those who create *Red Ink Behavior*—some are saboteurs and conflict creators in their own right. But many times, it's a personal style, habit, or an idiosyncrasy that drives coworkers and managers nuts.

My question for you now is: How much money and time are you willing to kiss off by refusing to search, seek-out and deal with bad behaviors?

The next chapter addresses Unwritten Rules, many which are cloaked in *Red Ink Behaviors*.

Summing Up

Most people "absorb" the *Red Ink Behavior* of other co-workers and staff. Rarely do they step back and evaluate how their own words and attitudes are impact others.

Those who are Red Ink Creators do not comprehend how their habits and idiosyncrasies impact themselves and their own productivity. Whether the creator or recipient, the bottom line surfaces—moneys go down the drain.

At times, with some fine tuning, including counseling, Red Ink Creators can mend their ways and become a key player on their team. And, at times, they need to be dehired—the sooner, the better.

Here is the bottom line—when Red Ink Behaviors are reduced/eliminated, patient safety and satisfaction skyrocket. A win-win—are you listening?

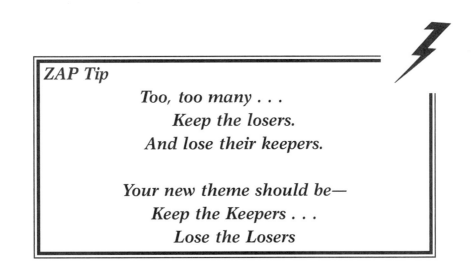

ZAP Tip

Too, too many . . .
Keep the losers.
And lose their keepers.

Your new theme should be—
Keep the Keepers . . .
Lose the Losers

12   The Unwritten Rules Rule

Several years ago, I spoke at an annual convention of a health care association on *Changing Conflict to Collaboration in the Toxic Workplace*. I usually bring copies of my books and audiotapes for participants to purchase if they so choose. Our policy has never been to pitch them; rather, they are available if anyone is interested. If no one wants to buy any, it's not a big deal. They are packed up and returned to my office in Colorado. If there are any sales, it's customary to make a donation back to the group for their foundation or other cause that the group has identified. My right to make books, tapes, and videos available is a provision included in my standard contract and agreed to by the sponsor in writing.

There were several pre-conference workshops going on at the same time as mine. The woman who had hired me was checking in on each one, to see how things were going. When she got to mine, she wasn't happy. In fact, she was very angry. The reason for her anger was a table displaying my books and audiotapes—the provision she had agreed to in writing earlier.

She could barely control her wrath. She said they had to be immediately boxed up and put away. Her unwritten rule was that no products could be sold (it didn't matter that she had already agreed to it!). At break time, everything was boxed up and put out of sight, a little jarring for the participants.

Since I was in the first quarter of an all-day workshop, I thought this would be a great example to use when I got to the section where I speak about unwritten rules. I told her I wasn't psychic. It was normal to have support tools and resources—books, tapes, videos—available, and this had not been excluded from our contract. My words were meaningless to her. I had violated her unwritten rule, and she forbade me to use it as an example in the workshop. She also forbade my giving any books away, which I normally do during certain activities in a program that involves audience participation. I did what she said.

In retrospect, I regret that I did not use her unwritten rule as an example. The situation was extremely unfortunate, but I learned a lesson: I now make sure that when I talk with the people in charge they really understand what is in my contract, and I ask what the specific rules are, if any, for their presenters—written and unwritten.

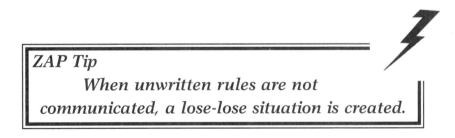

ZAP Tip
> **When unwritten rules are not communicated, a lose-lose situation is created.**

In my situation, we had three identifiable losers: the participants, who were angry because they could not purchase my books and tapes (even following me down the street when the workshop was over in an attempt to buy them at the hotel I was staying at); the association, because this woman created a great deal of ill will among the participants; and myself, since I had the hassle of shipping items that were not used, the disruption of boxing them up, irritation that her rule had not been explained to me, and the possibility that my performance would be affected by her negativism and her way of announcing her unwritten rule.

Now, when ever anyone in my office comes across a character or situation like this, we call it being "Mary Loued," the name of the woman who had zero flexibility, limited vision and unable to admit that she possibly screwed up. The good news was that the workshop participants gave great reviews for the program, ending in a standing ovation. The bad news is that this woman still works for the association and despite member praise for the program and requests from members to bring me back, she has blocked a return engagement. How much easier it would have been for all of us if the unwritten rule had been revealed before I was required to live and work by it.

Discovering the Unwritten Rules

The first time I conducted a workshop on conflict and sabotage in the health care workplace, I divided participants into different groups for a series of exercises. One of the exercises was to brainstorm in small groups of three to six individuals, in order to identify various unwritten rules in the workplace. I told them, "There are two identifiable rules in the workplace: go to work, and do the job. It's the one hundred plus unwritten rules that can destroy your working relationships and your work environment." Then, I gave an example of an unwritten rule: in the coffee room, the first person in makes the first pot, and the person who takes the last cup of coffee makes a new pot. Another was: in the copy room, if someone switches from regular to legal size paper, switch back to regular for the next person; if someone uses fuchsia paper for a flyer, the unwritten rule is to switch back to white.

These rules seem commonsensical, but when the un-written rules are not followed, they seed discontent. A single incident may not seem *important*, but over a period of time, many small infractions can make life a monstrous hassle.

Following are many unwritten rules identified by work-shop participants since 2000. Warning—some are reason-able, some silly, some contrary, some outrageous—but they are the reported rules that some health care professionals revealed. Unwritten rules that participants in our work-shops have identified include the following:

Bosses and Doctors *(for and about)*
Showcase the boss
Don't bug the boss when his or her door is closed
Avoid the boss when he or she is in a bad mood
The boss can do whatever he or she wants
Bosses are responsible for keeping employees and solving
   problems
In meetings, your opinions should follow the leader's
   (don't rock the boat)
Doctors can do anything
Doctors are king (this got a raspberry response from the
   group)
Don't undermine the doctor—she or he has the final say
Doctors are always right, it's someone else's fault
Call women doctors by their first names

Don't sit in the doctor's chair
Don't call a particular doctor to discharge a patient
Patients assume that all males are doctors
Doctors can't use nurses' or clerk's station
Doctors want all the credit
If doctors toss keys, back off
Don't wake ortho doctor
Doctors expect nurses to drop everything and do their
    bidding
Don't park in doctor's parking space
Tell doctor if he has BO, buggers or bad breath
Don't say no to the CEO or President
Be consistent with rules
Respect staff

Managers (for and about)
Managers work on their days off
Managers can fix things on short notice
Managers are on duty 24 hours a day
Managers always know what's right
White males are in charge
Women do not hold top-level executive positions
Managers don't take days off close to a deadline
Managers don't take two weeks of vacation time in a row
Managers don't call in sick on holidays or weekends
Managers don't walk their talk—are poor role models
Managers play favorites
Managers don't wear striped ties
If you socialize with the boss, you are brown-nosing
If the boss socializes with you, she is playing favorites

Nurses, Hygienists, Assistants & Staff (for and about)
Nurses are on duty 24 hours
Nurses should be willing to do anything

The best nurses take the worst assignments
The best nurses do things no one else will
Floaters always get the heavy work
Nurses always respond immediately
Full-timers should have more influence
Nurses should not take responsibility for peers; they
    should grumble instead
Whoever is stuck with the narcotic keys has to do the
    report
Never take pens out of the nursing office
The previous shift doesn't have to complete its work
Don't leave work undone
If there is a mistake, blame it on the student
If there is a mistake, blame it on the new nurse
Nurses with false fingernails can't do patient care
Don't call male doctors by their first names
Never call a resident between 7 A.M. and 8 A.M
Call residents by their first names, but with patients, call
    them "Doctor"
Avoid "Bertha" if she is floating
Don't sit in the clerk's chair
Always make rounds with doctors
Drop everything when the doctor enters
Doctors' wives get special treatment
Older nurses wages don't catch up
Nurses eat their young
New RNs must pay their dues
OK to dump on agency nurses
Don't dump on agency nurses
Do not ID a problem because you will have to come up
    with the solution
No shift rotation
Last person gets pulled
Last nurse in gets the worst patients

Don't expect to have the same patient everyday
Don't do transfers at shift time
If you are a pool RN, you are isolated
New person gets no breaks
Care providers don't say "oops"
If no charge nurse, the most senior RN steps in
Charge nurse covers the clerk for lunch
Charge nurse gets the best assignments
Charge nurse tells others when to go to
    lunch/dinner/breaks
If certain charge nurse doesn't like you, you get shit jobs
Tell coworkers if they have BO, bad break or buggers
Nurses are multi-talented—can do anything
Take report first, than wash hands
Be respectful

Teams (for and about)
Support all decisions of the team, even if you disagree
Rotate hard days
Don't cover up your mistakes or messes
Just do what needs to be done—don't wait
If not busy, help others
Act professionally at all costs
Bring out the best in other team members
Develop departmental loyalty
Cover for each other
Don't air the team's dirty laundry
Help another team member when your work is
    completed
Follow the chain of command
Don't brag
Be supportive
Give credit where it is due
Don't be a martyr; if you are busy, ask for help

Everyone should pitch in
If you come last, you lose
Whoever enters the last recording starts a new sheet
Let people know where you are
Look busy even if you are not
Part-time people can't refuse assignments
If it's not documented, you didn't do it
Doing extra work is brown-nosing
Cover your ass
Make up weekends
Don't be a whistleblower
Don't take side of nurses vs. non-nurses
Don't transfer patients at shift change
Don't check your patient at 3.45, 11.45 or 7.45
Don't challenge authority
Only certain people will help

The Workplace *(for and about)*
No handwritten signs
No tape on doors
Fill the soap dispenser
First one in turns on the copier
Return the copy machine to the regular setting if you
    change it
If the copier is empty, fill it
If you use it, put it back the way it was
Put the seat down
Keep areas neat
Return all dishes to the kitchen and wash the ones you use
Be the social butterfly
Deliver guilt
Squeaky wheel gets her way
The secretary makes the coffee
No one can drink coffee if the supervisor is present

Don't use someone else's coffee cup
Get a cup of coffee before you answer any questions
If it's broken, fix it
Reset the postage meter
Don't unplug equipment
Replace diapers
Replace TP
Flush the toilet all the way down
Don't use patient bathroom
Use Lysol when needed
Share lounge phone
Speak your native tongue in the lounge
Don't reuse disposables
Be courteous to co-workers,patients and their families
Don't talk to patients in the hallway
No gossiping with patients
Don't gossip about patients
Replace thermometer probe covers
Make new coffee for next shift
First one in turns the lights on; last one out turns
    them off
Clean up after yourself
Clean microwave
No TV on
Don't sit on the counters
Don't read newspapers or magazines at your desk
Don't move patient magazines to staff break area
Don't hassle front desk or clerk
Office property is everyone's; treat it so
Whoever stuffs it, empties it
Don't sit in someone's favorite chair
Don't touch someone's computer without permission
No gifts on birthdays; cakes only
If you smoke, pick up your cigarette butts

No coffee breaks at desk
Avoid "Bertha" at all costs
Stay out of clerk/receptionist/secretary's chair and space
If it's not yours, don't touch it
Come to work even when sick—spread it around
Food left around is free game
If you didn't bring food, you can't eat others
If you don't bring food, you can't share in potluck
Don't assume anything
Don't leave empty IVs
If you do IVs well, you will be the IV expert
Hang IVs for next shift
Don't leave empty feeding bags
Don't hang around in the office
Patient care always more important than office tasks
Lights off at 11 PM for midnight shift
Don't change thermostat
Only one person waters the plants
English should only be spoken at nurse's station
Don't answer phone 15 minutes before end of shift
No personal phone calls at work
Let the phone ring—someone else will answer it
Anyone can answer the phone
Turn down ER on the first call
Don't sleep at work
Be on time
Knock before entering
When there are certain re-admits—run
Don't leave things undone for the next shift

Co-workers *(for and about)*
Smokers can take more breaks than nonsmokers and get
  away with it

Smokers regularly take all breaks and lunches
Don't take extra smoke breaks
Certain people get specific time slots for lunch and
    dinner
Seniority gets first break/lunch/dinner
Rotate difficult patients with difficult RNs
Least senior person gets double shifts
Advise someone of your patient's status
Listen when some is talking
I show up at work, so should you
Don't expect to have the same patient every day
Get to take breaks with friends
Take breaks only during slow times
Night shifts don't take breaks
Night shifts get to do baths
Don't argue in front of co-workers or patients
Too many bathroom breaks are frowned on
Don't date co-workers
If you don't show up, you will be talked about
If you are sick, you get the silent treatment when you
    return
Give laxatives at the end of your shift
It's OK to eat patient's food
It's OK to combine lunch with breaks for a longer period
    of time
Give best assignments to friends
Parents can be on the phone more than nonparents
Parents get certain holidays off
Canadians work holidays
Parents don't have to work overtime
Parents can come in late and leave early
Parents can take time off
Parents can take more sick days off

Can't be sick in July (new residents start July 1)
Don't piss off a member of a clique
Belief—all midnight shifts sleep on the job
If midnight shifts don't do work—day shift will
Grouches should retire
If you've been there as long as the facility is old, you
    should retire
Be kind and courteous
Let person who is charting sit down
Keep messages
Return calls promptly
Answer the phone by the second ring
Stay by the phone if you page someone
Respond to boss' page immediately
Answer page in a timely manner
Personal calls are to be brief
No personal calls allowed

Miscellaneous (for and about)
Follow the Golden Rule
Anytime you go on a trip, you need to bring back gifts
All females on unit have to wear lipstick
Don't wear thong underwear with white pants
Don't wear jeans
Screen calls at home (they may want you to come into
    work)
It's OK to be late 5 minutes
Friday is dress-down day
Maintain a proper personal appearance
Be professional outside of the workplace
Don't bring the old culture back
No more than two Fridays off in a row
It's not the money that counts; you work to take care of
    others

If you don't take assigned work, you will get your hours
    cut back
If you do the work of a charge nurse, don't assume you
    will get paid as one
You don't get paid if you work overtime
If you cared, you would work more
Volunteer to keep notes at meetings
If you understand the form, it is time to change it
Always eat with the same people, or suffer
Tell someone she has lipstick on her cheek or teeth
Learn the "old boy" rules
If you take a risk, you had better be right
Tell me; do not surprise me
Do it the way it's always been done
Always act like a lady
If you volunteer, you will get picked on
It's not what you do, it's whom you know
Smile even if you don't like it
If you speak out, you are a complainer
You get feedback only when you grumble
The same rules should apply to all departments
Don't be happy or else someone will squash you
Give visitors directions
You cannot turn down a patient's request
You can sell (cookies, etc), but don't let Administration
    know
When their kids are selling candy, calendars, and
    cookies, parents can pressure you to buy them
Don't challenge authority
Unfreeze breast milk
New mothers can breastfeed
Don't chat outside of patients room
Don't adjust the vents
Be on time

Unrealistic Unwritten Rules

Every workplace has them. Sometimes there are different rules for different status, length of employment, even who you are aligned with!

Jill loves her patients, and she loves nursing. She also feels she would be better off if she could work in a vacuum because she has seen so many miserable things that established nurses have done to new nurses. She feels strongly that established nurses should open up during orientation so that new nurses will understand all the nuances of what is expected of them. If one of the unwritten rules is to blame "it," whatever it is, on the new nurse, her workplace is a perfect example. Jill adds,

> The older nurses expect a lot more of the newer nurses. They are brand new and are going to make mistakes. Why they expect them to know all the rules, all the requirements, and all the personalities of the other nurses on the floor is beyond me. There is a lot of bitching going on, and there are times I do not know why I do what I do. I love nursing. I just wish the atmosphere was more collaborative.

Lunchtime Is Not Personal Time

Holly is a health-unit coordinator with a large hospital in the West, working in a nonemergency sector of the hospital. She recalls a time when she decided to take care of some of her personal business during her lunch hour. Unfortunately, in Holly's workplace there were unwritten rules dealing with just how far she could wander during her lunch hour. She begins,

> I left the hospital premises to pay a bill. Later, I was informed that it was an infringement of hospital

policy to leave the premises during my shift. Dorian, who would normally cover my desk during lunch, had called down to say that her partner, Felicia, was leaving early because she was ill. Therefore, the two of us should go to lunch now, while Felicia was still there, so she could leave when we got back.

This did not make sense to me, since we could stagger our leaving times. I told her to go ahead and go, and I would go to lunch later because I had to pay a bill in the village. Dorian is not well liked within the hospital. She has a reputation for being bossy, and she likes to run things. I waited to go to lunch until she came back and offered to cover for Felicia so she could go home.

Our boss happened to call in, and Dorian told her that I was going to leave the premises to pay a bill. A few days later, I was called into her office and was reprimanded for violating hospital policy. When I responded that I did not know it wasn't allowed and was against the rules, I received no support. I've been with the hospital for fifteen years.

Holly was in a situation where a co-worker did not like her independence, and she was angry that Holly didn't do what she wanted her to do—take lunch when her co-worker thought she should. Holly wasn't aware of any policy that would have forbidden her to go the six blocks to pay her bill. Later, when Holly went to her boss's boss to inquire about the rule, she was told only that employees had to stay in close proximity to the hospital.

People can be very myopic and close-minded. They see only black and white, never shades of gray. It is understandable to ask someone in a critical-care unit or an emergency room to stay within a very short distance of the work station during breaks and lunch hours. Holly was a clerk. She was someone who would not have been involved in a life-or-death situation.

Until the rule changes, Holly will stay close to work on all breaks. For practical purposes, it would make sense for her employer to readdress and update this rule. After all, hospitals are about getting and staying well. Taking a walk is certainly healthier than sitting in a room or out on a bench.

Not in My Department

Sharon is director of surgical services with a hospital that is very family-oriented in terms of patients and employees alike. She remembers the time she fired two nurses. When the CEO found out, she was very upset. She told Sharon that she should have found a way to keep them, no matter what. The unwritten rule was that you didn't fire anyone.

What happens when a rule like *We do not fire anyone* exists? Simply this—employees experience lower morale and innovativeness and prevent the learning of new things. It can even encourage goofing off. It's like a disease that no one wants to talk about. Rather, people keep quiet, failing to recognize that such a rule can poison the whole work environment. She confided,

> I knew the hospital rule that you did not fire
> someone. I asked another department head to take
> two of my employees who I felt were unreliable and
> lacking in skills. She told me that she did not want to.
> I knew I wasn't going to keep them on my staff, so I
> had no choice. I terminated them. Now, I am viewed
> as a cold-hearted bitch. In my professional opinion,
> they were a liability to me, as well as to the patients
> I serve.

Unwritten rules that say *Do anything to retain personnel* create enormous problems. Many times, the person who is retained will be an older employee, one who is close to retirement. She may be slowing down or her skills may be substandard and outmoded. Management believes that because she has been with the establishment for so many years, she should be rewarded for her dedication and loyalty. The unwritten rule is that management owes this to the employee. But is that true? When someone is not required to maintain a level of continuing education and competence, such laxity can lead to mediocrity and even danger. Sharon had this problem in another instance, too. She continued,

> I recently had another serious breach of discipline, due to negligence. I believed that two more nurses should be fired. We had done a case in surgery where the instruments had not been sterilized. When I questioned the nurses, they said that they knew what they were supposed to do, but they just didn't do it. They never gave me a reason why. In fact, I found out that this was their normal practice. Because of the culture of the hospital, I couldn't fire them. I had to pass their mediocrity on to some other department and hold my breath that a lawsuit does not hit.
>
> I think that dedication and loyalty mean so much here that people who are problems are held on to and put into places where they cannot cause as many problems as before. At least, that's the theory.
>
> After I fired the first two nurses, there was a big meeting. It was the first time anyone had ever been fired from the operating room staff. Everyone was shocked. At the meeting, the CEO said she hated

getting up in the morning and coming to work when the staff was not happy to be working. I felt that her remarks were very inappropriate. After all, she can't be responsible for the staff's happiness.

Sharon is correct. People may be unhappy or happy for a variety of reasons, many of which may have nothing to do with the workplace. What the director or manager should be responsible for is creating an environment that is safe, meets various standards, delivers what it promises, and rewards competence.

Mandating Rules All

Natalie is a nurse who has one child and is expecting another. In her hospital, if the following shift looks short-handed, the nurse manager can mandate someone to work a second shift. Usually the person mandated to work is the low person on the totem pole. Her words,

> Normally, I work a three-to-eleven shift three days a week. I came on as an extra one day and was scheduled to work that shift. When the charge nurse said she was going to mandate me to work the next shift, eleven-to-seven, I told her that she could not do that, since I had agreed to work as an extra. She should then have gone and found the next appropriate person to work the night shift. But that person turned out to be a single parent with two kids. Because of that, the charge nurse worked the extra shift herself.

Natalie brings up a very sensitive point: she is married, and the other woman is not, but both are mothers. Just because someone is married, management should not assume that a spouse is available for child care. Natalie works the evening shift, and the assumption is that her spouse works the day shift—that should leave her available to fill in on the night shift if need be. After all, her husband could be with their child. She reported that he works the overnight shift,

> If the single mother had been mandated, she would have had two shifts and then had the responsibility for her child—but so would I. My experience with the unwritten rules is that single mothers get more understanding, leeway, and preference. On the days that I work, my husband and I pass each other in the night—he's leaving when I come home.

Natalie mentioned another unwritten rule. She is certified in chemotherapy, and the unwritten rule is that if you are so certified, you have to take on assignments. The exception is that if you are pregnant and in your first trimester, you do not have to do chemotherapy. During the time when Natalie was trying to get pregnant, there was a two-week period of uncertainty each month, until her pregnancy was confirmed. She shares,

> We were going through a staff shortage and had a bunch of open holes. If you knew chemo, you had to do it, even if you didn't want to or said no. If I had said no without a confirmed pregnancy, I could have been fired. Eventually, I transferred off the floor.

Use Your Head

Kim is a staff doctor in the emergency room of a medium-size hospital in the South. She says she did not realize how bright she was until she was in her thirties. That's when she decided to stop being a nurse and enroll in medical school. Kim feels that one unwritten rule should be *Use your head.* She has been with her present hospital for two years and finds that it is difficult to get rid of the old unwritten rules and let common sense prevail. She reveals,

> Sometimes I get aggravated with the nurses. We can have a waiting room full of people, and in comes a 26-year-old man who says he has chest pains, and they move a child with a temperature of 105 degrees to the back burner. The young man has waited three weeks to come in, and here we have a child with a high fever. It irritates the hell out of me.
>
> The nurses should have enough sense to make these decisions. I know that nurses have brains in their heads. I was a great nurse, and so were most that worked around me. When I questioned their judgment about bringing in the young man with chest pains first, they said, 'Well, he was here first.' My response to that was, 'This is not a damned bakery.'
>
> Several times I have made a general statement about the waiting room: children with high temperatures are seen first. My policy is not to let these children wait for three hours. I have found that if I go individually to the nurses and restate my policies, they feel that they are being singled out and discriminated against.
>
> My style is to be more blunt, but I have found that I have to change and be more subtle. If I don't, I could have a situation where somebody who is 60-years old, blue in the face, vomiting, and having massive chest pain will be held back while they bring in a child with a 102-degree temperature. It seems

absurd, but that's what happens. My rule is to use your head.

What Unwritten Rules Do You Work Under?

In every program I do on *Zapping Conflict and Creating a Collaborative Workplace*, an interactive section is presented on identifying unwritten rules. The entire audience—be it 50 participants or 500, are broken into mini-teams. The assignment—in 10 minutes, come up with as many unwritten rules as they can think of. Some are outrageously funny, some outrageously ridiculous and some outrageously scary or downright mean. As the group begins to share them with all, they are recorded on poster-sized paper and displayed for all to see. It's not uncommon to hear tons of laughter, even booing at some of them—it's also common to see heads nodding and vocalization of agreement that some are good, some no big deal and many, plain downright dumb, even dangerous.

In the Mid-west, I did a program on site for a facility that required all personnel from a specific department to attend. When I introduced the identifying unwritten rule activity, all were enthusiastic, except Mary. She just sat in the center of the room (we were in table rounds), with her arms crossed, slumping in the chair. Mary wasn't a happy camper and she made it plain that she didn't want to be there to all. She proceeded to say that there were no unwritten rules—everyone knew that you went to work and did the job. Period.

The advantage of leading the group is that I have the birdseye of the responses from others—many who were shaking their heads indicating that Mary was all wet—there were rules. In fact, by the time I was done, we found nine pages of them. Some, which were critical issues that management needed to deal with immediately.

Mary was a hostile participant that the head of the department told me prior to the program created problems among her co-workers. But, she was considered an extremely valuable employee—she always got good feedback from patients and customers (as some facilities call patients). Management felt that she was needed. Really?

Many of the participants had approached me throughout the day—could I get management to see the light about Mary? That her extreme negativity cast a cloud on all of them. The result being her attitude impacted their moods and their work. I did speak to management, expressed my concerns about her, as well as some of the feedback I had received. They acknowledged that Mary was a problem, but surely the others can just ignore her. They have—over half have left and gone to work for others.

Identifying the Unwritten Rules that Rule

Set aside 15 to 30 minutes over the next few days, and just ponder scenarios in your workplace. Identify the different individuals you work with, those in management or supervisory positions and those in senior management, including your CEO. Next, list the women and men you work with directly.

As you identify the women and men in your workplace, describe their tasks, their personalities, and the interactions you have with them. Ask yourself if they dress or speak in specific ways. Have the times when you had direct interaction with them been good, bad, or indifferent? Is your workplace stimulating and energetic, or is it a drag for you to show up each day?

Write down your thoughts about the various individuals you work with. When images of your boss, supervisor, or manager come to mind, are there any idiosyncrasies, mandates, or dictums that also come to mind.

Now think about your colleagues and co-workers. Do

you have rules regarding days off, break time, interactions, or housekeeping? No matter how minor they seem, write these incidences down.

Next, brainstorm with a trusted colleague to expand your list, or at least collaborate on one. In staff meetings, if there is time set aside for comments and questions, you can involve others in identifying various unwritten rules.

If your manager or supervisor is not open to this idea, she may perceive your suggestion as threatening. If so, or if you are unsure about how your manager will respond, it may be better to approach your manager on a one-on-one basis. Since your objective is to identify unwritten rules and make life in your workplace more livable, try saying something like this: "Since I've been here, I have noticed a series of things that many of my co-workers do."

Now, identify some of those things. It could be that everyone washes her own coffee cup, that certain coffee cups are not used, and that smoking is allowed only in specific areas. Everything you mention should be basically safe and nonthreatening. Continue with a statement like this: "If I had known that these were unwritten rules, it would have been so much easier for me when I started here. Has anyone thought about putting together a notebook of other rules that our team goes by? When we add new employees or have temps and floaters, this could give them a better understanding of what makes our unit tick."

A manager who declines to identify your team's unwritten rules, or who is insensitive to the need to do so, will be the exception. Encourage her to bring the topic up at a meeting, and reaffirm that if you had known some of the rules when you first arrived, you could have been more effective and efficient in your job.

Sometimes remaining anonymous is important, for personal or even political reasons, and a suggestion-type box can be used to collect the unwritten rules. And some of the rules that emerge will be absurd, sacred cows that everyone knows about and dislikes but that still are untouchable. Violation of unwritten rules can drive others crazy. If you or someone else continually violates or ignores them, enormous friction is created.

When I gave the sheets of unwritten rules obtained from a workshop for the staff of a 250 bed hospital in Northern California to one of the directors of a department—she planned on using them to begin a dialogue with her staff. They were a great tool to identify sloppy work ethics as well as a reminder for kudos for many of the things that they did that she took for granted.

Above all, have some fun identifying the unwritten rules of your workplace. Why not post an *Unwritten Rule of the Week* and have a good laugh with your co-workers? Give it a prize for the silliest . . . or even uncovering one that may be costing your department moneys that could be allocated in another area.

ZAP Tip

*Before assuming that an unwritten rule
really is untouchable or unchangeable,
ask why? If you are not sure, ask someone
you work with. Sometimes no one really knows
why some rules are in place. Identify those
rules and discuss them. If all agree, they
can be changed. (The group may also decide
to keep them, of course.)*

Summing Up

Every workplace has unwritten rules, and they are different in each one. Some may need to be changed. They all need to be communicated, passed along from those who know them to those who don't. If they are stockpiled and withheld from co-workers, increased conflict is the result.

As you learn the unwritten rules, speak up and circulate them. You need to pass them along to others. When you are oblivious to the unwritten rules, or when you don't speak out and circulate them, you set yourself up for a fall. You set others up, too, and everyone loses.

Keep in mind—it's not the written rules (show up, do your job), it's the unwritten rules that can make or break you and your workplace.

13 The Mentoring Way

If "nurses eat their young" is an unwritten rule in some facilities, the nurses who work in a Cape Cod hospital have nixed it from their workplace. Their rule is to "mentor the young—no devouring allowed." Their attitude was that if they didn't treat the younger nurses well and train them to the best of their abilities, they would be in deep trouble because—who else was going to care for them when they needed it? Smart thinking.

JB's Mentoring Thing

One Friday a month, I have a "Salon Day" at my office from one to six—participants refer to it as JB's Mentoring Thing! Invitations are done by email to a list I've accumulated over time. Those invites, in turn, get shared with others—it's a time that just about anyone can show up to pick my brain, get input or advice on a variety of topics that I have some expertise in. Sometimes there is a handful, others dozens. And, sometimes, I may not be sure, but someone within the group has had some experience in whatever is being questioned.

It does two things for me—first, it's part of giving back and second, I routinely get so many calls from women and men asking for advice that I get bogged down with my work. This way, I can easily say (and my staff)—let's talk on Friday, the 5ᵗʰ . . . here's my address.

It does three things for the participant—first, they usually have a good time; second, they get practical, hands-on advice that they can use and third, they usually make new connections by meeting others who they normally wouldn't in their own workplaces.

Some return time after time—a longer term mentoring; and others show up once or twice for a quick fix and then I don't hear from them for months. They know that I'm interested in their success and/or solving whatever they sought input on. They also know that once I probe into something and give feedback, it's not OK to keep recycling an old issue. And, I won't be their Mother and follow-up with reminders as to what I suggest they do. It's a win-win for all involved.

Being a mentor involves an interactive relationship with a mentee. A good mentor nurtures the evolving mentee. A good mother nurtures her young, too, but there is a difference between mothering and mentoring; what most women don't need is another mother in the workplace. Mothers often overprotect in their attempt to eliminate or reduce the risks their children encounter. A mentor empowers a mentee to take on the responsibilities and the risks that are in her path. MaMa management does not belong here.

> ## ZAP Tip
> *Men have understood the value, and necessity, of mentoring. Be it within or outside of their workplaces, they know that connections, affiliations, and advise from those in power or position can be critical to a career. Many women, especially those on a leadership track, recognize the benefit to their career when a mentor relationship is in play.*

A Mentor Is Your Advocate

Good mentoring relationships are always reciprocal. The mentee, the person who receives guidance from her benefactor or sponsor, responds with support for her mentor. She receives information and ideas from her mentor, and others whom she works for benefit as the ideas are implemented.

Mentors are teachers, sponsors, advisers, coaches, guides, and counselors. Sometimes they are friends. As teachers and advisers, they help chart career paths for their mentees. As guides, they walk those paths with their mentees. In a healthy mentoring relationship, the mentor has been through the school of hard knocks. As a counselor, she uses her experience to help the mentee avoid some of the potholes that surface in the workplace. As a sponsor, she expands networking capabilities within the professional ranks. As a coach, she supplies emotional support when pitfalls are encountered. Many view mentors as role models, but there is a distinct difference. A role model can be anyone; there does not have to be a direct relationship, nor interaction.

Types of Mentors

There are usually three types of mentors. The *traditional mentor* is usually older and more established in her career and in the organization. The *next-step mentor* is usually just one career level ahead of you and is closer in age. The *co-mentor* would be considered your peer and is often the same age. She or he is more of a collaborator on your career path.

Each type offers advantages. The traditional mentor brings power through her seniority. She has been around for a substantial period of time and is unlikely to lose out because of a political reorganization. When you are in a next-step mentoring relationship, all goes well if your mentor is "politically correct" in safe territory; otherwise, your relationship with her can be a handicap. One of the advantages of the co-mentoring relationship is that each woman brings strengths to the relationship, and they can propel each other toward whatever goals have been defined.

A mentor likes what she does. Her enthusiasm and energy are contagious. She is also very secure in herself and self-confident. She doesn't feel threatened when her mentee begins to outgrow the relationship—a common occurrence. If a mentee is bright and ambitious, or if her personal or career goals and visions change, her relationship with her mentor will change, and the relationship will need reassessment.

Who Should Be a Mentor?

Jeanne Watson Driscoll, a psychiatric clinical nurse specialist and former Dean of the University of Colorado Health Sciences Center School of Nursing, has been a mentor many times. She identifies several factors that enable a mentor to be helpful, including belief in the mentee, a commitment to investing her own time and expertise in the mentee's development, and the ability to recognize what the potential mentee can do for her.[1]

> Mentors have expertise in specific areas, and that's what mentees are looking for. Ideally, a mentor should be nonjudgmental and accepting of you as an individual, but it's not necessary for you to be her clone. Women who are excellent mentors encourage their mentees to move through their own space, with their own style. When the mentor looks in the mirror and is comfortable with the image that looks back, she can demonstrate her professionalism and leadership simply by being who she is.

Women who are Queen and Princess Bees, with the attitude that you need to make it on your own or don't compete with me, are women to be avoided as mentors. Phantom and Bumbler Bees referred to in Chapter 5 —women who believe that *no one* is as competent or qualified as they are— should also be deleted from your list of potential mentors. Women who are not team players should be avoided, too. They can't offer the give-and-take that this relationship requires. Ideally, it is a win-win relationship: a woman mentor will see her own leadership skills grow, and her own career planning and credibility may be enhanced.

Reaching out and offering her expertise and guidance to another woman encourages her to reevaluate her own career—where she is going, and what she wants to be at the end of the road. A healthy mentor encourages the mentee's transition from being nurtured to being empowered.

When a mentee stretches and begins to reach her goals, a mentor is pleased that she has been the cheerleader and advocate.

Mentoring Phases

In the beginning phase, the rules, written and unwritten, are laid out. Boundaries are determined. What's all right and what is not should be spelled out.

A woman who is a mentor is usually extraordinarily busy. You may not be the only mentee she has. Respect her time. Find out the best time to call her, and set up appointments. If you ask her early in your relationship how best to work with her, you will show her that you respect and honor her commitment to you. You can then adjust your time and needs to match hers. The odds of a successful mentorship will be significantly enhanced.

The middle phase is training. This is the time when you get to know each other. Your mentor does not have to be your friend. She doesn't even have to like you personally in order to respect you and recognize your potential. In the training phase, she is investing in you. Her words of wisdom and guidance during this time will become your tools, which will take you to your next level in the organization.

The final phase is termination. You may have outgrown your mentor, and it's time for you to move on. Or perhaps your mentor's goals, aspirations, or position with the organization has changed. It's highly probable that a friendship has grown between you. Although you will both go your separate ways, there is a bond. A friendship that grows from a healthy mentorship is a bonus.

The Toxic Mentor

As in any other kind of relationship, there can be problems. The relationship may become unbalanced: the mentee may become totally dependent on her mentor for approval or authority, or the mentor may become dependent on the mentee for attention, admiration, and support. A mentee may feel that she is being exploited by her mentor, or that her mentor is trying to control her and even sabotage her efforts. This kind of mentorship is clearly not healthy. For example, several of the women interviewed for this book had experienced a mentor taking credit for their work. Others said that their mentors were open, supportive, and encouraging but were mysteriously unable to offer help or information at the moment when it was needed.

Toxic mentors can derail your career, and they come in several varieties. *Cloggers* leave you out of the loop. *Wreckers* initially take pride in what you do and what you have achieved, and then suddenly nothing you do is right, and no matter how wonderful you think it is, they will find the flaw. *Castoffs* have a bit of the Queen Bee in them. Their attitude is often "Sink or swim," and when they finally decide to help, it's usually too late. *Escape artists* talk a good line. They tell anyone and everyone that they are mentoring you and have high hopes for your advancement, but they are never around when you need them.

Toward Empowerment

Women need to recognize their potential to be mentors, and they must be willing to be mentors. Mentoring is one key to eliminating some pitfalls of the workplace.

When a woman agrees to serve as your mentor, she puts you on the road to empowerment. But empowerment isn't something that can be given to you. It is *learned and earned* along your path. At times, you will get extra doses. At other times, you will have setbacks and feel disempowered.

A man can mentor a woman, women can mentor women, and in some cases, women mentor men. But when women mentor other women, it's quite positive. They demonstrate that they care about women's future and participation in the work force.

If you are new in your workplace, keep your eyes and ears open. Find out who has skills, expertise, respect, and power in your present environment, as well as in the area you would like to progress to. Find a woman (or man) you would like to emulate. Seek her out, and let her know that you respect and admire her. (Everyone loves flattery, as long as it's not excessive.) Ask for a 15-minute appointment, or invite her for coffee (and don't forget—you pay).

Many people feel that a woman in a strong position should automatically reach down and make time for other women. The woman herself may also feel that way, but she has a constraint—her time. Bear in mind that she is busy and has a lot of responsibilities. That's why she holds the position she does.

After you solicit her support and she agrees to act as your guide and advocate, remember that you need to support her and respect her time. Let her make the rules.

The Association of Women Surgeons created the Pocket Mentor several years ago. It's an excellent "how-to" resource. Go to the website at *www.womensurgeons.org* **or call 630-655-0392 for additional information.**[2]

Mentoring does take time and commitment. If you offer your hand to another woman, or to several, you have taken on a responsibility that is not light. Define your rules, just as your mentor did. Whether you are the mentor or the mentee (and many women are both), the relationship will be career-focused. If a friendship develops over time, congratulations. That's your bonus. It's not a prerequisite or a required outcome.

ZAP Tip

At the same time you're reaching up,
extend your hand down, and become
a mentor to another.

Summing Up

Mentoring is a tradition that has evolved over the Centuries—men do it and have done it—and now women are doing it. It's a way to continue a type of legacy . . . work that has commenced through the enthusiasm, actions and practices of the mentee, who in turns, reaches out and brings others along in the mentoring way.

When women (and men) take it upon themselves to act as mentors to other women, they ensure that women's views and voices will be actively and enthusiastically passed on to future generations—another step toward empowerment.

Star Teams—
Their Players &
Employers
of Choice

If you were to gather a group of managers from a variety of industries and organizations and ask them to identify the top three elements of creating an effective workplace for all—management, employees, and customers—being a team player and participating in teamwork would be on everyone's list. Team play, teamwork, and team members are interchanged continually in your workplace. Some teams have one member in one location; others have many members in numerous locations.

For many, the phrase *team player* almost has a tainted air about it. In the past, being a team player meant keeping your mouth shut, working long hours, and not speaking up when someone else took the credit. But today's work teams don't need to use sports metaphors to interact with each other. They do, however, need to understand that each member of the team has the potential to be a *Key Player*, no matter the size and number of locations of the team.

> A *Key Player* carries out her job at a peak performance plus. She can be found in at any level of an organization. She does any job with unswerving excellence, and her team skills make her an essential member of her team.
>
> A *Key Player* is confident, doesn't participate in the creation or spreading of rumors or gossip, shares unwritten rules of the workplace, acknowledges the work of others on the team, and is not a conflict creator or saboteur.
>
> A *Key Player's* unique combination of skills are essential and can't be easily replaced—she stands out. In the end, she has more leverage, is presented with extra choices and opportunities, and has greater autonomy in shaping her own career than her co-workers who merely show up and punch the clock.

As the health care industry evolves, teams will be a critical element—not just people coming together to work on a project or a report, but teams made up of *Key Players*. These teams become the *Star Teams*. Today's *Star Team* accomplishes its tasks with a high degree of energy, harmony and enthusiasm. It repays the effort of individual members by protecting and nurturing their careers and providing them with challenge, responsibility, opportunity, and—above all—recognition for their work.

The new-style team will win more than it loses. It will

focus on getting results, not just on personalities, processes, and rules. In the workplace, it will tap talent, time, and energy to get things done. Games, politics, and grand-standing don't belong, nor do they fit.

For any team to succeed, all the players must have a common vision and the desire to succeed at their goal. Players must complement each other, recognizing that not everyone has the same strengths and weaknesses, and being prepared to compensate for or offset others' weaknesses.

Imagine that you are a new member of a team. It looks as if civil war could break out at any time. The key problem is that conflicts can't be resolved and members are being pulled into opposing factions. Let's say that several problems have come to your attention, including—

- When one coalition or faction makes a successful presentation, the other reacts with hurt feelings.
- When ideas are brainstormed and offered, team conflict erupts, and members are told to forget what they are working on.
- When work is completed, members bury it, not telling the leaders that the project is done.
- New members of the team quickly learn that they have to align themselves with one of the factions (cliques).
- One of the team's co-leaders is angry because her protege, mentee or mentor doesn't receive respect from everyone.

Sound familiar? This could be your company, hospital, department, office or association. It could even be your family. No matter how successful a product, company, or organization is, a divided team is costly. Energy, money, talent, and time disappear into a black hole. Team warfare is crazy. It's destructive, stressful, and unproductive. Leaders and players must step back and assess their teams.

Phases of Team Development

Cohesive teams aren't created overnight. As a team develops, it evolves through phases. Teams in the first phase are usually individual centered, with each participant having separate goals rather than group ones. Individuals have no responsibility for others, tend to avoid change, and are not willing to deal with conflict. As the members get to know each other, new purposes and responsibilities are defined, the skills of various members are identified, and communication expands.

The second phase is more developmental. Individuals identify with the group. Purposes are clarified and expanded. Roles and various norms for working together are established. In this phase, a team tends to be leader-centered. The leader provides direction, assigns tasks, and evaluates performance. She is usually at the center of all communication.

In the third and final phase, the team is purpose-centered, and the members understand and use the purpose to guide action and decisions for the team as a whole.

No team is without problems. What happens when you are involved with a team and it just doesn't get off the dime, or when certain members don't carry their share of the load and others seem to dominate? On any team, whether newly formed or established, there will be breakdowns in communication, tasks, and cohesion.

Whether you are a member of a team, or it's leader, it's important for you to recognize problems when they are just beginning. Common problems include fragmentation, lack of productivity, lack of motivation, resentment, misbehavior, dominating and submissive personalities, overdependence on the leader, too much accommodation and too little challenging, lack of interest, and failure to deal with conflict. These are all problems that will surface at various times throughout the evolution of any team.

As a leader or as a member, you must not ignore any problem. Avoidance should be squashed. Arriving at the third phase of team development involves hard work. The adage "anything worthwhile is worth working for" applies.

Teams at Work

When interviewing Linda Miles, one of the leading consultant-trainers in the field of dentistry and author of *Your Key to the Practice*, she states that dentists are no different from doctors and managers—they hope that the problem/conflict, whatever it is, will simply go away by ignoring it.

Miles gets the same response that I do when she asks her audiences what happens when conflict is ignored—it festers. She also notes a significant difference between a medical and dental office. Linda's observation,

> I've found that communications among team members is stronger on the dental side. Medical doctors usually don't run the office and team—administrators are hired to handle them. Dentists usually have a far more active involvement with their office personnel, including planned continuing education programming for the entire office.

Lynne Kurth is Director of Operative Services with St. Mary's Health Care Center in South Dakota. I met her many years ago when she heard me speak on the toxic workplace. Since then, she has completed her thesis on managerial factors relating to turnover in hospitals. Her study (which won the Sabra M. Hamilton Award for Thesis of the Year at the University of Minnesota in 2002) revealed that employees wanted the opportunity to do their best every day.[2] She does everything she can to walk and talk what she found from the study to make her workplace a better one for all team members. She's building a Star Team. Lynne adds,

> There's been a high level of frustration from the staff—most feel that what they get from administration is lip service with no follow up. What they want is the opportunity to do their best.
>
> Over the past year, I've spent time evaluating my own strengths and weaknesses, as well as working with the staff to do theirs. For example, my strength is not psychology—I don't have the skills of others—I asked my staff to help me—tell me what fires them up, what makes them happy. I will do what I can to create that environment.
>
> I now know that there are certain people who shouldn't handle inventory, be warm and fuzzy, even starting IVs on difficult patients. It smacks against cross training, but the simple fact is some people are better at some skills than others.
>
> My group created our own pain management assessment long before the hospital created one, or even supported the idea.

Has it paid off for her team—yes. Her department has consistently won the highest marks in patient satisfaction. Patients aren't happy if they have to deal with grumpy personnel. Did management acknowledge her award from the University of Minnesota . . . or the fact that her team time after time gets tops in patient satisfaction surveys?—nope! It's good that she gets it, because they don't.

Brian Lee is the author of *Keep Your Nurses & Healthcare Professionals for Life!* and CEO of Custom Learning Systems in Calgary Alberta. He's an enthusiast for creating empowered workplaces and enabling employees to also do their best. He believes that there is a strong link between employee morale and customer satisfaction and often quotes Press Ganey, "A 1% change in employee morale equals a 2% change in patient satisfaction." Brian states,

> Give the staff the gift of empowerment . . .treat them as adults. A revolution is occurring that puts the value of staffs' attitude ahead of clinical competence when it comes to how managers treat staff and how staff treats patients (and/or customers).

Jo Manion, PhD, RN, CNAA is the author of *Change from Within* and has been a staff nurse, faculty member, director of nursing and administrator. Today, she also speaks and consults exclusively to health care organizations. She shares an experience where she was brought in as part of a recognition day for staff,

> The executive team was told that it was important to recognize staff by an outside consultant. The nursing managers were asked to identify those that were exemplary, then set up a big event to recognize them. Just before the Chief Nurse was introduced who in turn would identify the honorees, the CEO asked her to cut her remarks short. All the honorees heard and ended up getting a coupon for a free meal in the cafeteria. The Board adjourned to a private room for a catered lunch. It would have been better to have totally ignored them instead of treating them like cattle.

The above "pros" all favor empowerment, building trust, and practicing respect. They are true proponents of creating Star Teams in the health care workplace. Unfortunately, too many administrators, managers and staff aren't.

Here Today, Gone Tomorrow

After a merger, when staffs are combined and people are let go, problems often surface. Not everyone knows everyone else, protection of turf increases, and trust among co-workers has not yet developed. These phenomena are all normal whenever there are "new kids on the block." In the changing context of the health care industry, issues like these will be more and more common, as we'll see in the following case histories.

Georgia, a staff RN, works in a hospital that merged with another. Her manager was let go, and the manager from the other hospital was retained. She reports that her floor is swamped. Normally, the nursing staff was sufficient to cover needs and emergencies, but ever since the merger there has been more pressure on all the nurses. Georgia's previous nurse manager had gone out of her way to help and fill in, as necessary; an unwritten rule was that team members should offer that kind of support. But now, things have changed. She shares,

> I don't understand it. When we get busy and need help, she is gone. Since she has been here, it's happened three out of five days. It's awful.

Overstepping Boundaries

Marilyn is the head nurse of an intensive-care unit. During the process of selecting a new director of nursing, Marilyn and two others ran the department until the position was filled. The new nursing director didn't last long: she was fired after six months. Whatever got in her path ended up damaged, and it took more than six months to put the teams back together after she left. Marilyn said,

> The new director of nursing strongly believed in having people who were educated differently from the way I had been. She would place large, unacceptable expectations on people. It was virtually impossible to complete the tasks that she would assign. She constantly picked at you, and there was nothing that anyone did that was right, even though three of us had been functioning in her role for the past six months. Within six months, everyone had put in for a transfer. They just couldn't take it any longer.
>
> She was very aggressive and very demanding. There was no attempt to collaborate or get input from any of us. I believe that one of the factors in letting her go was that she overstepped the small-town atmosphere that our hospital had.

Marilyn identifies a key area of teams—managers need to seek out input from everyone within the team. When they don't, frustration surfaces and eventually staff throws in the towel and transfer to another unit or leave. Constant turnover fragments any potential team.

The Fear Factor

As a relief nursing supervisor, Nancy sees factions every-where. Mergers, hiring freezes, and layoffs have all had a substantial impact on the hospital where she works. With health care's changing marketplace, fear seeps out of every corner. When there is fear, it's difficult to work effectively as a team member or as a team leader. In her work role, Nancy has been able to observe firsthand the chaos and confusion of the past decade,

> I think hospitals are having a very difficult time. Administration is getting pressure from physicians, nursing staff, and the general public. It's as though everybody is against everybody else. The insurance companies are in one corner, administration is in another, physicians are in another, and the nurses are in another. Around the corner is the union, and then there is the general public.
>
> Everyone seems to want their own power, and factions position themselves with the belief that their way is best. Nobody wants to work together. It's like we have a bunch of special-interest groups.

What Nancy is reporting is quite common in hospitals today. A common remark I hear when I do internal programs for a hospital is that centralized communication is lacking.

It is impossible to build a team—whether it is a small unit, a floor, or the entire hospital—unless there is communication. Two factions that Nancy did not name are the government and lawyers. Each is a major contributor to the fear that permeates the hospital environment.

Hospitals Can't Be Assembly Lines

When change is in the air, the old rules often do not work. To create and build on new rules, people have to talk. Many hospitals today try to run their operations with an assembly-line or cookie-cutter approach when it comes to patient care. But patients come in all shapes, sizes, and colors. Some need a lot more care and attention than others.

In Natalie's hospital, however, the administration has developed a formula for patient loads. Her comments,

> Our hospital runs like an assembly line. We have HPPD—hours per patient day. It doesn't matter how acutely ill our patients are. They staff our floor with a graph. If it's the day shift, and there are thirty patients, you get so many nurses. In the afternoon and night shifts, you may have the same patient load, with the same number of acutely ill patients, but now you get fewer nurses. That's because of the assumption that most people sleep more during the night.
>
> On my floor, on any given day, there will be seven patients with leukemia. Leukemia patients take a lot of time. They may have just finished chemo, their counts have dropped, and they are continually given blood or blood products. Three leukemia patients could need the attention and care that ten others might need.

Closing the Ranks

As a certified nursing assistant, Sally feels that team efforts in health care are essential. But her observation is that few practice teamwork. If people did, the work load would be less overwhelming. Her observation,

> I feel we really have to talk to one another; it's a team effort. Some of the nurses don't realize that. When I'm working with an RN, I feel that part of my job is to tell her about any unusual things I notice about the patients. There are several nurses on my floor who act as though they are above everything. I know I'm not an RN. But when you

work closely with patients—whether it's bathing them, changing their bed linens, or helping them up, you tend to notice things that may not be apparent to nurses when they pass out the medication.

What Sally is experiencing is a form of professional snobbery—a type of caste system that is all too common in any profession. Managers look down on staff RNs, who look down on LPNs, both looking down on CNAs.

Breaking the Silence

If there is harmony in a workplace, and if a team is working effectively, members are more inclined to speak up when something is out of sync. Lorraine is a director of women's and children's services in a hospital in the Midwest. She recalls two instances when women in her group were up for promotion but got passed over. Lorraine revealed,

> The people who were conducting tenure reviews didn't have enough information about the contributions of these women. In one particular instance, several of us put together a meeting to review the situation.
>
> The meeting was not made up of people who were administrators and had power, but we did invite those individuals to join us. All of us wrote letters about what was happening and about how this woman was passed over. She eventually got her promotion and is now dean of the school of nursing.

Here was a group that rose to support one of its members, who had been overlooked. There may have been people in the group who wanted the promotion themselves, but the group's sense of fairness prevailed.

Who Was Here First?

When Gaye was promoted to head nurse, she had to lay off a member of her staff, and a little team support would have made a big difference. She remembers,

> Never in the history of the hospital had we let anyone go. My supervisor told me that the layoff would be by seniority and would be done in a month.
>
> When I had my staff meeting, I told the nurses that there would be a layoff in a month, based on seniority. They all asked who it would be. Without my naming names, they figured it out—Juanita was the last hired. She was very upset. I didn't want to lose her. I felt that she was very valuable, and I told her so.
>
> The atmosphere on our floor had a heavy cloud over it. I sharpened my pencil and started to move the nurses' hours around. With these manipulations, I estimated that if everyone would reduce her hours by four hours per month, I could retain Juanita's position. I felt very good about finding a solution.
>
> Then it turned out that the person to be laid off was not Juanita. It was Cheryl, who had been hired a week later. The next week, I called a meeting and put out my proposal to reduce everyone's hours and save the position. Juanita was the one who would not give up four hours to save her co-worker's job! And she ended up filing a complaint with the union.

If We Disagree ... You're Still OK

Change brings fear. When it happens to you, it's scary and intimidating. When you are an active participant, change can be exciting and exhilarating. Mary Ellen, a nurse manager of a mental health unit, is attempting to bring some of that excitement into the team-building programs she has implemented. Her words,

> We are doing team building throughout our whole unit. Communication skills are being taught. People are being shown methods for confronting conflict. We are really looking at a phenomenon that women seem to get stuck with, 'If I disagree with you, then you are a bad person, and I won't like you anymore.'
>
> With all the information we have about communicating, you'd think we would be skilled at it in our unit. But we get stuck, just like everyone else. Our next phase is to look at our various roles—what our expectations are of each other, and whether those expectations are realistic.

Initially, Mary Ellen met a great deal of resistance. It has taken her over a year to get the attention of the members of her team. All of a sudden, though, they are starting to move quickly, saying that things are better than they've ever been. She feels that, overall, progress has been excellent. Her unit had been notorious for its problematic staff. They had major crises, didn't know how to behave at work, and reacted negatively to the most minor events.

The change speaks well for Mary Ellen's leadership. She hasn't given up hope even during rough, nonresponsive periods with the staff. She has held to her vision and is beginning to see the rewards. Creating solid teams and introducing and implementing new skills and tools is not an overnight process. It takes months, sometimes even years, before it all gets in synch.

An Abnormal Teacher

As an instructor at the College of Staten Island, Laura Gasparis Vonfrolio discovered that some of her nursing students didn't do well on tests, even when they knew the material. Her solution was unique,

> When you take a test, you want to get the best grade. I found that there are students who do not do well, for a number of reasons. It may be that they don't study, but there are times when they just freeze up.
>
> My solution was to take the students who got B's or C's and pair them with the students who got As. The role of the A student was to work with the B or C students and make that student get an A. Once that happened, all my A students were exempt from any other exams. It almost always worked. Out of ninety B or C students, 83 eventually got an A and 7 got a B.
>
> But that is not the way it is in other classrooms. If you get a bad grade on a paper, the students who get A's won't associate with you. If they associate with you, the teacher might think that they are hanging out with stupid people.

This method sounds quite logical. The A student keeps on learning and has to study because she in turn becomes the advocate for her partner, as in a mentor-mentee relationship. The teaching cemented understanding of the material. The student's reward is exemption from testing. Meanwhile, she learns a lot about teamwork. Each member has strengths and weaknesses. Needless to say, Gasparis Vonfrolio got a lot of flack from her colleagues. Why? She did things differently. Her method was not the "normal" way of teaching. She continues,

> I didn't have the students do care plans, because all they needed to do was copy them from their books and have them typed. That's called being a secretary.

I would not allow any note taking in my classes. Instead, I hired a court stenographer. What she did was record my lecture and transcribe it that night. Then I would have copies passed out to the students. My objective was to create a network of support among my students, so that when they were out working in the nursing profession, they would expand their own networks.

Gasparis Vonfrolio taught at the college for eight years. She began her teaching in the associate's program and then was moved up to the baccalaureate program. I asked if she was able to measure the results of her methods. She said that when she began, students' scores on the state boards were low. When she implemented her teaching techniques, the pass rate increased from 73 percent to 92 percent.

When People Bug You

All of us, at some time in our careers, have worked with people who drove us nuts. Why? You name it—there's a long laundry list out there.

If you work with someone who bugs you, ask yourself why. Make a list. Most annoying habits and irritating mannerisms can be ignored. Quality of work cannot. If the issues have to do with work, you may have to confront her.

Then identify and list her strengths. Why do you think she was hired. What are her skills? Separate the personal issues from the professional ones.

Finally, ask yourself, "What's in it for me to work with her? What's in it for her to work with me?" Don't think about whether you want to be friends. Consider her talents instead. If her work involves your work, wouldn't you like to see her accomplish what she needs to do, before it all comes crashing into your arena? And, if her mannerisms, habits, or traits have no impact on whether she gets her job done or bugs others, then let go—this is not something you need to direct your energy toward. There's other battles that are more important.

ZAP Tip
When it comes to working and developing teams, you don't have to like the people you work with. And liking you is not in their job description, either. People's only responsibility is to complete the tasks and functions they were hired for.

Banish Geisha Behavior

If a Geisha is a girl or woman trained as an entertainer to serve as a hired companion to men, then a Geisha Nurse or Assistant is one who flirts with or displays physical or verbal affection or submissiveness toward a male, usually a doctor. In the nineties, I had the opportunity to speak and work with a group composed of women physicians. They covered every facet of medicine and came from almost every state. In a workshop focusing on confidence and crises, the term *geisha nursing* surfaced. Many of the participants in the group were familiar with the term. They rolled their eyes and shook their heads as several women began to discuss the topic. It was one that I was not familiar with, but the phrase alone intrigued me.

As I probed further, first by listening and then by joining in the talk, I found that geisha nursing was indeed a factor. Elizabeth, one of the women physicians we interviewed, said she also had a geisha receptionist. Her comments,

> She had discovered that her key way of getting along with men was to please them and be a flirt. I also find that women who display this tendency are the same ones I have the most conflict with.

Rosanne, chief of urgent care at a large health maintenance organization, had plenty to say. She had been an RN before going to medical school and had been a nurse manager. She said that if policies had been set by a male manager, no one would have questioned them. But because she was female, she felt, she was hassled. In her position, she was legally (and, in her opinion, morally) obligated to follow up on any reports of sexual harassment. When she did her job, she found that there were sometimes repercussions. Once, she told administrators that it was very difficult for her to work there as a woman. They suggested that she create a presentation that would increase the hospital's awareness.

She decided to interview all the women physicians in the facility, incorporating their concerns and feedback for the various departmental chiefs, all men. She titled her presentation "Geisha Nursing," primarily to get the administration's attention. She did and added,

> One of the key factors that the women physicians had identified involved working with nurses who preferred the 1950s style of flirtatious interaction. The women nurses reacted violently to the title and content of my presentation, but I found geisha nursing so prevalent that I didn't know any other way to deal with it except to bring it out in the open.

In my department, I had over fifty physicians who rotated in and out on any given day. Of these, the great majority were men. There were forty on the nursing staff. When I was working with both groups, trying to change some schedules, I uncovered a series of complaints from women providers who were not getting nursing support, especially from the flirtatious ones.

The emergency-room doctors often worked as lone cowboys in their departments. They had a bevy of nurses whom they pretty much ordered around and had follow them around, ready to respond to their beck and call. The doctors who cracked chests needed a great deal of one-to-one support, and they got it. Then there were doctors who worked in the clinic. They didn't get the support the others did. Anyone related with emergency and surgery was showered with support staff, who trailed after their every move.

The way the other doctors coped with the groups who got the support was to cultivate special and flirtatious relationships with the nurses, so that they would get increased attention and aid. When I brought this up at a routine departmental meeting, I mentioned that we had to divide up time equally or allocate time on the basis of the acuity of patients' problems. We couldn't allocate time according to personal preferences.

The nursing staff said, 'We are just nice to the people who are nice to us.' They viewed flirtation as being nice. I responded that we couldn't do that—this was a professional setting, and flirting was both demeaning and inappropriate.

I went on to say that I would deal with the doctors

and be an advocate for any nurse who needed help handling a doctor who displayed inappropriate behavior toward her. I wanted them to let me know, so that they would not have to succumb to the demands of power physicians. They were horrified. They rebelled and complained that I was souring the work environment.

What Rosanne is saying is that the 1950s are alive and well, still. When I delivered the keynote address at the Oncology Nurses Society and brought up the importance of banning geisha nursing, the audience broke out in loud applause—they knew what it was!

In the hospital environment, there is almost a caste system. One of the ways to move up and out of one's caste is to develop some type of bond with someone more powerful. In the hospital, doctors are powerful, and a nurse in a nurse-doctor liaison gets more status. Rosanne had assumed that the nurses would not want the doctors to flirt with them or take advantage of the intensity of the work environment. She assumed wrong. The geisha nurses liked it.

Rosanne also noticed that male doctors were allowed to display certain types of behavior that most people would call eccentric. A woman doctor behaving in the same way might find her job on the line.

Rosanne says that a lot of the nurses view her as a "mini-Hitler" a woman who's making their workplace a cold place to be in, and not as much fun as it used to be. She recently hired another physician to share her duties. At times she feels overwhelmed and realizes that if she had been in another setting, her responsibilities would have entitled her long ago to an assistant, or at least a co-chief. The administration finally agreed to hire another physician when Rosanne threatened to quit.

Word went out that a man had been hired, and many saw him as the man on a white horse—someone who would come in and make things nice again, the way things used to be and save them from the dreaded Rosanne. Her agreement with him is that she will play "bad cop" and he will play "good cop." Their objective is to support each other. She continued,

> It's difficult. The nurses want the female managers to be Mother-managers. They want mothers. They want to be overly personal. From men, they want sexual overtones. What's interesting to see is that many of the nurses act in a coquettish manner, and my co-chief doesn't respond to them, or at least not the way they expect. There are even rumors that I turned him into a bad person.

ZAP Tip

Geisha Nurses need to realize that their paychecks come from the combined revenues created by all doctors, not just a few men. Until then, it will be a negative factor in the workplace. Recognizing it, and confronting behavior that is inappropriate and that undermines all work relationships, is one way to begin ushering it out. With it, conflict will be significantly reduced.

When employees (women in this case) play games, we play them well. We have played them for centuries. It's not something that will be changed overnight, but it can be changed. Game playing that involves coquettish behavior is learned, not genetic.

As more and more women physicians and dentists enter the workplace, they will bring more of a no-nonsense approach. Verbal and physical harassment are being reported, and there is growing awareness that many women do not receive pay or promotions equal to those their male counterparts enjoy. More women are also entering surgery, including the macho field of orthopedics.

The Grumpies at Work

In every workplace there are morning people and night people. If you are a morning person and a few of your co-workers are night people and act like sourpusses when they come in each day, you have a problem. If you work with someone who seems to have a huge chip on her shoulders, then her style, her attitude, and her nonstop criticism may surround you like a giant thundercloud.

A bad attitude is not like a bad hair day. It doesn't change with something as simple as a shampoo and set. If you are the team leader, part of your responsibility is to keep the group's productivity at a certain level. If someone's actions are dragging it down, it's up to you to stop the behavior before other team members start turning on each other, as well as on her—and, believe it or not, on you.

Get out your note pad. Start to write examples down, and cite lots of them. You will need to confront her privately. Don't expect a one-time mention to change her. You will probably have to repeat your examples at a later confrontation. If she denies her behavior, don't be surprised. She has been doing it for a long time. It's part of her. The bottom line is that action is needed. When a co-worker has a bad attitude, it can destroy a team.

> **ZAP Tip**
>
> *Grumpy people don't make your day.*
> *They become the energy sucker of the*
> *workplace—always chipping away at something*
> *or someone. A Key Player, they are not.*
> *Do yourself a favor and minimalize your contact.*

Identifying Conflict Creators and Saboteurs in Your Midst

There is no question that team members can and do create conflict and sabotage others. Here are twelve questions you can ask yourself, to uncover a saboteur or conflict creator in your midst. A *yes* to any one of them demands that you go on the alert. If you answer *yes* to three or more questions, use extreme caution when dealing with the person.

Is There a Conflict Creator or Saboteur in the Midst?©

1. *Does anyone feel that her, or his, job is in jeopardy?* Whenever there is fear, anxiety, and change, many people overreact. For some, paranoia sets in—will I be next, will the mistake I made last month be my undoing, will my skill level not be high enough, etc?

2. *Does anyone stand to profit by another's mistake?* Any time someone makes a mistake, conflict creators and saboteurs relish the opportunity. They will be players in passing along the

"error" and may eventually benefit by a promotion or bonus, or at the very least by an enhanced reputation because of the mistake.

3. *Have new coalitions formed on your team or department?* It is commonplace for conflict creators and saboteurs to continually realign their "friendships." With each new realignment, they are often in the center, similar to the "movers" in a high school clique.

4. *Does anyone encourage gossip?* Most conflict creators and saboteurs are messengers—they can hardly wait to pass along damaging information about anyone or anything.

5. *Does anyone keep a tally sheet?* Everyone makes mistakes—conflict creators and saboteurs usually keep count and can make a huge mountain out of a molehill.

6. *Does information ever pass you by?* A typical strategy is to isolate others. The most common practice is to withhold information or interrupt an information pipeline that is relevant to your work.

7. *Is anyone on your team sometimes too helpful?* Until you really know how a group or team operates, an overly helpful or zealous player may not be what you think she or he is. This person may even ignore her own work, just to be in your physical space so that others can visually see that you need help.

8. *Does anyone routinely deny involvement in activities, yet know all the details?* Conflict creators and saboteurs are masters at working

the grapevine; they are also chameleons. They initially claim no knowledge of any specific incident, yet somehow they are able to pass along the details and information to anyone who asks, and, in some cases, doesn't ask.

9. *Does anyone encourage others to take on tasks that appear impossible?* When you or another fail at a task, saboteurs and conflict creators derive great pleasure from it. Your failure makes them look good, and even more savvy, for not taking on the impossible.

10. *Does anyone bypass your authority or go over your head?* Conflict creators and saboteurs will do almost anything to look good, including sidestepping a leader's authority or ignoring other team member's contributions.

11. *Does anyone routinely take credit for another's work?* Conflict creators and saboteurs rarely compliment or give credit openly for another's work. Women are more inclined not to speak up or out when someone hogs the limelight and/or takes credit for another's work.

12. *Does anyone discount yours or other co-workers' contribution to the workplace?* The style for conflict creators and saboteurs is more likely to discount participation by other team members and take credit for themselves. Openly cheering for another is almost an impossibility for them.

Source: The Briles Group, Inc. ©2002 Aurora CO All Rights Reserved.

Exhibit 14.1

> ## ZAP Tip
>
> *After you have identified possible or probable conflict creators and saboteurs, the next step is to deal with the agitator. Three things need to come into play at this point. The first is to* document; *the second is to* develop good communication skills *and the third is to* confront the person. *When you do confront, you need the facts to back up whatever your accusations are. Most saboteurs will do just about anything to avoid public exposure. They will rarely commit anything to paper, so you will need to have your facts in order.*

When a conflict creator or saboteur's motivation is redirected, you may be able to get your team back on track. They don't like to be left out in the cold for long and may actually attempt to make amends and rejoin your team.

Finally, the old saying "If you give her enough rope, she will hang herself" may apply. Once you identify your trouble maker, you must sidestep her games. Being a saboteur and conflict creator takes a lot of time, energy and commitment. Over time, their productivity should nosedive. The longer the game goes on, the less is produced, and the more likely the culprit will be exposed to others.

A Star Team Is Born

During the summer of 2001, I had done the keynote for the National Nurse Staff Development Organization and

met some of the mangers who worked at Kaiser Permanente in Hayward, California. I was asked if I would be
interested in speaking at the hospital and was told that
they were creating a new program. After exchanging cards,
we all went our separate ways with plans to keep in touch.

Several months later, I received a call from Debora
Zachau who introduced herself as the principal investigator
for an internal research application for Patient Care Services.
She is one of three Directors of Patient Care Services. The
funding that was being requested would be used to support
their current strategic nursing development program which
was designed to improve the work environment, nursing
recruitment and retention, professional development, care
of staff, and service delivery to members across the con-
tinuum of care. Her team's goal is to receive The Magnet
Recognition Program for Excellence in Patient Care Services
by year-end 2004, from the American Nursing Association.

In the spring of 2002, I had the pleasure of working
with Debora and Kaiser Permanente's Star Team—the program was called *May the Force Be With You* and focused on
conflict resolution, enhanced communication skills, team
building and confidence. We had a great time, spending a
week with the staff (multiple sessions) and the managers.

What started them on the excellence path was a survey—their facility had always been in the lower one-third
of the other hospitals within the Kaiser Permanente system. That was until they decided to focus on the employee.
One of the managers had a copy of *The Four Agreements* by
Don Miguel Ruiz. They used it as a starting point and values foundation for all the managers. Debora talks about
their first offering to the staff,

Our first outreach to the staff was the Healing Hands
Blessing, a wonderful ritual that was performed by

the Chaplain. After the blessing, they were given a laminated card with the words to the blessing and hand lotion. It was the first time the staff felt that they were cared for (and the managers totally underestimated how much Kleenex was needed). Word spread. The staff told their friends in the units, calling them at home to come in. There was over a 60 percent participation.

Debora and her Star Managers didn't stop. Other activities and events were now planned on a monthly basis with a special event every quarter. All managers must participate—they go to the individual floors, whether it's a tea, latte or ice cream cart they are pushing, cookies, even cold-care kits have been given out. At first, staff was suspicious. Now, they chase them down the hall to participate.

It was just a beginning—there's much more. They have offsite programs—presented by both local and national speakers like myself. Everyone has the opportunity to participate. They feed them at the events and found that communications opened up. They bring books (purchased) for everyone that participates—*The Four Agreements* was the first, *FISH* and *Don't Sweat the Small Stuff* are two others.

Traditionally, nurses in different departments are equivalent to a foreign country—nobody talks to anyone outside of their area. That all changed. Because they all get together every month, they face each other, communication skills are improving and distrust is reduced.

The management team at Kaiser Permanente knew that something had to change. They knew that it would cost money. Where hospitals have gloated about their slashing of education and training budgets and the coordinators and directors of education mouth gloom and doom, these managers knew differently—educational moneys were a necessity, not a frivolous expense. If they were to retain, retrain and grow their workplace, money needed to appear. With the overall support of the Director of Hospital Operations and the Physician in Chief, and all the managers, it was a go. With a two-year approved budget of approximately $900,000, the program went into high-gear.

And the financial impact the first year? Recruitment activities have improved significantly, turnover has been reduced from 17.1 percent in 2000 to 0.9 percent in 2001. They've actually had nurses leave other hospitals where they made more money and come to work for them for less. When a nurse has to be replaced, it can range anywhere from $20,000 to $96,000 for a speciality nurse. The Hayward facility factors in approximately one and one-half years salary for total replacement costs.

Let's do the math. With a staff of 450 RNs, a 17 percent turnover translates to 76.5 nurses. A reduction to 0.9 is equivalent to a turnover of 4.1 nurses. If the cost of replacement was on the low end of $20,000 per nurse, the cost of replacement at the 17 percent level is $1,530,000 and at the 0.9 percent level, $82,000 (a savings of $1, 448,000). At the higher end of $96,000 per nurse (Kaiser will be at the higher end due to its location in Northern California), the cost of replacement at the 17 percent level is $7,344,000 and at the 0.9 percent level, $393,600 (a savings of $6,950,400).

Money talks . . . It's the door to Administration listening.

The managers at Kaiser Permanente had a vision of what they wanted to be and where they wanted to go. They had to do something different from what they were doing. With their moxie and savvy, they created the roadmap to get there. The money that they have allocated for the program has come back many times over. Their facility isn't fancy, and it's very dated. Yet, it's become a place of choice to work for.

They've found that in order to save money and reduce their replacement costs, they had to spend money.

Education and Training Count

Since the mid-nineties, health care has slashed, and in many cases eliminated, moneys allocated to education and training. In the *Conflict Survey*, 34 percent of the staff/employee respondents said that the reduction of education and training was the reason conflict had increased in their workplaces. Only four percent of the managers and administrators thought it was an issue.

The managers of Kaiser Permanente-Hayward understand that education counts . . .and that it costs money. Period. It's paid off big time for them. The health care experts and consultants who travel North America throughout the year repeatedly say that educational training . . . or the lack of it, contributes highly to the increased conflict levels being experience. "But it costs money," Administration counters. "It costs far more if we don't," is your response. Then, do the math. The staff survey respondents are on the mark.

Dental consultant Linda Miles says that there is a different attitude toward education in the dental community. Her take,

Dentists view education along the line of the business model. It's an investment that takes money, not just an expense item. The entire dental team takes time off to update their skills—clinical and behavioral. The entire dental team practices teamwork.

Consultant and speaker Venner Farley, EdD, RN is not surprised at the increased levels of reported conflict. She's the author of several books including *Nurses Future Tense Or Tense Future* and *Pulling Together to Make a Difference.* Her decades of experience as an instructor, dean of a nursing school and now consultant-speaker fully supports the need for educational spending. Venner adds,

> Sure it cost money, but the dividends that are paid are long term ones—happier employees and greater loyalty. Both build a strong collaborative team. Staff and managers need rigorous training in dealing with conflict management as well as other skills—some of it together, some of it separate.
>
> Some facilities have inservice education coordinators or directors who deliver all programming—they may be cost effective, but they don't have the skills to really teach and demonstrate conflict management.

Farley points out a key issue—many hospitals will say that they do have training, and they do . . . kind of. But they fail to understand that outside voices are critical. Those voices bring new ideas, a perspective of what's happening (working and not working) in other systems, and hands-on expertise in a particular topic area. An employee who has read a book about the topic isn't going to have the practical application and experience needed to make a difference.

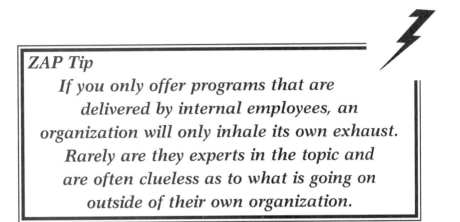

ZAP Tip

If you only offer programs that are delivered by internal employees, an organization will only inhale its own exhaust. Rarely are they experts in the topic and are often clueless as to what is going on outside of their own organization.

Summing Up

Teams, much less Star Teams, are not created overnight. Most take months or even years to pull together. As the entire health care system enters a phase of change, the development of cohesive teams becomes a critical factor in defining and redefining an organization's vision and mission. Hospitals, associations, institutions, and businesses all have stated missions.

Any organization that evolves from being individual centered (I know what to do) to being leader-centered (You tell me what to do) and to being purpose-centered (We have a joint mission) will survive, grow and thrive with change.

Active ingredients needed to create the right team stew include an environment that fosters respect, clear communication and conflict handling skills, trust at staff and administration levels, non-game playing, leaving negativity outside the workplace, empowering staffs to make decisions, and investing in their employees through training and educational programs.

The issue of staffing shortages always surfaces in team discussions. Managers need to learn to let go—get rid of marginal employees (as administration needs to let go of marginal managers). Marginal people bring down the group—they don't do their share, others step in to make sure the work is done (stretching and stressing in the process), and they cost any department a lot of money. Always consider the loss from the drain on total group productivity and turnover that is the fallout of maintaining incompetency. It's a lot of money.

The Round Up—10 Steps to Zapping Conflict

15

In previous chapters, you've read a variety of stories that inflicted pain and great disappointment. As I listened to the teller sharing them, there were many times when I wanted to jump in the middle of it. I felt angry at hearing what had happened—imagine how the teller must have felt when the event actually took place.

Many of the women and men interviewed—staff, managers and professional consultants to other health care professionals (see Speakers and Consultants Who Deliver Results in next section), offered specific steps that they believed would create a far better workplace. With that in mind, below are mine (and their) top ten ways to zap conflict from the health care workplace.

1. **Change is the Work . . . Work is the Change.**
   There's very, very little that you can do to stop

the change train—it's rolling and isn't going to stop for long before it starts down the change track again. What you can do is tune in, be alert and learn how to both grow and thrive with it. Certification, credentials and specific skills you may have today could be obsolete in five years. But, those same credentials and skills can act as a transition as in an evolution/revolution. Change today is noisy and distracting. Get over it. It needs to be embraced as normal and not broken when it occurs.

2. **Unwritten Rules Rule.** If you haven't started the exercise recommended in the chapter on Unwritten Rules, do it now. Every workplace has unspoken rules—rules that can make or break a team very quickly. Take the time to identify them, gather them from others and post them. If they are out of date, eliminate them; if they are hurtful or mean-spirited, delete them; and if they are inappropriate for your department, dump them. If they make the workplace more efficient, share them; if they reduce stress, broadcast them; and if they make your workplace a better place to be, look for other unwritten rules that can further enhance a workplace of choice and tell your colleagues.

3. **Speak Up and Out . . . Assertiveness Counts.** George Bernard Shaw said, "The greatest problem in communication is the illusion that it's taken place." Too many times, both speakers and listeners do a horrendous job in the attempt to communicate with each other. In a woman-

dominated workplace, the tendency is to not
speak directly out about any one issue; rather it
is to go back and share the injustice/concern/
problem/gripe with their co-workers. Staff and
managers need to learn to speak out and up and
to be more assertive about situations and issues
that impact their workplaces.

Communicate, communicate, communicate—
no one should be considered a doormat, or
enable someone to treat them as such.
Communicating clearly and effectively is an
essential ingredient in resolving any conflict.
Include doctors and staff. Too many doctors are
rude and patronizing toward staff. They need to
work with and respect them, not treat them as
though they are disposable.

4. **Delete Negativity Creators and Suckers.** Let's
   face it, we all know people who can rarely say
   anything pleasant, can always find something
   wrong with just about anything and everything and
   constantly have their "woe is me" sign up—"kick
   me" might be better. Just being in their everyday
   presence will have a significant impact on you—
   they will cause you to lose energy, enthusiasm and
   your good humor. People who constantly chip away
   and carry a chip around on their shoulders are
   energy suckers—they will literally drag you and
   everyone in a close range down. The result—you
   don't feel so well and your work suffers as well.
   Stay away from them—they aren't your friend and
   could need professional help.

   If you feel that you need to reach out . . . give
   them a name and phone number of a therapist

that could help them work through whatever ails them.

5. **Eliminate Marginal People.** Several years ago, a dentist shared that he had the dental assistant from hell on his staff. Because of the shortage (yes dentistry has shortages too), he didn't think he could let her go. I told him that I would assume that he was a good employer, paid well and wanted to create a harmonious workplace. I then asked the rest of the workshop participants if they would be willing to work an hour extra each day for the next six months if he would fire her the following Monday. Absolutely was the response.

   Why managers continue to retain employees and staff members that don't do their share of the work, grumble and gripe about anything and everything and make everyone miserable is one of the great wonders of the workplace. Marginal staff (and managers) are chronic—rarely do they get that they are the problem and they don't change. You'll know that you were right to remove them when you begin to notice that everyone breathes easier, smiles and walks more upright. Many marginal employees are often in the wrong line of work—their own fear of the unknown keeps them where they are. Set guidelines for both clinical and developmental skills—if they aren't met, move them on and out. No coasting allowed.

6. **Leaders Need to Lead . . . and Learn How to Lead.** Everyone at some point in time is a leader. It could be leading a patient through an info-

procedure—teaching them how take care of themselves or what is going to happen to them during a procedure. Ethics expert Diann Uustal notes that nurse leaders must include care and compassion in their vision for the organization as well as the patient. Leaders have to work to rid their organizations of the "us vs. them" culture that exists between frontline and management.

Speaker Brian Lee concurs. In his view, staff is desperately in search of a manager who can lead and that management needs to have quality leadership training. Leaders in turn, need to empower their staff to resolve problems without letting them fester to the boiling point. Part of that empowerment is to teach them conflict management skills. Jo Manion adds that leaders need to develop relationship skills—not just pay lip service to it. They need to work hard to develop their judgment skills and when to get involved and when not to.

7. **Understand that Everyone is Not Your Friend.** Nor is everyone friend material. One of the great challenges of the health care workplace is directly related to the disproportionate number of women to men employed. Women are more inclined to share personal information to almost total strangers, men will most likely withhold personal information. If information is misused, a sense of betrayal is often felt by the woman. Men bypass this issue by not participating in the open release of personal information. Women are more willing to trust; men hold back until they feel confident that the person is trustworthy.

8. **Carefronting® and Confronting Go Hand-in-Hand.** All the experts interviewed felt strongly that conflict resolution skills needed to be taught at all levels within the organization—managers, administrators, and staff. Tim Porter-O'Grady said that when a leader is comfortable with conflict, they view conflict resolution as a tool. The big problem, though, is that only a few recognize that it's normal and that there are skill sets, competencies, even the ability to anticipate it that can be learned.

    Learning how to confront another without creating the great divide in the workplace is a necessary skill for both managers and staff. Conflicts left alone or ignored, usually escalate in size and breadth, often taking on proportions never imagined. Before getting involved with a conflict, determine if it's a true conflict and does it warrant your time and energy. If a conflict is not addressed, your silence can condone it. It becomes your choice.

9. **Don't Leave the Education Express.** Health care organizations, mostly hospitals, have severely reduced moneys for education and additional training, especially in the area of nursing. The experts quoted throughout this book support education in both clinical and behavioral areas. They contend that they have equal importance and I agree. Most conflicts are fueled by bad and inappropriate behaviors along with poor communication skills—both considered "soft" skills and not critical by many in the hospital management setting.

When organizations support educational training, it is a statement of support, even caring— as in, we are investing in your advanced training. Business has long viewed further education and training as an investment for and of their employees (many businesses reimburse employees when classes are completed). Dentistry supports staff in advanced education, even doing a program as an entire office. My experience has been that it is not uncommon for a dentist to include his or her entire staff in a training or educational program. Not so for physicians.

Hospitals and doctors offices are more inclined to view it as an expense, something that can be eliminated. Recent contracts with nursing unions and hospitals stipulate that moneys and time be allocated for educational purposes.

Hospitals are now showing that spending money on education related activities can be a major factor in increasing their retention percentages and reducing turnover. Consultant and speaker Venner Farley believes that too many in administration ignore conflict and that vigorous training for both managers and staff is necessary— done separately and together. To Farley, the cost is minimal compared with the dividends that are derived—happier workers and increased loyalty, both adding to the collaborative workplace.

Speaker and consultant Sharon Cox adds that in order to have high patient satisfaction scores, it's necessary to have high employee satisfaction. When conflict subsides and employees are trained in conflict resolution, their satisfaction within their workplace rises.

10. **Put Fun Back in the Workplace.** I'm not talking about bringing a comedy act in—although some workplaces could use the facelift. Fun can be in the form of a management team delivering sundaes on a cart (as Kaiser Permanente did), to having quick neck and shoulder massages, a silly hat day or an outrageous story.

    Units, departments, teams, workplaces that laugh together survive and grow through change and conflict together.

11. **Bonus Step—Encourage Empowerment.** Years ago, I commonly used the word "empowerment" in the programs I presented for nurses and managers. Somewhere along the line, word came down from administration in many of the hospitals I worked with not to use the word—if the staff and front line nurses heard it too much, they would be harder to manage.

    What nonsense. True, empowerment is powerful. One of the most powerful things that an administration can do is empower their staffs—treat them as adults instead of taking on a parental role as so many employers have.

    When employees are empowered, they have the tools to give themselves permission to accomplish and succeed on their own. Empowering means enabling, authorizing, permitting, and giving power to. As a manager, with a model of empowerment, you give your staff the green light to pursue an exciting vision. One that is too often squashed by the higher-ups.

    Empowerment is not to be taken lightly. It's not a right, nor does it happen overnight. It's work and is earned. It is declaring, asserting and even demanding the right to be your true and authentic self. Within a group, empowerment requires a commitment from each member that enables all members to use collective strengths, abilities, and assets as resources. True empowerment will not exist unless there is an environment that allows and encourages the distribution of power. The development of your empowerment requires the roots of attention, belief, commitment, daring, and confidence.

One of the dark sides of the health care professions is that there are too many who are conflict creators and saboteurs. Low self-esteem, inferiority, anxiety, doubt, fear, envy, and jealousy all play a critical part in the damage that health care professionals can do to each other. Through empowerment, problems are identified and resolved. By committing yourself to solving them, you admit that they are there. You make a conscious effort to take responsibility for your own part in them, and you implement the changes necessary for eliminating them.

ZAP Tip

> *Resolving all conflicts will not happen overnight. The process takes time and commitment from all involved. When conflicts occur, stop and determine what your need is, find out what the other party's main need is—usually done by effective listening . . . answers are usually within your immediate walls/environment/room—and arrive at a solution that both of you can live with. It may not be ideal, but it's workable, which is the goal of conflict resolution.*

Speakers and Consultants Who Deliver Results

I spend over half the year on the road and have the opportunity to hear a variety of speakers and trainers. If you have a need for consulting, training, or speaking, the men and women in this section are stars in their respective fields. When planning a program, retreat or conference, any and all will deliver a dynamite presentation. Please call them.

Judith Briles, DBA, MBA
PO Box 460880
Aurora CO 80046
Phone: 800-594-0800
Fax: 303-627-9184
E-mail: Judith@Briles.com
Website: www.Briles.com

Judith Briles is an international speaker, consultant, coach and author. She has published over 20 books, including the award winning **The Confidence Factor, Stop Stabbing Yourself in the Back, Woman to Woman 2000, 10 Smart Money Moves for Women, Smart Money Moves for Kids** and **When God Says NO. Zapping Conflict in the Health Care Workplace** is her second book dedicated exclusively to the unique health care organization.

Judith's expertise is the female dominated workplace. She has conducted five national studies on workplace issues in groups that have a higher female population. With the results, she has structured several books and presentations that solely address the type and levels of conflict that surface within health care based on her research. Judith has spoken to over 1000 nursing, medical and dental groups.

Her most requested programs are *The Confidence Factor—Cosmic Gooses Lay Golden Eggs, Zapping Conflict in the Workplace, Thriving with Change, Creating a Collaborative Workplace* and *Smart Money Moves for Health Care Professionals.* Bi-annually, she chairs the Confidence Working Cruise for Health Care Professionals in the late summer/early fall.Information is available at www.Briles.com.

For further information regarding consultation or speaking engagements, please contact Judith Briles at 800-594-0800 or Judith@Briles.com.

Leslie Charles
TrainingWorks
PO Box 956
E. Lansing MI 48826
Phone: 517-675-7535
E-mail: leschas@aol.com
Website: www.lesliecharles.com

Leslie Charles' mission is to make a difference. She combines practical ideas with a personal touch and encourages people to take new steps toward realizing their potential. Leslie has been speaking to groups across Northern America for over 20 years to rave reviews.

Leslie is an expert at distilling complex subjects into an easy-to-digest and comprehensible form. She is the author of seven books including **All is Not Lost, Why is Everyone So Cranky, The Instant Trainer, The Customer Service Companion, Stick to It!** and **Rule #One.**

Her most popular programs are based on her books, including *Why is Everyone So Cranky?, Creating Your Future, Going for the Gold, Team Building and Communication and If You Don't Take Care of the Customer . . . Someone Else Will.*

For further information regarding consultation or speaking engagements, please contact Leslie Charles at 517-675-7535, leschas@aol.com or www.lesliecharles.com

Sharon Cox, MSN, RN
Cox and Associates
5115 Albert Drive
Brentwood TN 37027
Phone: 615-371-0215
Fax: 615-371-0577
E-mail: sharon@esharoncox.com
Website: www.esharoncox.com

Sharon Cox has over 30 years experience in health care ranging from staff nurse and department management to faculty and administrative roles in academic health centers. Since 1987 she has conducted over 1500 workshops and consulted in 350 hospitals in the US and Canada in the areas of management development, team building and culture change.

Her workshops are designed for staff and managers who want to expand their skill sets in dealing with relationships, difficult behavior or morale issues. Sharon stresses practical approaches, using a step-by-step "how to" style so that program participants have approaches for next day use in the real world of health care. She is a nationally known speaker in numerous convention settings and is on the editorial board of *Nursing Management Magazine.* Her most requested programs include *Motivation and Morale—Beyond a Quick Fix; Out of the Comfort Zone;* and *Staying Positive When Working with Pearl and Grumpy.*

For further information regarding consultation or speaking engagements. please contact Jim Cox at 615-371-0215 or jim@esharoncox.com

Mimi Donaldson
Mimi Speaks, Inc.
269 So. Beverly Dr.
PMB 327
Beverly Hills CA 90212
Phone: 310-577-0229
Fax: 310-577-0020
E-mail: mimi@mimidonaldson.com
Website: www.mimidonaldson.com

Mimi Donaldson excites, educates and entertains audiences all over the world. Her approach is humorous and practical, aimed at improving communication and teamwork. Her background includes 10 years in human resources and a master's degree in education.

She is co-author of the international best-seller, **Negotiating for Dummies.** She is currently at work on **All Stressed Up and No Place to Blow.**

Mimi routinely has her audiences in stitches, and at the same time, make points on critical topics that can make or break a workplace. Her most popular presentations are *Men and Women: Can We Talk?, Four Steps to Managing Anyone, Don't Wait—Negotiate!,* and *Managing Stress in Times of Change.*

For further information regarding consultation or speaking engagements, please contact her at 310-577-0229, mimi@mimidonaldson.com or www.mimidonaldson.com.

Venner Farley, EdD, RN
6512 E. Kings Crown Rd.
Orange CA 92669
Phone: 714-744-2814
E-mail: vennerm1@aol.com

Venner Farley is a national consultant on leadership development in health care (nurses, physicians, administrators), professional practice development (true partnerships) in nursing, curriculum re-design and motivational speaker. She is widely recognized as a presenter at national and international nursing conferences and is noted for her ability to speak to complex issues enlightened by a wise sense of humor. She has served on multiple boards of health care institutions and nursing journals.

Venner is the author of **Pulling Together to Make A Difference** and **Future Tense or Tense Future.** She is currently at work on the third book in the series. Her most requested topics are *Nurses are Due: Self Management; "Boss" is a Four-Letter Word;* and *It Is Time the Elephants in Nursing Learned to Tango.*

For further information regarding consultation or speaking engagements, please contact Venner Farley at 714-744-2814 or vennerm1@aol.com.

Richard C. Ireland, President

The Ireland Corporation/The Snowmass Institute
8694 East Mineral Circle
Centennial, CO 80112
Phone: 303-771-5501
E-mail: snowinst@eazy.net
Website: www.snowinst.com

Richard Ireland is President of The Ireland Corporation in Centennial, Colorado—an organization that specializes in management, marketing, strategic and organizational development issues in healthcare and higher education.

He is also founder and President of The Snowmass Institute, a division of The Ireland Corporation, which specializes in women's health, service line management, and healthcare conferences and is also the publisher of a nationally recognized newsletter, *The Ireland Report on Succeeding in Women's Health*, and the *Service Line Leader* newsletter.

Ireland designed the highly acclaimed Succeeding in Women's Health conference and the Succeeding in Service Line Management conference.

He has been a leading consultant on marketing, strategic development and planning for women's health service line projects, organizational and leadership development to healthcare organizations for the past three decades. He has more than 200 successful strategic development projects to his credit and has led dozens of workshops, board and management retreats, and special assignments with more than 400 health care and higher education organizations, professional groups and associations, and corporations in the United States, England, Mexico, and Canada.

For further information regarding consulting, educational services, and speaking engagements please contact Richard Ireland at 303-771-5501 or snowinst@eazy.net.

Linda Larsen
Linda Larsen Communications Inc.
PO Box 15204
Sarasota FL 34277
Phone: 800-355-4420
Fax: 941-927-4722
E-mail: linda@lindalarsen.com
Website: www.lindalarsen.com

Linda Larsen is a dynamic, funny, high energy keynote speaker who can jump start a conference and leave participants inspired, motivated and equipped with creative, practical information. She is a formal professional actor who understands the unique combination of entertainment and information delivery.

She is the author of **True Power** and the audio program **12 Secrets of High Self-Esteem.** Forthcoming books include **How I Did It,** and **How to Get Men to Behave.**

Linda's most popular programs include *Winning the Mind Game, Innovative Thinking—Incite & Ignite!, Keeping Your Cool with Difficult People, Visionary Leadership,* and *High Impact Communicating.*

For further information regarding consultation or speaking engagements, please contact her at 800-355-4420 , linda@lindalarsen.com or www.lindalarsen.com.

Brian Lee, CSP
Custom Learning Group Systems, Ltd.
#200, 2133 Kensington Road NW
Calgary, Alberta T2N 3R8
Phone: 800-667-7325
Fax: 403-228-6776
E-mail: Brian@customlearning.com
Website: www.keepyournursesforlife.com

Brian Lee, one of North America's leading experts in the field of World Class Healthcare Patient Satisfaction and Employee Retention, is the author of **Keep Your Nurses & Healthcare Professionals for Life** and known as health care's "Mr. Customer Satisfaction". Relaying over 20 years experience in the field of professional speaking and training, Brian and his team work with over 150 hospitals and health care associations in the USA and Canada.

His attitude is that for any culture change to work, it must be led from the top and the front line. Brian's programs are dedicated to that goal. His most requested programs include *Keep Your Nurses and Health Care Professionals/ Providers for Life, The Service Excellence Initiative, Winning with Difficult People*, and *The Physician/Nurse Communication Effectiveness Seminar.*

Brian is Chairman of the Health Care Service Excellence Conference, held annually the first week of October. The conference features 3 days of exceptional keynotes, seminars, round tables, and workshops attended by service oriented health care providers from across North America. Visit www.healthcareserviceexcellence.com for information.

For further information regarding consultation or speaking engagements, please contact Brian Lee at 800-667-7325 or Brian@customlearning.com.

Jo Manion, PhD, RN, CNAA, FAAN
Manion & Associates
5725 Oak Lake Trail
Oviedo FL 32765
Phone: 407-366-6506
Fax: 407-366-6521
E-mail: jomanion@sprintmail.com

Jo Manion is founder and principal of Manion & Associates, an organizational development consulting firm. She is a nationally recognized speaker and author as well as a senior management consultant whose expertise has provided practical problem-solving assistance to hospitals, health systems, and other health care organizations across the country and internationally. Her work focuses on human resources and development both for leadership staff and the diverse teams they lead. Developing positive, emotionally intelligent workplaces is a primary area of focus. With over 30 years of health care experience, her practical, down-to-earth approach is appreciated by both colleagues and clients alike.

She is the author of several books, including **Change from Within, Team Based Heath Care Organizations** and **From Management to Leadership**.

Jo's recent work reflects the current upheaval and challenge in health care workforces including the effects of downsizing, job shifting, turnover, institutional mergers and consolidations, and all the stress these and other organizational changes put on employees. Her most requested programs include *Creating Community in the Workplace; Retention Strategies That Work—Creating a Positive Workplace;* and *Healing Trust & Betrayal in the Workplace.*

For further information regarding consultation or speaking engagements, please contact Jo Manion at 407-366-6506 or jomanion@sprintmail.com.

Eileen McDargh, CSP, CPAE
333465 Dosinia Drive,
Dana Point CA 92629
Phone: 949-496-8640
E-mail: mcdargh@aol.com
Website: www.eileenmcdargh.com

Eileen McDargh connects with mind, heart, and spirit with her audience. She is one of the most sought-after speakers in North America and draws upon practical business know-how, life's experiences, and over 20 years of consulting and facilitating to national and international organizations, including hospitals, international pharmaceutical companies, nursing associations, and practice managers. Her programs are loaded with content, humor, interaction and authenticity.

Eileen is the author of the award-winning **Work for a Living & Still Be Free to Live** and **The Resilient Spirit.**

In the health care setting, her most requested programs are *Engaging Spirit in the Workplace* (also a video tape series entitled Engaging the Spirit of Nurse Leadership), *The Resilient Spirit: Staying Rightside Up When the World is Upside Down,* (www.theresilientspirit.com) and *Work for a Living & Still Be Free to Live.*

For further information regarding consultation or speaking engagements, please contact her at 949-496-8640, mcdargh@aol.com or www.eileenmcdargh.com.

Tim Porter-O'Grady, EdD, PhD, FAAN
Senior Partner, Tim Porter-O'Grady Associates
Associate Professor, Emory University
529 Crystal Creek Rd.
Otto NC 28763
Phone: 706-746-7575
Fax: 706-746-6585
Website: www.tpogassociates.com
E-mail: info@tpogassociates.com

Tim Porter-O'Grady and his associates offer health system consultation services in health settings throughout the world. The focus of the consulting services is on issues of governance, leadership, conflict, staffing, system's structure, shared governance (including Magnet recognition preparation) and mediation activities. The practice has been operating for 17 years and has offered health consultation services in over 750 settings throughout the world.

Tim (and select other associates) also speaks and lectures internationally with emphasis on nursing and health futures issues, shared decision-making models, governance, leadership, and conflict resolution. He is the author of several books including **The Nurse Manager's Problem Solver** and co-author of **Leading The Revolution in Health Care**. His most requested programs include *Innovation & Creativity—Living in a Transformed Health System; Chaos & Complexity—New Rules for Leadership;* and *Preparing Today for Tomorrow—Nursing and HealthCare Transformation.*

For further information regarding consultation or speaking engagements, please contact Mark Ponder at 706-746-7575.

Robert W. Wendover
Managing Director
The Center for Generational Studies
15200 E. Girard Ave, Suite 400
Aurora CO 80014
Phone: 800-227-5510
Fax: 303-617-7209
E-mail: wendover@gentrends.com
Website: www.gentrends.com

Bob Wendover has presented customized training and keynotes for industry, education and government for the past 15 years. He specializes in assisting organizations understand the challenges of working with the new generations.

His publications include **From Ricky & Lucy to Beavis & Butthead: Managing the New Work Force, Smart Hiring, Two Minute Motivation** and **Handpicked: Finding and Hiring the Best Employees and Recruitment and Retention.**

The Center for Generational Studies conducts research, produces seminars and publishes resources on how the generations relate to one another in the American workplace. Its premier program, *From Ricky & Lucy to Beavis & Butthead,* has received rave reviews from employers throughout the U.S. Other requested programs include *From Newspaper Ads to Jobs.com* and *From the Lone Ranger to a Pierced Stranger.* For a complimentary subscription to the Center's newsletter, GenTrends, go to www.gentrends.com.

For further information regarding consultation or speaking engagements, please contact Dan Ereth at 800-227-5510 or ereth@gentrends.com.

Diann Uustal, EdD, MSN, BSN

2168 S. Shore Acres Rd
Soddy Daisy TN 37379
Phone: 423-451-0011
E-mail: dbuethics@aol.com
Website: www.dbuethics.com

Diann Uustal is a nationally and internationally recognized educator, author, and consultant in health care ethics, caring for the caregiver, and value-based leadership. Dr. Uustal earned her BS and MS in Nursing, a doctoral degree in Education, majoring in values and ethics in healthcare.

Diann has authored countless articles, written the script for an award winning film and has nine books to her credit. Her books include **Clinical Values and Ethics in a Changing Healthcare Environment** and **Caring for Yourself ~ Caring for Others: The Ultimate Balance**, and the co-edited **Cutting Edge Bioethics: A Christian Exploration of Technologies and Trends.**

As a clinical-ethicist, she is experienced in consulting with hospital ethics committees, conferring in problematical clinical-ethical cases, reviewing and writing policies, and helping establish new ethics committees.

Diann is a highly sought after educator, author and keynote speaker, known for her dynamic and thought provoking presentation style. Her most requested programs include *The Ethic & Spirit of Care in Healing Relationships & Healthcare; Caring for Yourself ~ Caring for Others: The Ultimate Balance; Living in Balance in a World on Fast-Forward;* and *Attitudes are Contagious: Value-Based Strategies for Enhancing Staff Morale & Collegiality in Nursing.*

For further information regarding consultation or speaking engagements, please contact Diann Uustal at 423-451-0011 or dbuethics@aol.com.

Recommended Readings

Briles, J. *The Confidence Factor.* Aurora CO: Mile High Press, 2003.

———. *Woman to Woman 2000.* Far Hills, NJ, 1999.

———. *Stop Stabbing Yourself in the Back.* Aurora CO: Mile High Press, 2002.

Buckingham, M and Coffman, C. *First, Break All the Rules.* New York: Simon & Schuster, 1999.

Charles, Leslie. *Why is Everyone So Cranky?* NY, Hyperion, 2001.

———. *All is Not Lost.* East Lansing, MI: Yes! Press, 2002.

———. *The Customer Service Companion.* East Lansing, MI: Yes! Press, 2002.

Chesler, Phyllis. *Woman's Inhumanity to Woman,* New York: Nation Books, 2001.

Covey, S. *The Seven Habits of Highly Effective People.* New York: Simon Schuster, 1989.

Donaldson, Mimi and Michael, *Negotiating for Dummies.* Chicago, IDG Books, 1996.

Dowling, C. *Perfect Women.* New York: Summit Books, 1988.

Duck, J. *The Change Monster.* New York: Crown Business, 2001.

Eichenbaum, L., and Orbach, S. *Between Women.* New York: Viking Penguin, 1988.

Farley, V. *Pulling Together to Make A Difference.* Los Angeles, CA: iUniverse, 2000

———. *Future Tense or Tense Future.* Los Angeles, CA: iUniverse, 2000

Forward, S. *Toxic Parents.—Overcoming Their Hurtful Legacy and Reclaiming Your Life.* New York: Bantam Books, 1989.

French, M. *Beyond Power—On Women, Men, and Morals.* New York: Ballantine, 1985.

_____ . *The War Against Women.* New York: Summit Books, 1992.

Glass, L. *Toxic People.* New York: St. Martin's Press, 1997

Harragan, B. L. *Games Mothers Never Taught You.* New York: Rawson Associates, 1977.

Heim, Pat and Murphy, Susan. *In the Company of Women.* New York; Tarcher Putnam, 2001.

Helgesen, S. *The Female Advantage—Women's Ways of Leadership.* New York: Doubleday, 1990.

Hyatt, C. *Shifting Gears.* New York: Simon & Schuster, 1990.

Hyatt, C., and Gottlieb, L. *When Smart People Fail.* New York: Simon & Schuster, 1993.

Jeffers, S. *Feel the Fear and Do It Anyway.* New York: Random House, 1988.

Jeffries, E. N. *The Heart of Leadership.* Dubuque, Iowa: Kendall/Hunt, 1993.

Jongeward, D., and Scott, D. *Women as Winners.* Reading, Mass.: Addison-Wesley, 1983.

Kaminer, W *I'm Dysfunctional, You're Dysfunctional.* Reading, MA.: Addison-Wesley, 1992.

Kreigel, R. J. *If It Ain't Broke . . . BREAK IT! New* York: Warner Books, 1991.

Larsen, Linda. *True Power.* Sarasota, FL: Brandywine Publishing, 2000.

Lee, B. *Keep Your Nurses for Life.* Calgary, Alberta: Mastery Publishing, 2001

Leonard, G. *Mastery.* New York: Dutton, 1991.

Lerner, H. G. *The Dance of Anger.* New York: HarperCollins, 1990.

_____ . *The Dance of Deception.* New York: HarperCollins, 1993.

Manion, J. *Change from Within.* Kansas City, MO: American Nurses Association, 1990.

_____ . *From Management to Leadership.* Chicago, IL: American Hospital Association, 1998

_____ . *Team Based Heath Care Organizations:* New York: Aspen Publishers, 1996.

Marone, N. *Women and Risk: A Guide to Overcoming Learned Helplessness.* New York: St. Martin's Press, 1992.

McDargh, Eileen. *Work for a Living & Still Be Free to Live.* Portland, OR: Book Partners Inc., 1997.

Miles, L. and Hailey, W. *Your Key to the Practice.* Myrtle Beach, SC: Dental Dynamics, 1998.

Popcorn, F. *The Popcorn Report.* New York: Doubleday, 1992.

Porter-O'Grady, T. *The Nurse Manager Problem Solver.* New York: Mosby, 1994.

_____ . *The Health Care Team Book.* New York: Aspen Publishers, 1999.

_____ . *Leading the Revolution.* New York: Mosby, Inc, 1998.

Schaef, A. W *Women's Reality.* Minneapolis: Winston Press, 1985.

Schapiro, N. *Negotiating for Your Life.* New York: Holt, Rinehart & Winston, 1993.

Schwartz, E *Breaking with Tradition.* New York: Warner Books, 1992.

Scott, G. G. *Resolving Conflict.* Berkeley, Calif: New Harbinger Publications, 1990.

Shames, K. H. *The Nightingale Conspiracy.* New York: Power Publications, 1993.

Summers, C. *Caregiver, Caretaker.* Mt. Shasta, Calif: Commune-a-Key Publishing, 1992.

Tannen, Deborah. *You Just Don't Understand.* New York: Quill, 1998.

Tavris, C. *The Mismeasure of Women.* New York: Simon & Schuster, 1992.

Teal, J., and Walker, L. *The Battered Woman.* New York: HarperCollins, 1979.

Uustal, D. *Caring for Self, Caring for Others.* Greenwich, RI: Educational Resources in Health Care, 1997

_____ . *Clinical Ethics and Values,* RI: Educational Resources in Health Care, 1997

Wilson, L. and Wilson, H. *Play to Win,* Austin, TX: Bard Press, 1998.

Notes

Chapter One

1. *Is the Nursing Profession a Toxic Work Environment?,* Rehabilitation Nursing, Volume 20, Number 5, Sept/Oct 1995.
2. *Taking Off the Rose-Colored Glasses: The Need to Find Remedies for Toxic Workplaces,* Rehabilitation Nursing, Volume 21, Number 2, Mar/Apr 1996.
3. Briles, Judith. **GenderTraps**, McGraw-Hill, NY, 1996.
4. Briles, Judith. **Woman to Woman 2000**, New Horizon Press, NJ, 1999.

Chapter Five

1. Deal, T. E., and Kennedy, A. A. *Corporate Cultures.* Reading, MA: Addison-Wesley, 1982.
2. Kanter, Rosabeth Moss, **Men and Women of the Corporation**, Basic Books, NY, 1977, pp. 77, 82, 134.
3. Gilligan, Carol, **The Birth of Pleasure**, Knopf, NY, 2002.
4. Briles, Judith, **The Confidence Factor**, Mile High Press, Aurora CO, 2003.

Chapter Six

1. Dunn, Herb and Budin, Wendy, *Horizontal Violence: A Possible Link with Job Satisfaction in Operating Room Nurses,* Nursing Research II, 2001.

Chapter Eight

1. *The Pentagon Declares War on Electronic Slide Shows That Make Briefings a Pain,* The Wall Street Journal, April 26, 2000.
2. Tannen, Deborah. *You Just Don't Understand.* New York: Quill, 1998.

Chapter Thirteen

1. Driscoll, Jeanne Watson *Mentoring in Nursing* (Philadelphia: Wyeth-Ayerst laboratories, 1993). For information on obtaining this video, write to the company at P.O. Box 8299, Philadelphia, PA 19101, or call 215-971-5872.
2. *The Pocket Mentor,* published by the Association of Women Surgeons. To purchase a copy ($15), write to the association at 414 Plaza Drive, Suite 209, Westmont, IL 60559, call 630-0392 or contact at www.womensurgeons.org.

Chapter Fourteen

1. Kurth, Lynne, *Managerial Factors Related to Employee Turnover in a Hospital Setting,* Credential of Advanced Studies in Healthcare Administration, 2001.

Acknowledgments

While it is an author with a vision who conceives a book, that book cannot be delivered without the help of a birthing team. The first book dedicated to the health care community began in Glens Falls, New York. This book, carrying over key elements from *The Briles Report on Women in Healthcare*, than adding a new survey and new steps and material for unraveling conflict in the workplace, had seedlings throughout North America.

The thousands of women and men who work in the health care field have been generous with their time and insights beyond anything I imagined. I thank the survey respondents and those who agreed to be interviewed. Their voices make this book. All names have been changed to respect these women's requests and the need for confidentiality. My health care encouragers, cronies, conference pals and meeting planning visionaries—Jo Manion, Diann and Tom Uustal, Venner Farley, Ellen Tryon, Kathy Petrucelli, Brian Lee, Sharon Cox, Tim Porter O'Grady, Linda Miles, Paula Szyer, Leslie Brock, Cherie Mee, Karyn Cousart, Richard and Peggy Ireland, Leslie Charles, Eileen McDargh, Linda Larsen, and Mimi Donaldson all make being "on the road" so much easier.

The thousands of men and women who took the time to complete the survey and the hundreds who participated in real-time interviews including Debora Zachau, Herb

Dunn, Robert Wendover, Steve Lee, and Lynne Kurth a big, big thank you.

I thank Vic and Nancy Cruikshank for their eyes, ears and sage advice.

To the book creators who are wonderful—Ronnie Moore, Mikell Yamada, and Karen Saunders. Thank you all for being there.

And of course, none of my books are created without the support of my staff John Maling, Shari Peterson, and Karen Zuppa. Angie Pacheco creates the glue that links my office with our clients. As always, all my books are started and finished around water. True to form, this one took shape at my daughter Shelley's home in Chesapeake Beach MD. I thank them all.

Index

About the Author

Judith Briles, DBA, MBA

Dr. Judith Briles is CEO of The Briles Group, Inc. a Colorado based research, speaking, training and consulting firm. She is internationally acclaimed as a keynote speaker and recognized as an expert in solutions to workplace issues. Her clients include hospitals and healthcare associations and organizations throughout North America. In 2002 and 2003, her company was selected as one of the Top 100 Women Owned Businesses in Colorado by *ColoradoBiz* magazine.

She is an award winning and best selling author of over 20 books including *The Confidence Factor (winner of 2002 Best Business Book from the Colorado Independent Publishers Association), Woman to Woman: From Sabotage to Support (winner of The Chicago Tribune's Business Book of the Year), The Briles Report on Women in Healthcare (featured selection of the Nurses' Book Club), 10 Smart Money Moves for Women (winner of the 2001 Colorado Book Award for non-fiction), Smart Money Moves for Kids (winner of the 2001 Colorado Independent Publishers Association Award for Self-Improvement/Parenting), The Dollars and Sense of Divorce, GenderTraps,* and *When God Says NO.*

Dr. Briles has been featured on over 1000 radio and television programs nationwide and writes columns for the *Denver Business Journal, Colorado Woman News, and Zenith magazine.* Her work has been featured in *The Wall Street Journal, Time, People, USA Today* and *The New York Times.* She's a frequent guest on *MSNBC, CNBC* and *CNN.*

She is a Board member of the WISH List, President of the Colorado Independent Publishers Association, Gilda's Club-Denver; serves on the Advisory Boards of *Colorado Woman News, Zenith* magazine; and is a past director of the National Speakers Association, the Woman's Bank of San Francisco, Colorado Women's Leadership Coalition and the Colorado Nurses League.

For information about Judith Briles' availability
for speeches, the Judith Briles Health Care Leadership
Forum, or information about her annual health care
confidence cruise and subscribing to her newsletter,
contact her at:

Judith@Briles.com
www.Briles.com

303-627-9179 ~ 303-627-9184 Fax
The Briles Group, Inc.
PO 460880
Aurora, CO 80046

Also from

Dr. Judith Briles . . .

Stop Stabbing Yourself in the Back

A complete analysis of the problems of self-sabotage—such as blaming others, procrastination, excuse-abuse, not taking responsibility, perfectionism, excess loyalty, change-a-phobia, fear of failure, fear of confronting, ego, etc., etc. Identifies 21 ways you can undermine yourself and create the right antidotes to correct them.

Book   **$25**

When God Says NO—Finding the Yes in Pain and Disappointment

Overcoming adversity and adapting to life's unwanted changes are challenges that everyone faces. Understanding that a "yes" is behind the "no" will help guide you through your maze of hurt and sorrow. Pain is inevitable. Misery is not. Perfect for anyone hurting.
     Book   **$15**

Smart Money Moves for Kids—The Parents' Complete Guide

For parents and grandparents—everything you wish you knew before you became a prarent—covers ages from three to the Boomerang-ers: allowances, jobs, college cars, weddings, collecting, investing, leaving home, the Internet—money and parenting resources, quizzes and games. ~**Award-Winner!** ~

Book   **$22**

New! Coming in 2004!
Caution: Women at Work—
The Man's Guide to Managing & Working with Women

Is there a difference in managing women? Working with women? Yes— This books is a compass for those navigating the obstacle course. Stories and strategies from both genders are included—a true eye-opener! *Reserve your copy today!*   **$25**

"I am a Woman of Confidence" Big Shirt/Sleep Tee

Now that you <u>are</u> a Woman of Confidence, tell the world to watch out, because here you come! Our oversized purple tee is emblazoned in white: **"I AM A WOMAN of *Confidence...*Beware"**

Long Shirt   **$20**   **Short Shirt**   **$15**

All prices are subject to change. To order, please check our website at www.Briles.com or call 800-594-0800.

The
Judith Briles
Health Care Management
Leadership Forum

Superior Management Skills for Health Care
2-Day Intensive Skills, Coaching & Mentoring Forum
(Up to 23 Continuing Education Units)

The Judith Briles Health Care Management Leadership Forum delivers an intensive training that focuses on the soft people skills that just don't come naturally: *Red Ink Behaviors, Confidence-building, Mentoring, Conflict, Confrontation, Management/Resolution, Change Management, Resolving Retention Issues, Effective Communications, and Leadership.*

The goal of the Forum is to create an environment where new and nearly new managers and supervisors can learn a variety of skills that can be implemented *immediately.* The end result is the creation of a workplace of choice, high retention, and minimal conflict. As documented in **Zapping Conflict in the Health Care Workplace,** *over 70% of participants reported they had quit a position because of <u>abusive behavior from their manager!</u>*

Regular sessions are conducted by Dr. Judith Briles at her offices in **Denver, Colorado.** Participants come from a cross-section of hospitals nationwide.

At the conclusion of the Forum, participants are prepared to apply their newly-learned skills to deal with workplace issues. They are able to communicate, anticipate, trouble-shoot, and provide solutions—**they are able to manage!**

Space is limited to only <u>16</u> participants. Register now!
Dates and Fee information available at www.Briles.com/forum
Group Rates are Available! Please call us: 800-594-0800

Dr. Judith Briles

... *The Speaker That Makes a Difference*

Keynotes, General Sessions and Workshops

Especially for Health Care!

Zapping Conflict from A to Z

Health care is unique because of its gender dominance, practicing cultures that do not mirror the written mission of the organization, and the wild card – the patient. Participants are taught how to identify the initial problem, its underlying causes, the impacts, and the effects on patient satisfaction and the bottom line. Finally, solutions are delivered to zap conflict. Based on **Zapping Conflict in the Workplace**, a 2003 Nurses Book Society Best Seller.

The Domino Factor©—How to Get out of the Game and Focus on Patients

When distractions like gossip, scandal, conflict, sabotage, promotions, and impending change enter the workplace, the result is worry, speculation and guesstimating outcomes. While men typically hang around the "cooler" then go back to work; women tend to continue to dissect the latest as often as they can throughout their duties—often within the range of their patients, colleagues, and patients' families. It's called the *Domino Factor©* and when it's in play, productivity takes a dive. As a manager, you need to acknowledge that it exists, determine its roots and work on resolution before it costs you more red ink than it already has. Learn how to anticipate the *Domino Factor©* by understanding the distractions that put it into play, and what steps to take to get your employees re-focused on their patients.

The Savvy Worker's Guide to Personal Finance

Too often caregivers take care of everyone but themselves. In this workshop based on Judith's award-winning books **10 Smart Money Moves for Women** and **Smart Money Moves for Kids**, participants learn 10 smart ways to secure their financial future. Ideal for an extended breakout session, the program is presented interactively and delivers information that can be used immediately. Judith's business background includes more than 11 books focused on financial topics!

Creating Confidence Out of Chaos or *The Confidence Factor*
(General Sessions Only)

Confidence is **the** Career Maker or Career Breaker. Based on the best-selling book, **The Confidence Factor**, you'll learn that confidence is acquired, not inherited. Woven around the *Ten Steps to Building Confidence*, this stimulating and humorous speech is guaranteed to motivate and inspire audiences.

To book Judith Briles for your next speaking engagement, call 303-627-9179 or visit us online at www.Briles.com.

Leading with Confidence
Leaders need to know how to manage, yet lead; managers need to know how to lead, yet manage. Both must be confident to be successful within their organizations and teams. Learn the key tools to creating and becoming a Confident Leader.

Changing for the Better: A Collaborative Approach
When your unit is in need of change and it's your task to figure out what to do and how to do it, where do you start so that the result is happier, not resentful employees? In this 2-day session, Dr. Briles takes your staff and leaders through separate assessments to determine who still belongs – in the unit, the facility, even the profession. By revealing the "unwritten rules" of the workplace, the real drivers of the current culture will be discovered and strategies will be formed based on new knowledge of what works – and what doesn't.

Communicating with Confidence and Clarity for Credible Leadership
Are you communicating? You might think you are, but only your colleagues know for sure! Rarely is a communication style <u>wrong</u>, just different. Participants will learn the four steps to effective communicating—both as a listener and speaker—and identify the factors that impede successful communication such as gender, age, culture. Learn how to avoid the pitfalls of sharing too much information and why listening is the key to resolving conflict and to successful negotiation.

Thriving & Empowerment in Health Care—From Sabotage to Support
Over 80 percent of survey respondents reported that they had been undermined by co-workers. Can women be bullies? Is the workplace fair? Should one be more cautious of women or men in the workplace? Based on the entire body of Judith's pioneering research into workplace issues –including five of her books—participants will learn the *Ten Steps To Build a Collaborative Workplace,* how to identify *Saboteurs in the Midst©* and how to use the *Conflict Management Style Survey©*. Ideal workshop for longer and all-day sessions.

Keep the Keepers...Lose the Losers
Retention is the key to any recruitment program. Too often, hospitals have created a "bait and switch" strategy to recruit new hires. The secret is not in adding numbers, but in creating an environment and culture that keeps and attracts the best while eliminating marginal employees. Creating cultural changes and reducing conflict-inducing behaviors are key factors in keeping your keepers. This program shows you where to start and gives you the tools to keep going toward the goal of "Employer of Choice—of <u>Choice</u> Employees."

Thriving with Change When Thriving Doesn't Feel Like an Option
Change is everywhere. Some changes are no bigger than gnats, others the size of a Mack truck. Either way, the thought and implementation of changes can demoralize, even destroy those going through it. Participants will be able to identify the five stages of change, access their resistance to change and create an action plan to grow through it and thrive.

To book Judith Briles for your next speaking engagement, call 303-627-9179 or visit us online at www.Briles.com.